Don't miss the ~~other~~ **unforgettable true stories from the files of BigHugs.com . . .**

Love Lost and Found
True Stories of Long-Lost Loves—Reunited at Last

Share in the romance of these touching true stories of lovers divided by time and distance, and reunited by their hearts.

Together Again
True Stories of Birth Parents and Adopted Children Reunited

Three extraordinary true stories celebrating the joy of reunion between birth parents and adopted children.

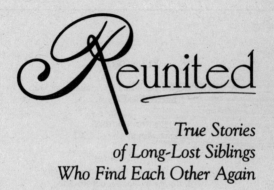

Reunited

True Stories
of Long-Lost Siblings
Who Find Each Other Again

Carolyn Campbell

BERKLEY BOOKS, NEW YORK

REUNITED

A Berkley Book / published by arrangement with
International Locator

PRINTING HISTORY
Berkley edition / April 2002

Visit our website at
www.penguinputnam.com

ISBN: 0-425-18401-3

BERKLEY®
Berkley Books are published by The Berkley Publishing Group,
a division of Penguin Putnam Inc., 375 Hudson Street,
New York, New York 10014.
BERKLEY and the "B" design
are trademarks belonging to Penguin Putnam Inc.

PRINTED IN THE UNITED STATES OF AMERICA

10 9 8 7 6 5 4 3 2 1

This one's for my kids:
Aaron, Chris, Colin, and Alyssa
Hold on tight to your dreams

The Brother He Never Forgot

Chapter 1

∞

Michael was terrified. Here he stood in this unfamiliar place called the courthouse, surrounded by more people than he had ever seen before in his eight-year-old life. Conversations buzzed around him like bees. None of the others waiting in this hallway outside the courtroom were kids. There were tall men in gray, black, and brown suits and a few women in Sunday dresses. The hum of their droning voices and the worried looks on their faces fascinated Michael. No one looked at him. Even Mama stared over his head and whispered with the black-suited man he knew was her lawyer. Every few minutes, Michael felt her long, painted red nails dig into his shoulders.

"I don't like it here," he said to his mother. "Let's go home."

"We can't go yet." Suddenly her hand clamped his shoulder like a vise. "Remember—do what I told you." She paused and faced him, moving nearer until her brown eyes bored into his blue ones. "If you don't do what we talked about, Scary Jack will get you. He'll hurt you or kill you."

Again, the fingernails dug. Michael stared across the hall to the tall, blue-eyed man in the gray suit. He'd heard frightening stories about this man all his life. Michael knew this man was Scary Jack—his father. Michael couldn't remember the last time he'd seen him, but Scary Jack did look familiar in some way, like a stranger you saw on the street and thought you knew.

"Don't look at him," Mama hissed now, again bending close. "Don't let him see how scared you are."

Michael quickly averted his gaze, staring instead into the sea of suits and dresses. He took a deep breath and smelled tobacco and the dusty staleness of the city. He and Mama hardly ever came to the city—or anywhere else where she thought Scary Jack might find them. They moved to one apartment after another, staying each time until Mama thought Scary Jack might know where they were. Then they moved again, sometimes even leaving their clothes and Michael's toys behind.

Now Michael couldn't believe that Scary Jack stood just five feet away, across the hall, where he could stare at Mama and Michael as long as he wanted. It was the most frightening moment Michael had ever known. "We have to go in the courtroom any minute now. Remember, do what I told you or he'll get you." This time, Mama's fingernails grazed his neck.

Jack stared across the courthouse hall at his slim dark-haired son, Michael. It seemed like he'd waited forever for this day. He longed to walk over to the boy, hug him, and tell him how much he'd missed him. It had been three long years. His son was in second grade when he saw him last. He still remembered the boy's innocent face, round blue eyes and apple cheeks. They had been together for one rare and precious afternoon, which Jack now relived every day, and lots of nights when he couldn't sleep. The two of them spent a quick hour at the park. During most of their time together, Jack hid his tears, still believing that a man shouldn't cry.

Now did he even dare hope there was a possibility he might get to see Michael again? Were these few minutes during the hearing the only time he'd lay eyes on his own boy?

Jack turned to his attorney. "What are my chances?" he asked. "How often do they give custody to the father?"

His attorney looked away, then coughed behind his

hand. "I won't lie to you," he began, then paused and shuffled his feet.

"Not very often." Jack shook his head in despair. "I knew it."

"Not ever with one of my clients." said his lawyer. "Not once in my twenty-year experience."

Jack shook his head.

Now the lawyer cuffed Jack's shoulder. "It's time to go in."

Jack stood next to his lawyer and glanced across the courtroom where Michael stood next to Amanda. She wouldn't look at him. Even from here, he could see her eyes were filled with fire. She knows she won, he thought. And she's still furious with me. But I can't help wanting my own son. Could Amanda ever guess how much this separation hurt him inside? Could she find a shred of compassion for him, anywhere in her heart? Didn't she know he loved Michael, too?

"All rise," said the court clerk.

Jack stood and held his breath.

The black-robed judge glanced alternately at both of them. Jack watched his lawyer shuffle his feet.

"After weighing the testimony, documents, and circumstances presented earlier this week, I have reached a decision." The judge paused, again glancing out into the courtroom through gold wire-framed glasses. "After receiving testimony and proof regarding allegations of noncompliance with visitation orders, neglect and public intoxication on the part of the child's mother, I have decided to award permanent custody to the child's father, Jack Dutton."

"What?" Jack gasped in disbelief. Then he felt his heart pound as tears flooded his eyes. Relief and happiness poured over him in waves.

"You won." His attorney cuffed him on the arm. "I never told you, but I would have bet a million to one against this verdict."

Jack sighed with relief. "I can't believe it. Do you know

how happy I am? Do you have any idea how much I wanted this?"

His attorney patted his back, and the two men hugged. "You got it. Now you just need to sign the papers." The lawyer pointed him in the direction of the clerk.

Jack only took one step before Amanda yanked at his sleeve. Her bitter voice spat, "I don't know how you did this to me—"

He caught his breath. It was like the whole court paused within the wrath of her venom. Why did she hate him so? Before he could respond to Amanda, his lawyer stepped between them.

"It was the judge's decision, ma'am." The attorney's tone was brusque. "Based on—"

"I don't know who you paid—or what you did—but you won't get away with this. In the meantime, I'm saying good-bye to my son alone. I'm taking him out in the hall for a minute and I'll be right back."

Before Jack could protest, Amanda flounced away, her hand firmly gripping Michael's arm.

"Should we let her take him outside like that?" Jack's brow furrowed with concern.

His lawyer's voice was calm. "Don't worry. There are officers there. She'll be back." The two of them stood and waited.

Jack's lawyer nudged him. "Bet you're glad you saved him from that . . ." The attorney spoke under his breath and shook his head. "Boy's a lucky kid."

"Let's get the papers signed so I can take my son home. My wife and daughter are waiting," Jack said. "Michael has been through a lot and now we can at least have a normal life." He felt weary suddenly, but the hope and relief inside buoyed him enough to approach the clerk's desk.

"You're the boy's father?" A thin man behind the desk smiled at him.

"Yes, I'm happy to say. Always was and always will be."

"First father I've ever had sign as the custodial parent.

And I've been here twenty-five years—since 1932. Right here, sir, on the bottom line. Congratulations. You won."

"I sure did." Jack shook his head. "Never knew I'd have to fight for my own boy."

"At least you got him. Your son is lucky to have you."

"I hope he feels that way."

Jack sat on the bench beside his lawyer and waited. Four, maybe five minutes crept by before an alarm went off inside him. Panic gripped his mind.

"Where's Amanda?" he asked suddenly. "She said she'd be right back."

Both he and the lawyer stood instantly.

Michael saw it was time to run. Mama patted her hair, at the back of her neck. That was the signal. All week she told Michael to run like the wind the second she touched her hair that way. As an electric charge of fear filled him, Michael ran. He dashed through marble halls and surged down two flights of stairs. Then there was another hall, filled with closed doors. He ran to the end, where there were still more stairs. Wasn't there a door in this place? How could he get out of here? He panted and felt a ribbon of sweat drip down his chest.

Where should he go now? The building felt like a maze with no way out. Michael glanced down a flight of stairs that lay ahead and saw a sheriff standing guard at the bottom. He turned and rushed back down the hall. He was out of breath, and an ache filled his side, but he couldn't stop now.

"Come back here, boy," the sheriff called out, thundering after him with thudding steps. But Michael remembered that Mama told him to run, no matter who followed him, no matter what anyone said. His legs kept moving. Down the hall, turn right, down another flight of stairs. Then he found himself alone in a big room with a long table in the middle and a chandelier on the ceiling. He dashed back to the door of the room, then heard the sheriff's feet against the marble floor. There just had to be another door someplace. Maybe at the other end of the table . . .

Michael gasped as someone grabbed his collar and yanked him backward. He gagged and coughed, and the person finally let go.

Michael was sure it was Scary Jack who choked him. "Please—" he begged.

Mama said Scary Jack would hurt Michael bad if he didn't run away as soon as she said to. She said that he was running for his life. Mama told him that Scary Jack had already hurt him when he was little.

Now iron-strong hands yanked him around and mean eyes stared at him.

It was the sheriff.

Other sheriffs and men in suits hurried up beside him.

"Your mother ever tell you to listen to a policeman, boy?" The sheriff's strong arms clamped his. Michael shook with fear as the sheriff's craggy face bent close. "Don't you ever run from the law again, kid."

Michael's tongue froze in his mouth.

Mama had said not to talk to anybody, not to say a word.

Now Michael couldn't talk even if he wanted to. His mouth felt swollen shut. Where was Mama? Had Scary Jack already gotten her?

Two other sheriffs walked toward him. He remembered Mama's words—that he should run, no matter what. He held his breath and counted to three. He ran about four steps before the sheriff grabbed him again and shoved him toward the other sheriff.

"Take him back to the courtroom," the sheriff barked.

They were giving him to Scary Jack. He was a dead kid for sure. He knew it. Sheriffs didn't care if he got hurt—sometimes they hurt people, too. Mama told him that. What would Mama tell him to do now? How could he possibly get away?

The sheriff kept a hand on his arm and led him back

to the courtroom. Mama was there, and although she hugged him, her grip was rough and her eyes, cold. Michael shook within her hold as the judge's voice boomed and echoed in the high-ceilinged courtroom.

"I will not tolerate an outburst like that again. I'll hold you in contempt if you can't control your son," the judge thundered at Mama. "You are in violation of the terms of my orders if you don't control him sufficiently to deliver him to his father. He can't be allowed to run off—"

"I told my son what might happen," Mama said, in what Michael called her fakey sweet voice. "He just jerked himself away from me and ran off. He does not want to go with his father, Your Honor."

Mama told him she might tell a lie today—if she needed to save him. She said Michael just had to keep his mouth shut and let her talk.

"Let me emphasize once again that no visitation is included in this judgment. I've granted sole custody to the boy's father, Jack Dutton. Now you must control your son sufficiently to see that my words are carried out."

Mama's lawyer stood. "Your Honor, never in the history of this county has sole custody been given to a father . . . without visitation."

"My judgment is now declared," said the judge, hitting the bench with his gavel.

Michael heard Mama break into sobs. He felt his own throat close in terror. Fear filled him as he saw the sheriffs walk toward him. He huddled close to Mama, who looked up at the officers.

"Please," she said softly. "I didn't know it would be sole custody. My son is terribly upset. That's why he ran away. Since I'm never going to see him again, I need to explain that he can't run away. He's scared of all the sheriffs in this room. We'll just go out in the hall there"—Mama pointed—"And I'll bring him right back. I'm afraid he'll run away after I'm gone if I don't talk to him now."

The judge shook his head in exasperation. "Five minutes. And send a guard with her."

Mama sounded calm, but she squeezed his hand hard. "Just watch me," Mama said to Michael under her breath. As they stepped out in the hall, accompanied by a guard, she began to rummage through her purse.

"What are you doing?" Michael asked.

"Shh . . ." she said, and he watched as she took a fifty-dollar bill—all they had left this week—and held it out to the guard.

"Look the other way," Mama said. "That's all I'm asking. Ten seconds. You turned your head and you didn't see me leave."

"Ma'am, I could have you arrested for this—"

"He's my boy," Mama hissed. "His father has abused him. He's already paid the judge or we wouldn't be here."

Michael saw the guard hesitate. "I could lose my job."

"If you don't let me go, I'll lose my boy."

The guard wavered. "Ma'am, we could both get in serious trouble."

"My boy gets abused if you don't let us go."

The guard stepped back, raised his hands. "I'm going in that courtroom right now to tell the judge you tried to bribe me. And you're coming with me."

"No—we're going," Mama said, and to Michael's surprise, the guard didn't stop them. She yanked Michael's hand and they headed down the hall.

Before he knew it, they came to the big, glass double doors that led outside the building.

"Mama—we're not—"

Mama let go of his hand and clapped her fingers around his mouth. "Shut up!" she hissed, pulling open the heavy door and pushing him outside. "Go to the car!" she whispered in his ear and the two of them ran across the parking lot. Michael expected a sheriff to grab him like before, but no one did.

They made it to the car, a beat-up rusty Corvair that broke down every other week. Michael climbed in, and Mama gunned the engine.

"You won't get us, Scary Jack," she called out, looking back over her shoulder at the courthouse as the car sped away.

"You won't get me," Michael called out, and he and Mama laughed together.

Yet Michael's heart pounded as he sat next to Mama on the front seat.

He expected to hear a siren any minute.

This time the sheriff might put him in prison.

Chapter 2

 озо

"She tried to bribe me and then she ran—" the guard panted.

"They're gone!" a sheriff yelled. "All units head out."

Jack's heart sank lower than he ever remembered. How could this happen? Here, of all places, in a building filled with sheriffs, judges, and lawyers. His attorney's hand found his shoulder. "Sorry, man. What was he thinking? He should have handcuffed her or something. I have another hearing to go to, but you need to talk to the police."

"This place is full of police," Jack said, discouraged. "All the sheriffs saw what happened. She stole him right from under our noses."

"But you still need to file a report. This is kidnapping."

Jack had never felt so sad or weary.

Minutes later, after he picked up his wife, Mary, and daughter, Stephanie, at the house, the three of them sat in a conference room at the police station.

"Tell me everything you know about how to find this woman." The officer's hand was poised to write on a yellow pad.

Jack ran a tired hand through his hair. "I haven't been able to find her in years. And neither has anyone else."

"He searches for her all the time," Mary said. "We just haven't had any luck."

The officer sighed. "We'll give it one more try. Do you by any chance have an address?"

"I've got a pile of them at home. Every time the police get close, she moves."

"How do you mail the child support?"

"I send it every month if I find an address. She moves again and again. No one can catch up with her. The mail just comes back."

"Phone number?"

Jack sighed. "Didn't even bother to write them down after a while. If I call once, it will be changed the next time. I always wait for her to call me."

"And does she?"

"Still calls every month to scream at me. Makes threats. Tells me I won't get near Michael." His sigh was heavy. "I guess she's probably right."

"Don't have much to go on here." The officer shook his head. "What about her work. What does she do?"

"Typist, mostly. Temporary jobs. Makes it easier for her to move from place to place."

"Any family members she's close to?"

"A sister. In Sebastian, Florida."

"You know how to reach her? Give me her number. She might know something."

Jack reached inside his wallet. "Just tell me—do you think there's any hope of finding my kid? I feel like I've been trying to catch up with him my whole life."

Now the officer shook his head and looked down at the pad in front of him. "I gotta tell you, mister, there's not much here. Can't believe your lawyer let her get away with—"

"I work at the phone company." Mary's voice broke through. "I'll see what I can find out."

"Do anything you can," the officer said. "I gotta say,

this woman is a pro. Stealing a kid from the courthouse . . ." He shook his head, stood, and shook hands
with Jack. "Do whatever you can. Send us any information you have."

Mary spoke up. "Do you think you'll find her?"

"I couldn't say, ma'am." He paused and looked at the
two of them. "But if anything else crosses your mind,
don't hesitate to call it in. Anything."

"Thank you," Jack said, although thankful was hardly
the way he felt now. "Please let us know as soon as you
hear anything."

"I'll call you right away."

They were walking down the steps outside the police
station when Mary finally spoke again.

"They're no help at all." Her voice was bitter.

"We have to trust them—what else can we do?" Jack
asked. He put his arm around his wife's shoulder and the
two of them walked to their car, feeling too hopeless to
say another word.

It was one week since their escape from the courthouse
and they were living in some motel in some town. They
were shopping at a drugstore when Mama suddenly turned
and stared at him. She frowned as she looked at his hair.

"Is there a bug on my head?" Michael asked. He
reached up and swatted at his hair.

"No bugs, but we need to do something about that hair
of yours." Mama's fingers sifted though his hair at the
same time as she made a face, as if his hair were dirty,
though he'd taken a shower that morning. "What color do
you want your hair to be?" Mama's voice sounded happy.
Her mouth smiled, but her eyes held that scary light of
anger. It was a look Michael knew could mean mad, fiery
anger, or the sad anger when she said everyone in the
world hated her and life was just rotten and maybe she
wanted to die. Michael never knew what he was supposed
to say when Mama was angry. Sometimes, if he said noth-

ing, she screamed and threw cans or glasses or anything close to her. He never knew what would set her off.

Michael didn't answer the question about his hair. He hardly thought of his hair unless Mom told him to comb it. It was always that dark color, like the "Special Dark" Hershey bar, like Scary Jack's hair color. Mama's hair was red.

"Come on . . . what color?" The anger light still raged in Mama's eyes, and her smile paled a little, which he knew meant she was getting impatient. She grabbed his shoulder roughly and led him toward a shelf with hair dyes.

"Go on—pick one!" She pushed his shoulder.

He leaned up to whisper in her ear. "You're not really going to dye my hair, are you?"

Now the push from behind was hard. "Choose one," she hissed at him. "We can't hang out in here forever. Someone will see."

Who? Michael wondered, looking quickly over his shoulder. Did she think that Scary Jack could somehow find them in his little bitty town more than a hundred miles away from the courthouse?

"Pick one." Her breath flowed hot against his ear as she shoved him ahead until he nearly collided with a shelf of hair colors.

The box covers showed pictures of women. Women with happy faces and perfect hair, slender hands and long fingernails, like the women who presented the prizes on TV game shows.

Suddenly Mama pulled his ear.

"Choose," she hissed.

His head swam with fear, anger, and bewilderment. He never, not once in his eight-year-old life, pictured himself with a hair color other than dark brown. The idea was weird, like being in a science-fiction movie, where you might wake up and discover that you suddenly had purple eyes. But Mama was mad. And when she was angry, Mama meant business. His mind floundered.

Blond, he thought, suddenly. The Beach Boys were blond, those guys that drove all around California and stopped their woody wagon only to play their guitars and sing songs.

"Blond," he said.

"Which one?" Mama's words were iron. Without stopping to check the color, he grabbed a box and shoved it at her.

Mama took the box from him and walked to the checkout line. Then she piled all the supplies on the counter.

No boy he ever knew changed his hair color. Was she really going to dye his hair?

Neither he nor Mama spoke all the way home. But when she turned the car off, he saw she was looking at him.

"I don't want to do this to you, either," she said. "You can thank Scary Jack. He'll get you if we don't hide everything the best we can. This will be like a disguise. You can pretend you are hiding out. Like somebody on TV."

"Like the Lone Ranger? Do I have to wear a mask?"

"No mask." Mama shook her head and opened the car door. "Just change your hair."

Would that hair coloring stuff burn his head? Would there be sores and scrapes? Michael shivered, even though it was Labor Day, and still hot in the car.

"This won't take long," Mama said, "and then you'll be a whole new kid."

An hour later Mama washed the thick paste from his head. Michael looked in the mirror and gasped. His hair wasn't blond.

"It's orange!" Michael's heart sank. He looked like Bozo the Clown.

"That's because your hair is so dark," said Mama, toweling around his neck.

"It's blond on the box," he protested.

"Your hair wasn't the right color for blond."

"I don't want to go school with orange hair," Michael protested. "Kids will tease me."

Mama's voice registered impatience. "They won't even know you. And you'll probably have to change schools again before there's time to worry about it." Mama stood back and surveyed his new look. "It's different from what you had before. We have to do this so Scary Jack won't find you."

"Can't we buy another box and make it blond?"

"I can't put coloring on again right away," Mama said angrily, as if he should know. "Your hair will fall out. You'll be bald." Mama's laughter fell on Michael like stones. He felt torn with emotion. He didn't know which was scarier—Scary Jack or the kids who would laugh at him at school.

Jack and Mary sat in the police station. Sighing, Jack leaned forward. "Is there any word? Any word at all?"

"The all-points bulletin is still out. I have to admit, I'm surprised we haven't seen a report on her car. Does your former wife have more than one car?"

"I wish I knew." Jack shrugged in frustration and felt Mary squeeze his arm.

"We saw her so seldom," Mary said. "And she never brought Michael over the way the visitation order said. We went to her house to pick him up—and she still didn't give him to us."

"That's why we got custody. But now I can't even visit." Jack knew he sounded discouraged. He looked up when he heard the sheriff's voice.

"Mr. Dutton, I feel I need to ask. Your wife seems very determined to keep the boy away from you. Is there any special reason why?"

"I wish I knew that, too," Jack said truthfully. "We had our differences, but I don't think they should get in the way of my seeing my boy." His voice rose with determination. "And I'm here today to try to see that they're not." He paused. "Alabama—were you going to check there?"

"We'll need to file for a writ of habeas corpus to search out of state."

"Again? That's three hundred more dollars."

"Each new state requires one. That's why I wondered if there is any additional information you have that might place her in a particular city."

Jack shook his head. "I'm sorry. I don't know how she keeps a step ahead of everybody."

"Do you want us to file in Alabama, then?"

"I guess so. Can't really afford it right now, but if there's a chance—"

"Go ahead," said Mary. "Anything you can do."

"I'll let you know next week," the sheriff said. "Wish there was more news now."

"Takes time, I guess," Jack said sadly.

Mary held Jack's hand as the two of them walked out of the police station.

They were standing by the car when Mary suddenly turned to him. "You know," she said, a puzzling twinkle in her eye, "it would be nice if we found Michael in time to meet his new brother or sister."

"His new brother or sister?" Jack frowned.

"Yes." Mary's smile broadened.

Jack felt an incredible thrill fill his body. "Now wait a minute," he said as a grin lit up his face.

Mary slipped her hand out of his and marched around to the other side of the car. Then she looked at him out of the corner of her eye and nodded.

"You're going to have a baby?"

"In March." Mary nodded, then rushed back around the car to hug him.

Jack felt tears on his face. Another son. Or a daughter to be with Stephanie, the daughter Mary brought to the marriage, who was now twelve and who Jack thought of as his own.

"Oh, I can't believe it," he said. He took Mary in his arms.

"Now, if we could just find Michael, we could all be a family together," Mary said.

Jack knew what she meant. No matter if he had ten children, or twelve or fifteen, there would always be a special place in his heart for Michael. He would never forget, not for a day, that Michael was missing, leaving a hole in his home and an ache in his heart. He put his arm around Mary.

"We'll find him," he assured her. "We'll never give up."

Chapter 3

∞

Michael was watching TV when he smelled something burn-ing. The chili on the stove. Michael leaped to his feet, dashed out to the kitchen, and yanked the pan off the burner.

Where was Mama? An eerie fear filled him.

"Mama?" he called out, louder than he needed to in the four cramped rooms. She'd started leaving him alone after school, now that he was almost eleven and she was off doing secretary work. "Don't answer the phone or the door until I get back," she'd say, powdering her nose and brushing her long red hair. She'd always finish in the bathroom by smiling at herself in the mirror, a wide-open smile so that her teeth showed. But this time she didn't say she was leaving. And he didn't hear the door shut. Where was she?

"Oh!" Mama cried out suddenly. From the echoing

sound, Michael knew she was in the bathroom. What was wrong? He ran to the door and knocked, remembering how she spanked him if he walked in on her.

"Mama!" He heard the fright in his own voice.

"Go away!" Mama sobbed, a long, panicked, echoing sound.

"What's the matter?" His hand went to the knob. He turned it half an inch before it stopped. Locked. "Open up," he called, pounding on the door.

"Go back to your TV."

"Come out," he shouted. "The chili was burning. I pulled it off the stove."

Silence. "I'm not eating," Mama said.

"Just come out," Michael insisted. "I'll give you a hug."

She laughed nastily. "Too late for that now."

Something in her voice sounded an alarm inside him. He heard the rustling sound of fabric in the bathroom, as if she were getting dressed. His hands pounded on the door. "Mama, come out and talk to me."

"Just remember that I love you."

"Come out and tell me."

"I'll tell you this, I can't stay in this world anymore. You'll find someone to stay with. Just keep running and don't let Scary Jack get you. After I'm gone—"

"Gone? Mama, where are you going?"

"I'm going to stay right in this room until God takes me."

He frantically rattled the knob and kicked the door. Usually, Mama would spank him for that, but now the silence was scarier than her words. He finally stopped kicking the door and listened to the eerie nothingness. His voice wavered. "Mama? Open up."

"No, I don't want you to see me like this."

Like what? "Let me in, Mama."

"No. I'm ready to die. You're better off without me."

"Die? What are you talking about?"

"I'm going to leave this world, son. I can't take care of you like a mother should."

"No, Mama, stop!" He frantically pressed his ear to the door and heard Mama moan. "Come out!" he shouted. "Come out now!"

"I can't fix what's wrong with my life. With my brain. I messed everything up."

"Come out and we'll fix it."

A breathy, mournful laugh. "Like a little punk like you could fix anything. Just leave me alone."

"Mama! At least let me kiss you good-bye."

"Just tell me you'll miss me."

Tears streamed down Michael's face. "I don't want to miss you. I want you to come out here and be with me."

He felt panic when only silence answered him. "Mama!" His voice suddenly burst forth in a cry. He kicked and hit the door in a frenzied rush of fists and feet. Then he heard a retching noise, like Mama was throwing up.

"Help!" he shouted, to anyone who might hear him. With one last pound of his fist, the door opened.

"I threw up, you little brat," Mama snarled. "I can't even swallow pills right." Mama sniffed and shoved him aside.

She ran into her bedroom and slammed the door shut behind her.

He stood outside the door, scared and alone, listening to his own heaving breath. After what seemed like forever, he walked out to the kitchen. His stomach growled as he scraped himself a bowl of the dried and blackened chili. He ate the whole potful, then lay awake on his bed the rest of the night.

He wondered what would happen if he ran away or called the police or told someone about Mama. Would Scary Jack find him if he told someone he was afraid that he might come home someday and find his mother dead?

Jack and Mary and their pastor watched baby Dan crawl across the living-room floor.

"We sure love him," Jack said to the pastor.

"Now Stephanie has a baby brother," the pastor said.

Mary watched a cloud of sadness gather on Jack's face. She saw that the minister caught his look. "I have to tell you, as thrilled as Jack is with the baby, neither of us can look at Dan and forget that he has a brother that should be there, playing on the floor along with him."

"A brother?" The pastor looked at Jack.

Mary nodded. "Yes. Jack's son was kidnapped by his mother, almost two years ago."

Jack shook his head. "I couldn't sleep for months. I'm trying to give the situation up to God, and think that if he wants me to find my boy, he will." Jack felt tears on his face.

"Of course, we're trying everything we can think of, too," Mary said. "I think I may have found his ex-wife's phone number. The police are checking it out. We've got our fingers crossed. We're hoping we can raise the two boys together."

The pastor shook his head. "My prayers will be with you—and with your son who is missing. What is his name?"

"Michael," Jack said, and the word scraped against his throat. He hardly ever said his other son's name out loud. Michael is a name I should be saying every day, Jack thought. Catch the ball, Michael. Eat your soup, Michael. Time for lights-out, Michael.

Instead, he said it mostly in his mind. And in his prayers.

It was a beautiful spring day and the air smelled fresh and clean. Michael took Gilligan, the yellow dog Mama let him have to keep him company, to the park, remembering Mama's admonition to be home early in the afternoon.

"Home at four-thirty. Not one second late." Mama's

words still echoed in his mind. "Or you won't go out for a month."

Now he walked over to the school at the edge of the park and pressed his face to a classroom window, hoping to see a clock. It was four-twenty.

Yet, as he and Gilligan trudged up to the house, he caught sight of Mama standing before the front window, her face set in a frown.

"I'm home on time," he protested.

"Just barely."

"I've got five minutes."

"No, you don't. Be ready to leave in two." Mama flounced away, red hair flying behind her.

"Where are we going?" he asked.

"Shopping," Mama said, but she wouldn't meet his eyes.

He sensed tension in Mama's posture as she drove downtown, her arms rigid at the steering wheel. Yet at the same time he smelled the floral scent of her perfume and saw that she wore earrings and lipstick. What was going on?

He was near panic when Mama stopped suddenly in the middle of downtown. "Here it is," she said. Michael looked out of the car window into a sea of tall buildings and people walking fast along the sidewalk.

"Where are we?" he asked.

"Downtown," Mama said impatiently. "You've been downtown lots of times."

"Where are we going?"

"Time to go. You're going to miss it!"

What was she talking about? "Miss what?"

Mama didn't answer.

He wanted to go home, where he could watch TV or ride his bike if he wanted. "I want to go home—" he ventured.

"I said, *come on*." There was impatient urgency in Mama's voice. He knew that tone; it often preceded a slap.

Michael followed Mama past tall buildings, men in suits, women in fancy dresses. Suddenly Mama stopped. Michael saw they were at a theater. Even though it was only five-thirty in the late afternoon, the neon lights already flashed the theater's name.

Rialto. Michael rolled the name around his tongue. Rialto. Was Mama taking him to a movie? She strode ahead of him to the ticket window while he stared at the flashing neon letters.

"One." He heard Mama's determined voice.

One ticket? What was this? Seconds later she came back to him and pressed the ticket hard into his hand.

"Go on in—show starts in ten minutes."

"Aren't you coming with me?"

"I got my own plans. Just go enjoy the show."

"I want you to come with me."

"Listen," she hissed. "You're ten years old. You know how to watch a movie."

"Where are you going?"

"None of your business. I'll be back later."

"When will you be back?"

Mama inhaled harshly, angrily lifting her wrist to glance at her watch. "I'll be back at ten P.M. Sharp. On the dot. Does that suit your royal highness?"

Michael's stomach growled. "I didn't get any dinner."

"Here—" she spat, and pressed a five-dollar bill into his hand. She pointed at the theater. "Eat all ya want . . . in there."

"What if I need you?"

"You're such a baby. I'm back here at ten."

He thought she was going to hit him, but a group of men strode by right then. Mama walked off suddenly, leaving him there with the ticket in his hand.

He instantly felt small and alone on the bustling downtown sidewalk in the dimming twilight. He was tall, he knew, for his age, but he had never gone to a movie alone before. And now he had nowhere else to go.

With a sigh, he walked to the theater and went inside.

As he watched the previews and then the newsreel, the warm darkness of the theater became oddly comforting. Tarzan dashed onto the screen, tossed aside snakes, leaped onto an elephant's back, and drank coconut milk.

That would be a fun life, Michael thought. No school. No Mama. Tarzan would toss Scary Jack aside as if he were a water snake.

Michael laughed and cheered along with the audience, and really began to enjoy himself.

But it wasn't long before the movie was over. Michael looked at the clock. It was only seven forty-five. Mama said she would be back at ten P.M. What should he do now? He wandered out in the lobby, read the posters, bought more candy and popcorn, and played a pinball game. He washed his hands in the rest room, drying them under the air machine.

He sauntered out to the lobby again. Mama was nowhere in sight. With a sigh, he went back into the theater and sat. The newsreel, previews, and Tarzan all over again.

When the movie was over, he walked out to the lobby once again. The clock said ten-ten. Oh no! He was late. Mama was probably standing outside the theater waiting, tapping her foot, getting madder by the second. Michael ran past the concession stand and pushed through the heavy glass doors. It took his eyes a moment to adjust to the darkness after the blaring lights inside the theater.

He waited. No one rushed up to him. People walked past without stopping. There was no familiar face. He shrank against a building and waited. Minutes crawled by. There was no sight of Mama. He sat on a ledge and waited, staring out into the darkness and listening to the rush of passing cars.

His back grew tired as he leaned against the hard, jagged bricks of the theater. Anger, and then fear, poured over him in waves. Where was Mama? Why wasn't she here? And what was he supposed to do now?

Reluctantly, he strode back toward the theater. He

pulled open the heavy glass doors when someone yelled at him.

"Ticket, please!" The woman who called out to him was heavy, angry, and loud, with mean, scowling eyes.

"I just went out to see if my mama was here yet," Michael said.

"No one gets in without a ticket."

"But I was just here."

"You can't reenter without paying."

Michael patted his pockets in the hope that money would somehow materialize inside them. The cloth under his hands was flat.

"Please—" He realized his voice was quavering. "My mama isn't here. She told me she'd be here at ten. I left the movie so I wouldn't miss her."

"How do I know you're not just saying that? Just want to get in free."

"I can tell you everything that happens in the movie, about Tarzan—"

"Maybe you came yesterday. Or last week. Can't let you sneak in free."

"Please. It's dark. And it's getting cold."

"Stay in the lobby the next time you need to wait for your mother," the woman said, picking up a phone. Was she calling the police? What would Mama say if she came back and found him in big trouble? She had warned him about getting in trouble. She said that Scary Jack could find them if he got in trouble with the police.

Michael went back to the ledge and sat. He felt tears start behind his eyes, then shame, because he was too old and big to cry. As minutes crawled by, parts of his body felt numb. His legs went to sleep, and then his back. He had a headache. Lying down on the ledge, he was wondering if he might fall asleep when someone jabbed him in the shoulder.

"Hey you, kid."

Michael was on instant alert. Mama always told him not to talk to strangers who came up to him. She said that strangers who talked to you first were the scariest strangers. Those kind of strangers might be friends of Scary Jack.

When Michael didn't speak, the man leaned close to his face. Hot breath surged across his cheeks. Michael smelled liquor, a scent he recognized from one of Mama's boyfriends.

"Got any money, kid?" The man leaned into his face again.

"No." Michael's voice broke. "Spent it all." His heart pounded. When the man didn't leave, Michael stood and turned his pockets inside out. A dime buried in the seam of his pocket lining fell to the ground and rolled along the sidewalk. The man grabbed it and rushed off without looking back.

Michael ached all over. Tears filled his eyes. He was thinking that maybe Mama had left him here forever when she suddenly materialized out of the blackness.

"Come on," she said, yanking his hand, sounding like she was mad at him instead of being sorry for being so late.

"Where have you been?" His voice was a weak whimper in the darkness as he followed her down the night-black street.

"Never you mind." How had she managed to get so angry with him already? Her harsh words silenced him briefly. They walked for several blocks. Each step seemed to heighten his exhaustion.

"I'm tired," he said weakly, finally giving way to tears. "I waited for hours. I thought you left me." He stomped his foot in daring protest as she opened the car door and gestured for him to get in.

"I told you I'd be back," she snapped. "Do you think I'd lie to you?" She turned the key, the engine roared to life, and the car sped down the street.

"You said ten o'clock," he protested, surprised at his own courage.

She leaned and cuffed the side of his face with an annoyed swipe. The car swerved. She swore. Now each word was edged with fury. "Something came up. It took longer than I thought. I got here as soon as I could."

"You took too long." He flung the words at her, then slid near the door as she reached for him again.

"I'll decide how long I take. I don't need to hear crap from you." This time her slap reached him, but he hardly felt it through his anger.

As the car lurched down the street, he yelled at her profile. "Someone tried to rob me. Someone could have kidnapped me. I was scared."

"You say one more word and I'll beat you black and blue." There was frightening menace in her low voice. He flung his face away and stared out the side window so she couldn't see his tears.

After they got home, he saw that someone had been in the apartment while he was gone. There were two dinner plates on the dining-room table, two tall glasses with stems, and a big salad bowl.

Mama had had a date and didn't want him around. The thought made him madder and sadder than ever.

Chapter 4

∞

Mary was clearing the table when the phone rang.

"Gimme Jack." It was a woman's voice, angry and raspy.

"May I tell him who is calling?"

"Just give him to me—"

"Jack—phone for you." Mary set the phone on the table, then went to get her husband. "Somebody who sounds mad," she whispered to him, then watched as he picked up the phone.

"Hello?"

Mary could hear the woman's screams from across the kitchen. She watched as color drained from Jack's face. He looked up, their eyes met, and he frantically gestured for her to give him a pencil. She rummaged through the drawer, finding a pen and an old grocery list, handing them to him.

"No—no—I didn't. You got that wrong," he was saying. Glancing up at Mary, he frantically scrawled, *It's Amanda.*

Ask her about Michael, Mary wrote, but Jack waved her away.

"No, you're wrong there, too. I didn't do anything like—"

Mary went to the other room, planning to pick up the extension.

"I know I won't." She heard Jack strain to keep his voice calm. "But he's my boy, too. I deserve to see—"

Mary lifted the receiver just in time to hear Amanda hang up. She rushed back to the kitchen. She planned to ask Jack what Amanda had said about Michael, but the question froze on her lips when she saw he was crying.

He sighed, then wiped his eyes with the back of his hand. "Lost my temper," he blurted.

"What did she want?"

"Just to tell me not to try to find Michael. Said for me to leave him alone."

"We haven't bothered him—or her. We don't know where to find them."

"Well, according to Amanda, we'll never lay eyes on him again."

Mary was surprised at the fire that rose inside her. "That's what she thinks," she said, and the determination in her voice caused Jack to look up at her. "Amanda doesn't know everything."

"She's pretty good at hiding out."

"Well, it's not over yet."

Jack walked over to Mary and put his arms around her. At his touch, she began to cry and the two of them held each other for a long time.

It was two weeks later, and Michael's anger had partially but not completely died down. They were in the car.

"Where are we going?" he asked, feeling brave.

"Just for a little ride."

The fake airiness in her voice was scarier than if she had really gotten mad. He waited as the car turned three corners and headed in a familiar direction. Now he saw the movie theater in the distance.

"Could you take me back home?" He gave it one last try.

"No, I can't." The lightness left and she was just plain mad. "I have an appointment and I'm late."

He sat back hard against the seat, then cringed with the thought that nothing could change her mind and she might hit him again. The car wove its way downtown. This time she stopped at the curb in front of the theater but didn't get out of the car. Without a word, she slammed a ten-dollar bill in his hand. Ten dollars. He had never had that much money of his own—not once in his life. But he looked at the limp bill with fear, not excitement.

It probably meant she'd be gone a long time. The thought of hours in the theater filled him with bleak despair.

His voice burst out. "Please, Mama—I'll stay home. You can go wherever you want. I won't leave our house. No one will see me."

Her look was filled with fury. "You'll stay where I put you. And you're right, you won't go anywhere else."

A car honked behind them.

"Get out of this car now," she said between clenched teeth. "And I'll be back."

The heavy woman with black curls sat behind the ticket window.

He handed her the ten-dollar bill.

"Brought money today, did you?" she asked without looking at his face. He nodded as his throat suddenly filled. He pushed the bill closer in her direction and looked off to the side.

"How many admissions?" the woman demanded. "Five people can get in for ten dollars."

He fought to clear his throat. "Just me," he said.

"One?" the woman asked.

He nodded at her, not trusting his voice.

She handed him the ticket and counted out his change. "You know it's not good to go to the movies alone. Never know who's in there." She nodded her head toward the theater. "You should bring a friend."

"My mom won't let me bring anybody," he said.

"You tell her this isn't safe." The woman's eyes held a mixture of anger and sadness.

"I'll tell her, if you don't tell anybody else I'm here alone." His heart pounded.

The woman sighed in frustration. "I won't tell on you, and it's not your fault. But you tell your mother to quit leaving you alone before something bad happens."

He nodded, afraid his lip would quiver if he said another word, and he rushed inside the warm, bustling theater. He bought popcorn and a drink, thinking he would buy candy later, when he got hungry again.

Again, the darkness of the theater comforted him. He bought Milk Duds after he watched the movie the first time, and a hot dog after he'd seen it twice. By now, he knew most of the movie by heart. It was at the end of the third show when he suddenly glimpsed long legs standing beside him. He felt a startle of fear as he looked up. The usher looked nearly as tall as the high-ceilinged theater.

Michael stared.

"Young man?" the usher addressed him.

Michael touched his chest, flustered. "Me?"

The usher frowned. "Is someone coming to pick you up?"

Michael nodded.

"Are you sure they're not waiting for you?"

"Yes." He had checked every time, between shows, and sometimes if the movie got boring. Mama was nowhere in sight.

Now the usher knelt and looked into his eyes. "I walked into the theater in back of you—at the beginning of my shift. That was six hours ago."

"I know." Michael swallowed.

"Where is your mother?" Was that worry or anger in the usher's frown?

"I don't know."

"But she'll be coming for you?"

Another swallow. "She always does."

"She's done this before, then . . . dumped you at the movies?"

Michael nodded slowly.

Now the usher stood and looked around. "I probably should tell someone—"

"No! No!" Now Michael jumped to his feet. "Don't tell anybody."

The usher eyed him. "You'll get in trouble at home if I tell . . . is that it?"

"Well . . . that or Scary Jack will get me. . . ." Michael caught his breath. He never mentioned Scary Jack to anyone. Mama said not to even think about talking about him. Someone who knew Scary Jack might tell him where they were.

"Scary Jack, huh? Who is that?"

"I can't tell you." Michael was embarrassed when his lip quivered. "Mama would kill me." He clapped a hand across his mouth, knowing he'd said too much. Suddenly the usher knelt beside him again.

"Kid, I don't know what's going on here. But I'll tell you one thing: leaving a kid like you in a theater alone for six hours is dangerous. Your mom could probably get arrested for that."

"And Scary Jack would get me." The words burst out before he could stop them.

"I don't know about any Scary Jack. But your mom shouldn't leave you without someone to look out for you. What if you fall in the dark and get hurt? What if you get sick? Don't you get hungry?" The man's eyes seemed to bore into him.

Michael breathed. "She gives me money."

The usher shook his head in frustration. "Okay, kid. I gotta get back to work. The show's about to start. But I'll leave it up to you. I think your mom is leaving you here way too long. And if you want me to do something about that—so she won't keep dumping you—I want you to come and tell me."

"But—"

"I won't tell Scary Jack. I'll tell someone who can help you."

"Who?"

The usher looked at him. "I have a feeling you don't want it to be the police, either . . ." he said slowly.

"No police."

"Okay. Someone else who can help." The usher patted his shoulder and stood.

No one ever helps me, Michael thought. I am all alone.

Jack was getting ready for work. The white shirt, the tie . . . By now, after twenty years at the railroad, Jack knew how was he was supposed to look. He had started working there way back when because Amanda said they needed more money. He had taken another job, too, and didn't get home until eleven o'clock at night.

The phone rang.

"Mary?" he called out, his tie half tied.

"Be right there." She was in the bathroom.

Feeling rushed, he picked up the phone.

"Was that you hanging up on me last night at midnight?" Amanda's anger chilled him to the bone.

"No. I don't know your phone number. You see to that. Couldn't call you if I wanted to. Now——"

Suddenly Mary was there, right under his nose, making shushing motions and holding out a pad. She wrote, *Keep her talking, then ask her where she is.*

Distracted from his train of thought, Jack shrugged helplessly. What could he say now?

Jack stammered, "Where's my boy?"

"He's not yours. Not anymore."

"I'm his father. He's half mine."

"You'll never see him again."

"I will if the judge gets hold of you——"

He heard a click. Jack's heart froze; he thought she had hung up. But then he heard background noise.

"Wait! What do you want, Amanda!" he called out.

"I want you to promise me you'll leave us alone. I know you called the other night."

"I didn't call," he said in exasperation. "But I'll never forget my boy. Just tell me he's all right."

"I'm not telling *you* anything."

The phone slammed. Mary and Jack stared at each other in the silence.

Chapter 5

∞

After a few times of being "dumped" at the movies, Michael caught on to the pattern. His mother would usually leave him for five or six hours. If he acted upset, she gave him ten dollars. She always said she'd be back long before she ever was, and never told him where she was really going. And he didn't leave the lobby of the movie theater anymore, no matter how late it got. The usher, who he now knew was named Ed, nodded, or waved at him occasionally, which left him both relieved and nervous. Would Ed actually tell someone about him?

Once he was in the theater in his favorite seat, fifth row from the front, three seats from the aisle, he began to feel he was in his second home. He discovered that after he watched the movie once, he began to focus on other parts besides the story. How the camera could focus on a scene outside in a jungle, then switch to a group of men sitting around a conference table. How a puff of smoke emerged from a smokestack and clung to the sky as a train chugged around a mountain. He found favorite scenes in movies— scenes where the characters moved around frenetically and scenes that were pastoral and still. He found himself waiting for his favorite scenes again and again as he watched a movie, once, twice, three times. He found himself wondering what it would be like to capture scenes like that, to work on a movie set, to plan the scenes and choose where to aim the camera.

Then there was the day when he and Ed walked out of the theater together. "Good-bye, Michael," the usher called to him. Michael saw Ed glance over his head at Mama, whose eyes burned with the familiar electricity of anger.

Why was she mad at him now? It was twelve-fifteen, after midnight. He'd waited patiently through three showings of another Tarzan movie. Mama yanked his arm and led him to the car with frantic, jerky steps.

As soon as they sat down in the car, she turned to him, her face angry outlines in the satiny black night.

"Who was that man?" she spat at him.

"Man?" Michael was bewildered. He was still thinking of Tarzan and Jane and Boy.

"That man in the theater."

"Oh, the usher."

"Yeah, the usher." She made an angry face.

"He works nights." Michael swallowed. "I see him there sometimes."

"I heard what he called you."

What the man called him? "He didn't say anything," Michael protested.

"I heard him. He called you *Michael*."

Michael blinked. "I guess so," he admitted.

"When did you tell him your name?"

"I don't know . . ."

"How does he know who you are?" Her face, hot and angry, moving close to his.

"I don't know."

"Didn't I tell you to watch out? Scary Jack is looking for you. He's looking for a ten-year-old boy named *Michael*."

Mama yanked the car into gear and surged out of the parking lot, glancing around and turning on backstreets.

"If I told you once, I told you a million times—"

"I didn't mean to tell him my name. I don't remember if I ever did."

"Well, he knows it. That's for sure."

Mama set her mouth then, and drove home quickly, slamming on her brakes at the red lights and stepping on the gas as soon as the light turned green. Michael felt his own rising fear. What would happen when they got home?

Back at the apartment, he rushed to his bedroom, threw off his clothes, then lay awake in his bed and listened to Mama, cursing and banging things around the apartment.

It was the next morning, early, when Mama woke him. She flicked the lights on angrily, then yanked the covers off his bed.

"You can't have your name anymore." The electric anger in her eyes bored into his.

"What?"

"Now that you gave your name out to someone downtown, you have to change it."

He stared at her. "I can't."

"What did you say to me?" She drew up to her full height, then rushed at him, grabbing his shoulders and forcing her angry face an inch from his.

"I'm Michael at school," he said softly. "My teacher calls me Michael. All my friends—" He swallowed. "I can't tell them I'm not Michael. They won't believe me." Tears that he'd held in all night threatened to spill. Mama remained still a moment, hovering over his bed.

She paused in angry thought. A full five minutes passed before she looked down at him again. "Your last name, then. We'll say I got married and you have a new name."

"Why?"

"You stupid thing! Because you told your name to somebody downtown who's an inch away from the police! Why didn't you use your brain!"

He didn't answer. A different name. Deep down, he knew he'd already lost part of his name. Michael Scott was the name he used at school. But Scott was really his middle name. Now Mama said he was going to change his name again. Michael felt anger and sadness surge inside him. He'd already lost one name. His other two names seemed like the only two things that belonged to him after they ran away.

"Well," she said. "Tell me what your new last name is going to be."

He didn't want a new name. He couldn't think of any name he'd choose besides his own. His mind was blank.

"Tell me now so I can go to the school with you and let them know." She stepped toward him and fear forced his words out.

"I don't know."

"Choose one. Before we leave this house this morning."

She left the room and Michael lay in his bed. Choose another name?

He looked around his bedroom. Wilson, on the tennis ball. In the bathroom, Crest, Pepsodent, Ajax. Ivory. His shoes, Keds. And P.F. Flyers. His underwear, Hanes.

None of them names he would choose.

He heard Mama, banging pans and dishes in the kitchen, and frantically racked his brain. He put on his school clothes and picked up his books. Math, English, history.

History. Lots of names in there. Washington, Columbus, Lincoln.

But now they were studying Indians. Native Americans, as his teacher called them.

Sitting Bull. Cochise. Pontiac. Sequoya. Geronimo. Hiawatha. Black Hawk.

There was that one Indian. Quanah Parker. His mother was a captured white settler, his father a Comanche war leader. Michael knew Quanah was a great warrior himself, leading a battle when American soldiers rushed into Comanche land to keep the Indians quiet. Quanah led his band, the Quahadis, in battle, and also helped them hide away from the soldiers for years. When they were forced to surrender, he led them onto the Indian reservation and into a new life. Quanah knew how to make his old enemies his new friends.

Scary Jack couldn't catch Quanah.

And if he did, Quanah would turn him into his friend.

Michael combed his hair and brushed his teeth.

He walked out to where Mama waited expectantly.

"My name is Michael Parker," he said.

"Parker?" she said, looking at him from the corner of her eye. "Where did that come from? A Monopoly game? Parker Brothers?"

"No," he said, suddenly angry, as if she were making fun of him. "You told me to choose and I did."

"Don't get smart with me," Mama warned. "Just remember that name. You picked it and now it's yours."

Mary half heard her son's voice as she stirred the soup on the stove.

"Let's play ball, Daddy . . ." She watched as Jack instantly set his newspaper aside to follow his four-year-old

son outside. Did Dan ever notice how he didn't have to
ask twice?

Did anyone, anywhere, play ball with Michael? Mary
couldn't help thinking that if there were two boys here,
they could throw to each other.

The phone interrupted her thoughts. "Jack Dutton," said
a woman with a gravelly voice. Mary's heart thudded.
Was this Amanda calling? Could it be? Mary couldn't tell
and she didn't dare ask.

"Phone, Jack," Mary called out.

"Who is it?" He looked up at her with a slight frown,
not wanting to leave the ball game.

She tried to keep her voice light. "Don't know. Some
lady. Dinner's almost ready."

She saw Jack pause at her words. "Better go in," he
said to Dan. "We'll play again after supper."

Mary busied herself with dinner but listened carefully
to Jack on the phone.

"Hello?" She watched him shift his feet, then suddenly
hold still. "Hello," he said again.

Suddenly Mary heard loud noises coming from the
phone. Jack pulled the phone away from his ear.
"Amanda, you're drunk," he said. "You're not making
sense, Amanda." Another pause. "No, I didn't call you.
Where's my boy?"

She saw him recoil and slam the phone back on the
hook. He looked at her and shook his head. "I know we
agreed I'd try to let her talk. But she was just screaming
and I couldn't help thinking of poor Michael."

Mary held her breath. "Just think of him and keep her
talking, and maybe she'll say something about where they
are especially if she's drunk."

"It's her drinking that caused all this trouble. She
wasn't like this when I met her. She was the prettiest
woman at church, and she was so sweet. Sure, when we
got married she wanted me to make more money. There
was never enough for her. Little did I know that the
money was going to booze."

"I just hate to think about what she put you through."
Mary's voice was bitter.

Jack shrugged. "When the drinking started getting bad—
when I found out about it—I wanted to get her help. I,
thought I could help her. But then she started to get abusive. She got so angry when I wouldn't give her money to
buy alcohol. She even called the police once, and told them
I was abusing her. I couldn't stay with her after that. I just
couldn't live with her. I didn't realize that her anger would
be so great that she'd never let me see my son."

Mary was about to say something, try to comfort him,
when Dan walked into the kitchen.

Jack scooped up the boy and hugged him tight.

When are we going to tell him he's got a brother? Mary
wondered. How long should we wait? We have to tell him
eventually. Especially if we get Michael back. How could
they say, *Hey, Dan, meet your brother that you've never
heard about before*.

We have to tell him someday, Mary promised herself.

Chapter 6

∞

*They moved again, just far enough for Michael to have to
change schools. Mama said they didn't have to unpack
after dinner—they could wait until morning. Instead of
watching TV, Michael watched Mama, sitting on the
couch beside him. The light from the single table lamp in
their apartment living room bathed her face in a golden
glow. He watched her breathe, the shallow rise and fall
of her chest. What was she thinking now, at the end of a
long day?*

"Why is Scary Jack so bad?" The question was out of his mouth almost as soon as it entered his mind.

Mama jerked her head toward him. Her eyes blazed. "Did he call here? Did you talk to him?" Her hand gripped his shoulder.

Puzzled, he shook his head. "No . . . I . . ."

"Did he come here? To the door?" Now she grabbed his shoulder, turning him to face her.

Yanking himself away, he wished he'd kept his mouth shut. "No," he managed.

"Tell me." She cupped his chin and forced his face close to hers.

"I didn't talk to him, he didn't come here." Michael's voice broke. "I don't remember him at all."

"Good thing you don't." She looked away from him, back at the TV.

"Tell me why." Again, the words burst from his mouth before he could stop them.

"Oh—I don't want to say anything."

Something in the tone of her voice changed. He had a feeling her words were rehearsed, as if she knew they'd have this conversation someday, and she had planned what to say to him. Curiosity burned inside him. "No, go ahead, tell me."

"Oh, all right." Her next words burned into his brain. "He attacked you."

"What?"

"He hurt you—in a way an adult should never touch a child. The wrong way for a dad to touch a son."

He felt totally bewildered. "I don't remember."

"Because you were too young. And you didn't know what was happening."

"Where were you?"

"I went to the store, then I came home and found him with you."

"He was hurting me?"

"You were in the bathroom . . . he took off your clothes."

Michael glanced at her with total bewilderment.

"He is a pedophile, a man who goes after little boys. I had to save you. That's why we ran away."

Michael felt sick inside. "Then why did he get custody of me? That time in the courtroom?"

Her voice thundered at him. "Because I didn't want to tell anyone what he did. I didn't want them to hold it against *you*."

His head swam with both upset and misunderstanding. Why didn't he have any memory if something like that had happened? "Why would he do that to me?"

"He's sick," Mama said. "That's why we have to stay away."

She stared into his eyes for a long moment, then, with a pat on his shoulder, she stood and went into the kitchen. Michael's mind was racing. Was it his fault that Scary Jack had hurt him?

Michael lay awake all night, wondering about that terrible day all those years ago. But he couldn't remember anything. Shouldn't he remember? If Scary Jack hurt him so badly, shouldn't he remember it? He remembered every slap Mama gave him.

What was wrong here? Had Mama lied to him about this? She lied to him lots of times, he knew that. But would they really be running away and hiding forever if what she said wasn't true?

Was he kidding himself? Was the memory of that day buried inside him, somewhere deep? Maybe he didn't really want to know.

Mary and Jack were driving home from Dan's Little League game. The boy had stayed behind to celebrate the victory with his friends.

"He was great out there today." Jack beamed.

"He certainly was." Mary smiled, but then her expression turned serious. "How I wish Michael could have been playing with him today."

"Mary, don't do this." Jack sighed.

"I just wish—" Mary paused. "We really should tell Dan about Michael."

Jack slammed his hand on the steering wheel. "We've discussed it, okay. When he gets older."

"When, Jack? I don't want it to be a shock to him."

"When he's old enough to understand."

"I never told you—" Mary began. "I went to a support group."

"What?" Jack frowned. "What kind of group?"

"It was for birth parents." At his puzzled look, she continued. "You know, parents who have given up their child for adoption."

"Hey, wait a minute. I never gave—"

"But it's the same thing. We have a child who is being raised by another family."

"Family." Jack shook his head. "I don't know that I'd call Amanda a family."

"Do you know what they said?" Mary waited until Jack turned to look at her again. He shook his head. "They said that you should tell the children in your family about the situation as soon as possible. So that they grow up with it naturally. So that it isn't a shock."

Jack sat straighter in the seat, shifted his shoulders. "I don't want the boy to carry the pain, that's all. I don't think it's fair to burden him."

"The situation isn't fair. But it's not your fault. And it's reality. The way things are."

Jack sighed. "He's just a boy."

"And he's stronger than you think."

Jack just nodded.

"So I think we better tell him," Mary said.

"He'll ask why we didn't say anything before."

"And we'll just explain everything to him."

Jack shrugged. "I don't know. Guess I always thought I'd find Michael before I had to worry about telling Dan. I hoped they'd grow up together."

Mary squeezed his arm. "Don't give up hope," she said.

Chapter 7

∽

Something was different when Mama picked him up on time from the movies. She arrived right at ten, just when he was thinking of buying another hot dog. Her cheeks were red and there was a smile on her face.

As she drove, Michael stared at her. When they stopped at a red light, she turned and saw that he was looking at her.

"What?" she asked, her tone light, almost playful.

He shook his head quickly, turned away.

"Michael—" Mama's hand reached out to try to tickle under his chin. He slid to the other side of the car before she could touch him. The light changed, and she pressed on the gas, throwing him forward.

"Move back before you fall out the door." Her words were commanding, but not scary, the way they usually were when she got mad at him. There was a lightness about them, like Mama was suddenly happy. What was going on? Moments later she turned the car down a different street, one that didn't lead to their apartment.

"Where are we going?"

Her smile grew, but she didn't speak.

"Aren't we going home? It's late."

Without looking at him, she said, "I want you to meet someone."

"Who?"

"You'll see." Again, the words sounded strangely light for Mama.

Michael sat like a stone as his thoughts raced. Who would Mama want him to meet?

Moments later the car jerked to an abrupt halt, and Michael peered out. In the growing darkness, he saw a row of dull, gray-looking office buildings bordering an alley.

"Where are we?"

"Just come with me." She stepped out of her side of the car, walked around, and opened the car door beside him with a flourish.

"Come on." There was enough steel in her words to draw him out into the night. She took his hand, also a rare happening now that he was thirteen. Without a word they walked down the street and turned the corner to where light poured out the windows of a small café and pooled on the sidewalk. The only light on the street.

"What's this?" Michael asked.

"He's in here." She gestured with her head. "The man I want you to meet."

Before his thoughts could register, they were inside the café. Through both the subdued lighting and his worry, Michael saw that the man in the booth was big. Bulky, bulbous, and full of muscles. He had piercing brown eyes and, Michael guessed by the assortment of scars and tattoos on the man's arm, he had lived an eventful life. Probably been in the army or something.

To his surprise, Mama walked over and sat on the man's lap.

"My son, Michael," she said, turning to the man and giggling as she tickled the man's cheek. She twisted a lock of hair around her finger and smiled at Michael.

The man wore a leather vest, through which Michael caught glimpses of an assortment of more tattoos. Michael was studying a tattoo of a knife when he realized the man was also looking at him.

"How old are you, boy?" The man's voice emerged from deep in his chest. There was a feeling of power about him that made Michael draw back. He was afraid, and his voice ventured out timidly. "Thirteen, sir . . ."

Was he supposed to tell the truth now? Mama said nothing, but a grin still filled her face. "Fourteen in July," she said.

"Think you're old enough to travel across the world?" The man tilted his head, waiting for an answer.

"I . . . don't know. I never thought about that. Never traveled much." Just moved from place to place when Mama decided it was time.

"How far away you been so far?"

Michael thought. Should he tell the truth? "Georgia," he said. Memories of that fateful day in the courtroom brought chills.

"That's no place."

"Florida."

The man wavered. "Nice beach, but not far."

"Alabama," Michael said, glancing sideways at Mama.

"Hop, skip, and a jump." The man sounded bored.

"Virginia, once."

"Still the South."

Michael had a sudden thought. "Where have *you* been?"

The man sat up straighter, and his chest seemed to swell. "Caribbean. The Orient. Europe. All of them. Every country there is, practically."

"Are you a pirate?" The words were out before Michael could stop them. He cringed, awaiting a slap from Mama. Yet she and the man burst into gales of laughter before the man kissed Mama's cheek.

"Guess I look like one, don't I, boy? Tell you the truth, there's a trouble with gettin' tattoos like this." He held up his arm so that the knife tattoo nearly touched Michael's cheek. "You might decide you'd like a knife on your arm on Wednesday . . . and be tired of it by Saturday. By then there's not much you can do." He and Mama laughed again. "Got this one in Seoul." He held up his other arm, and Michael saw a tattoo of a long thin, Asian-looking woman. "Wanna see her dance?" The man flexed his muscles and the tattoo on his arm flexed, too, as if the woman were doing the hula.

The man and Mama laughed together. Michael stared. His voice quavered. "What did you do in Korea?"

"Michael, Hank is in the army. Important guy," she said as the two of them began to laugh again. "He's a big shot. He travels all over."

"Wish I could travel," Michael said, thinking about the places he saw in the movies. Tarzan went to Africa. James Bond went from country to country in a silver jet, always stopping back in London to pick up his new car with the new gadgets.

"He wants to travel. He's a man of the world," Mama said, laughing and patting Hank's arm. Soon the two of them couldn't stop laughing.

Michael stared. Finally Mama caught his glance.

"Actually, you *are* going to travel. We're going somewhere," she said, in a sort of half-pleased, half-smug tone that caught his interest. "We're leaving next week."

"What about school?"

She waved her hand at him, as if he'd never have to worry about school again. "There'll be a new school where we are. And maybe you'll learn another language there . . ." She looked at Hank and the two of them laughed together.

"Adios, amigo," said Hank, and this time Mama's head fell back as she laughed with the big man.

"Taco tico," she said, and the two of them giggled again.

Michael felt fear in the pit of his stomach.

"Where are we going?"

Now Mama put her arms around Hank's neck and leaned up so that her thin, slender face pressed against the man's fleshy one. "Hank and I got married, Michael. We're moving to Spain."

"Married? Spain?" He couldn't tell which was the bigger shock. "Am I moving, too?"

The two of them laughed at him again.

"When did you get married?"

"Last week."

"Why didn't you tell me?"

"We're telling you now—"

"Why didn't you tell me before? Why wasn't I there?"

"You were at the movies." A scolding tone filled Mama's voice, as if he had chosen to go to the movies on his own and missed the wedding.

Michael's head swam. "What about school?"

"You'll go to school in Spain."

"What about my bike?"

"We'll get you a new one."

"I don't want a new bike."

Mama gave him a warning look. "We'll get you one. Just like the old one."

"But I still don't want to move. And I—what about Gilligan?"

He thought of his dog's familiar, comforting presence. The one friend he could talk to and feel safe with. He wouldn't leave without Gilligan. He would run away himself. It was as simple as that.

"You can't take the dog, son," Hank said. Michael didn't know what to say. And why was this man calling him son? No one had ever called him son in his whole life.

"I'll stay here—with Gilligan." His words sounded hollow, even to himself.

"We'll get you another dog." Shreds of anger were in his mother's voice.

He had lost the home where he lived when he was little. He lost his name four years back. Now he was going to lose his dog—and his home—all over again.

"Please let me me stay here. I can go to school and be with Gilligan."

"You'll go where I tell you."

Michael knew he was going to cry. He moved to walk away, but the man's hand—firm as an iron pipe—closed over his arm.

"Wait a minute, son. I got a buddy stationed out at the base with me. He's been lookin' for a watchdog for his place. Why don't I get him to take care of Gilligan until we get back?"

He wasn't ready to feel relieved, but somehow he did. "Could I stay here and live with him?" Michael asked.

"No." The man shook his huge head. "But I'm almost positive he'll take Gilligan. And we can call while we're there and see if Gilligan is all right."

Mama looked at him warningly.

"Can we find out for sure—and can we get Gilligan when we come back?"

"Yes," said the man. "I'll tell him Gilligan is only stationed at his place temporarily. He owes me a favor or two. I think he'll do it."

Michael left the café with an odd mix of feelings. He never imagined Mama getting married again. He always thought it would just be the two of them, running away to a new state if they thought there was any chance Scary Jack might be somewhere nearby. He remembered an odd remark from years before—when someone said that Mama was pretty. He'd looked at her with new eyes, tried to see her as something other than the woman who both protected and frightened him. He decided long ago that the scariest thing about Mama was that she was unpredictable—you couldn't tell what she would do next. Like the first time she dumped him at the movies. Like the night she said he had to change his name, and the day she dyed his hair. Like tonight, when suddenly his whole life was yanked away and she was married to this guy he'd never seen or heard about before.

The next day, as they packed their belongings and piled boxes in the living room of their apartment, Michael said to his mother, "Scary Jack won't find us now, will he?" He tried to laugh, but his laughter came out high and thin.

"You don't need to ever think about him again," said Mama. Why did the tone of her voice sound more like a warning than a comfort.

Spain. He didn't speak the language and he could barely find it on a map. But Mama was right—after a few months living in a foreign place, he quit thinking Scary Jack was hiding out around every corner.

Chapter 8

∞

"Hello?"

There was no answer, and Dan was about to hang up when he heard someone gasp.

"Who in hell's this?" It was a woman's voice. She was angry and she sounded scary. Was the woman mad at him? What should he say now? He was too afraid to hang up.

"I said who are you?" the woman yelled. When he didn't answer right away, she swore.

"This is Dan Dutton," he ventured.

"*Dan* Dutton?" she spat. "What are you doin' at Jack's house?"

What was he doing here? "I live here," he said simply, still scared and puzzled by this woman's anger.

"You live with Jack? That . . ." The woman's words descended into a sea of curses. Dan frowned as he thought of his dad, a calm and gentle tower of strength. What on earth had Dad done to make this woman so mad?

There was a silence. Then the woman snarled, "Is Jack there?"

"No, he's not. He's at work."

"Then what are you doing there?" The woman flung the words at him.

"This is my house."

"What do you mean, your house?" The words felt like slaps against his face.

"I live here. I'm Jack's son."

"His son? You're a liar, boy."

"No, I'm not. He's my dad."

"You mean he's got another son?"

"What? Another son?" Stunned with shock, Dan waited to hear the woman's next words.

"Jack never told me he had another boy. Then what's he doin' tryin' to find Michael? You tell him he'll never get within *miles* of Michael. I'll never let that—" Dan shrank against the curses. "He'll never lay a hand on my boy."

"Dad never hits anybody," Dan protested.

"I'll see that he doesn't." The woman slammed the phone down, leaving Dan's ears ringing while the rest of him was numb with shock.

Another son? What did the woman mean? Dad didn't have another son. All his life, he was the only boy. There was Stephanie, his half sister, thirteen years older. But she wasn't his friend the way a brother would be. He longed for a brother to play ball with, climb trees with, walk to school with, and talk to late at night while he was trying to fall asleep. Man, if he had a brother, he'd know it.

And this woman said he had one. She sounded crazy, but she had gotten his dad's name right. Jack Dutton. And the phone number, too. This was Jack Dutton's house.

Then who on earth was Michael? The rest of the day, Dan numbly cleaned his room, played his guitar, and waited. He didn't want to leave the house in case his mom and dad got back. He waited, hoping that angry woman didn't call again. Maybe he didn't want to find out who Michael was . . .

But if he was his brother . . . Dan paused, his fingers still on the guitar. How could he have a brother he didn't know about? He thought of Dad and Mom and how they loved him and Stephanie. If they had another son, that son would be sitting with them at Thanksgiving dinner, and they'd have a cake for his birthday, and they'd go hunting and fishing and play ball. They'd go to church together, and maybe even play guitars together.

So who on God's green earth was Michael?

Dan got tired of playing the guitar, so he just waited for someone to come home. He heard the door open and shut and he knew it was Mom, back from shopping. He was about to leap up and go ask his mother if he had a brother, but something stopped him. He wasn't sure why, but he thought he should wait until his dad got home from work and ask him.

That night at dinner, Dan stared at his father across the table. He watched his dad's warm blue eyes, freshly slicked black hair, and calm smile. Could he really be keeping such a major secret from him? While Dan was speculating, Jack looked up and caught his glance.

"More potatoes?" he asked. "I've been kind of hogging them down here." Mom and Dad laughed good-naturedly. Still, Dan thought he might have caught a flicker of worry in Dad's eyes. He wasn't sure, but before he could think much more about it, the words dropped from his mouth like two cold stones.

"Who's Michael?"

His dad's mouth froze midchew. He sent a long stare in Dan's direction.

"Michael who?" Dad asked, slow and tentative.

Dan saw his parents exchange a worried glance.

"I don't know," Dan started. His father's stare was penetrating. "A woman called here today. Mad as blazes. Sounded like she was mad at you when she called. Then she screamed at me. Kept yelling about some guy named Michael."

"What did she say exactly?"

Dan felt his heart beat with fresh recollection of the woman's sullen anger. "She said Michael is your son." Now his gaze held his father's.

Dad blinked and looked away. As Dan studied his father's face, he felt Dad's warm fingers reach out and wrap around his own.

"Guess I gotta tell ya. She's right, son."

"What do you mean?" How could that frightening, furious woman be right?

"Michael is my son."

Chills draped Dan. There was a stunned, speechless silence.

"She said I have a brother. Are you saying that's true?"

Dad nodded. Mom said, "We always planned to tell you—"

Dan raised his voice without thinking. "How come nobody ever told me about this?"

Now Dad looked away. "I planned on telling you—when you got older."

"But I'm fourteen."

Dad sighed. "I just kept hoping things would be different by the time I said something. I didn't want you to find out the way you did."

Dan felt blown away. "So if I've got a brother, where is he?"

Dad shook his head. "I don't know."

"Well, why isn't he here tonight? How come his clothes aren't in the closet and he doesn't go to my school? Why isn't he sitting here having dinner with us?"

"His mother kidnapped him."

"His mother?"

"Amanda—my former wife."

"The woman who called here . . ." Dan confirmed, just to settle things. He had known, dimly, in the back of his mind, that Dad was married before, long before he himself was born. But they never talked about it. And he never pictured Dad sitting at another kitchen table with a different family . . . where there was another son.

"That woman has Michael?"

Dad nodded. "I hope and pray every day that he's all right."

Dan stared. "Why don't you go get him back?"

"I've tried. I can't find him. But I won't give up."

"Can't you call the police?"

His dad's smile was painful. "I call them about every six months, son."

"What do they tell you?"

"They don't have any luck. She's too fast for them. Always stays one step ahead." Dad reached in his back pants pocket for the worn, brown wallet. As Dan watched, Dad flipped the wallet open to a picture of a small, dark-haired boy dressed in pajamas. The boy was smiling and sitting beside a Christmas tree. Dad silently handed the wallet to Dan.

"This is Michael?" Dan stared. He ached for this father's sadness.

Then a sudden thought struck him. Was there any way he could find Michael? Maybe his dad had given up—but he wouldn't. He'd look for Michael, and when he found him, he'd finally have a brother. He handed the wallet back.

"Eight years old," Dad said. "The last day I saw him."

"So now he's . . ."

"Twenty-two," Dad said, without stopping to figure or count.

He's been gone fourteen years, Dan thought. He was kidnapped right before I was born. Dad's been searching for Michael for fourteen years.

Spain was exciting, and Michael grew close to Hank. For the first time Michael began to feel like he had a normal family—a mom and a dad, and a regular life. For the first time in a long time Michael felt happy.

But the happiness didn't last long. Mama and Hank started fighting, and she started drinking a lot. It wasn't long before they left Spain and moved back to the States, to Georgia.

Soon after their return, Mama dropped the bombshell.

"I'm getting a divorce," she said.

"No!" Not from Hank, the only man who ever looked out for him.

"It's none of your business!" Mama's eyes filled with fire.

"Then I'm leaving home!"

"How can you leave me! After all I've been through." There was fear in Mama's eyes, and suddenly Michael realized she could no longer tell him what to do.

"I'm going to have my own life." Michael knew he sounded braver than he felt.

"You're being selfish."

"I'm old enough. I'm twenty-three," he said. "I need to be on my own."

"I still need you." Their eyes met, and Michael knew, for the first time, that Mama *did* need him. All these years, all the time when she acted mad and like she wished he would go away and leave her to her own life, she had needed him.

Michael swallowed. "I love you," he said, the words closing his throat. No matter what Mama did to him, he still loved her. "But now I'm grown up. I'll still visit you."

"Don't do me any favors."

"Did you think I'd stay here forever?"

"I didn't think you'd leave me if I asked you to stay."

"I've stayed long enough." Yet his heart pounded even at the thought of going. Mama was the only constant in his life, and even if they yelled, they each knew they had no one else.

So he didn't move far. He still saw Mama. And now that he was back in the United States, every once in a while Scary Jack crossed his mind. Was it possible that Scary Jack still looked for him, even after all the years that they were gone? Would he even recognize Michael now, tall and slim and all grown up?

Michael had to get on with his life. He got his own apartment, a job selling suits in Nordstrom's, and for the first time in his life he felt in control of his destiny. He didn't have to worry about Mama. He didn't even worry about Scary Jack. He was finally on his own.

Erin and Dan had a date the night before. He could have talked to her then. So why was Dan writing her a letter? They had been dating for six months and they talked almost every night. So why did he feel like he needed to write to her? Was there something he thought he couldn't tell her in all the nights they talked on the phone? Curious, Erin slid a fingernail under the flap and drew out two sheets of paper.

> *Dear Erin,*
> *There's something I never told you.*

Oh no, thought Erin. She felt her pulse quicken. The first time she saw Dan, back in high school, something had torn loose in her heart. He had a wonderful smile, and better than that, he was really a nice guy. The nicest guy she'd ever met. So what was this letter?

> *I have a brother.*

A brother? So why was this a big deal? Why write a letter? What was so earth-shattering about having a brother? Erin had two brothers herself, which she mentioned every once in a while if the conversation happened to steer itself around that way. A brother. Why was this front-page news?

> *I better back up. My dad was married before.*

Oh. Still no big deal, right? But did he think that she wouldn't want to date some guy who was from a family where there was a divorce? That sounded like the Dark Ages, Erin thought. What family didn't have at least one divorce nowadays? Why didn't he think he could just tell her all this, some night on the phone?

My brother is from his first marriage. He's nine years older than I am.

That made sense. She knew Dan and Stephanie and his mom and dad. And she'd been to their house a few times without seeing any photos of anyone else.

My dad's divorce was messy.

Weren't most of them?

My brother's mother (would she be my stepmother, even if she got a divorce from my dad before I was born?) kidnapped my brother from the courthouse right after my dad got full custody.

His dad got full custody? Way back in the . . . Erin calculated in her mind, way back in the fifties? Or maybe the sixties? That might be something interesting. And kidnapping someone from the courthouse? It sounded like a *Movie of the Week.*

We haven't seen him since then. I mean my dad hasn't. I've never seen him. I guess I just thought I should tell you just in case . . . well, just in case.
 Love, Dan

Just in case? Just in case what? Erin stared at the end of the letter again. It felt like it was unfinished. Staring at it again, she picked up the phone.
 Hearing Dan's familiar voice, she said, "It's me . . ."
 "Oh." He sounded nervous.
 "I got your letter."
 "You did?"
 "Yeah . . . it was interesting."

"Didn't know what you'd think."

"Uh . . . this brother?"

"Yeah?"

"Have you ever tried to look for him?"

"Well . . . there's something else I didn't tell you."

Erin felt a sinking feeling, but her curiosity was stronger than that feeling. "Just tell me this time. You don't have to write a letter."

"His mother, my dad's former wife—I think she might be crazy. Or even violent. So I don't know what she'd do."

"How would she know?"

"Well, if I ever got close enough to actually find him, I might run into her. She used to call and threaten my dad."

"Someone threatened Jack? Who would do that? He's one of the nicest guys I ever met."

"I know, but this woman is crazy. Really. So we don't know if my brother's okay."

"I think you should find out. Surely your dad's thought of—"

"He told me he thinks about him every day."

"Then you need to find him."

"Dad said he ran out of money trying to look."

"But we don't need money. We'll just look in places that are free. Like the library."

"Okay, I guess. Maybe. I don't know . . ."

"You don't want to?"

"I don't want my dad to get hurt. If his ex-wife is . . . you know."

"Think how hurt he's already been."

"I know . . ."

Chapter 9

∝

Michael was a natural salesman. And at Nordstrom's, he
learned about the suit business. Fabrics and weaves. Cuts,
lines, and styles. More than anything, though, he learned
that men didn't really want Nordstrom's to behave like
Nordstrom's. They really wanted to shop for suits at 7-
Eleven. Hurry in, get what you want, and leave. They
might want one line of conversation, such as "How'd you
like the score last night?" Or "Nice weather we're
having." But they didn't really want to try on ten suits
and spend hours deciding on the appeal of each one, like
women. They wanted to buy their suits and go. Like
Nordstrom's was a drive-up window.

That understanding helped him, and the commissions
started coming in. He had more than enough for rent, and
a few of his own Nordstrom's suits. He even bought
something he'd longed for a long time. A camera. He
laughed at himself. Who did he think he was going to
become? One of those big movie directors? Cecil B.
DeMille? Dino De Laurentiis? He only knew that when
he aimed his camera and took a shot, it reminded him of
those long-ago days in the movie theater, when he tried
to figure out how moviemakers captured scenes on film.
He tried to visualize how the final photo would look after
he took the picture. Sometimes, he was totally off. Some
of his pictures were out of focus, lacked contrast, or were
shot at too great a distance to have the impact he wanted.
Others were right on target. He bought an album and kept
them all, reviewing them at night and on weekends.

He really enjoyed the photography, but he didn't have as much time to take photos after he met Corinne. He saw her several times at a restaurant where he went on his lunch hour. Michael stared at her for weeks without getting up the courage to say hello. But one day she walked right up to him and said hello.

"Do you eat here every day?"

"Not Sundays and Mondays. Not on my days off," he said.

She laughed, though he didn't think he'd made a joke.

"I see you here all the time," Corinne said. "You always stare at me."

He felt himself redden.

"Do I know you?" she asked, peering into his face.

"No." The word stuck in his throat.

"Then why do you stare at me?"

He swallowed. "I didn't know I was."

"Are you ever going to ask me out?"

A fresh blush warmed his cheeks. "I don't know." As he shrugged, he saw the smiling expectant look leave her face, and she turned to go back to her own booth.

"Wait." he said quickly. "Will you go out with me?"

"Sure," she said.

"Okay," he said.

"When?" Corinne prompted.

"Uh . . . this weekend? I don't get off until nine on Fridays. But Saturday night—"

"Saturday night would be fine," she said. "But there's just one thing . . ."

"What?" Michael asked, instantly worried.

"If we go out to dinner, could we eat somewhere besides here?"

After he and Corinne started dating, Michael realized for the first time that he'd been lonely before he met her. There was just Nordstrom's, his camera, and long, solitary hours in his apartment. After they dated for several months, he knew he didn't want to be without her. From the moment she first spoke to him, Michael felt there was a world for just the two of them.

Now, after today, he hoped he would never be alone again. There was just the two of them here at the courthouse. No Scary Jack. No Mama. No one from Nordstrom's or the dental office where Corinne worked. No one to tell him he couldn't be here, or that he'd have to leave when they said he needed to go.

Just them.

"Any witnesses present?" the justice of the peace asked.

Michael cleared his throat. "We didn't bring anyone."

"That's okay. I can get someone from down the hall."

Michael sighed with relief.

Corinne smiled at him. After the justice left the room, she asked, "Shouldn't we call your mother? Wouldn't she want to be here?"

"I don't know," Michael said. "I think she'd say I'm leaving her." He hadn't told Corinne everything about Mama yet.

"But won't she be mad when she finds out?"

"It will be too late then. We'll be married already."

Corinne smiled that grin he loved.

He asked her, "What about your mom and dad?"

"Mom would want a big church wedding. I think she'll be secretly relieved when I tell her she doesn't have to sew my dress and plan a reception."

The justice of the peace bustled back into the room. "I found two witnesses. Ten dollars extra. Just kidding. No wedding guests?" the justice asked.

Michael shook his head.

"Sometimes it's better that way." The justice looked down at his book. "We'll get started, then."

"Do you, Michael Parker, take this woman, Corinne Bell, to be your lawfully wedded wife, in sickness and in health, for richer for poorer, as long as you both shall live?"

"I do." Michael looked in Corinne's eyes and thought, Do I ever.

"And do you, Corinne Bell, take this man, Michael Parker, to be your lawfully wedded husband, in sickness and in health, for richer or poorer, as long as you both shall live?"

"I do," Corinne said.

Michael felt intense love flood over him. But a deeper worry nagged. What was he afraid of?

"With the authority vested in me, I now pronounce you man and wife. You may now kiss as husband and wife."

Michael took Corinne in his arms. Her lips felt warm and sweet under his. So what was this nagging fear he sensed? As soon as the kiss was over, he looked up.

"I wish you a long and happy life." The justice of the peace smiled.

Michael didn't even hear him. He was preoccupied, wondering why he should he worried on the happiest day of his life.

As they were leaving, he caught sight of the heavy courthouse doors and it hit him. "I know what's wrong," he said.

Corinne looked at him quizzically. "Something's wrong already? We've only been married five minutes," she joked.

"It's this place."

"Seemed fine to me. Nice enough guy. Didn't even charge us the witness fee—if there really is one."

"No, it's my problem. I couldn't figure out why I felt . . . scared to death."

"Well, thanks a lot." Corinne dropped his hand.

"No, it has nothing to do with you—it's me."

"So what's your problem?"

"I felt like running out of here. I didn't know why. But now I do. It's just that—I hadn't been in a courthouse since I was kidnapped from one."

"Kidnapped?" She raised her eyebrows.

"My mother kidnapped me from a courthouse once." Michael felt guilty for not confiding in her before now.

"Why did she need to kidnap you? Didn't you live with her?"

"I did . . . but my dad got custody."

"How did that happen? Wasn't it unusual for men to get custody back then?" Corinne asked.

"I don't know how it happened," Michael said slowly.

"You mean you never asked your dad?"

"I never saw him again."

Corinne's face was serious. "Why not? If he got custody."

"After Mom kidnapped me, she told me he would hurt me . . ." Michael was surprised to feel the old fears coming back. "So we kept running away."

"Maybe you ought to find him. You're probably bigger than he is by now."

Michael shuddered slightly. "She sure knew how to make me scared of him. I've actually been running from him my whole life. But I don't know why . . . or why he'd hurt me."

Sensing that Michael's mood was turning somber, Corinne tried to change the subject. "I'm the one that's kidnapping you this time." She reached out and took his hand. "Where do I send the ransom note?"

He held her hand all the way out to their car in the parking lot.

His heart was still pounding as they drove away.

"I need to tell you something." Dan reached for Erin's hand.

There was her smile, warm and accepting.

"My degree will be in music, but I've always had the feeling I might want to be a pastor someday."

Erin's face fell instantly. "No. I can't believe you just said that."

He watched as she shook her head. What was she thinking?

"I have a strong belief in God."

She squeezed his fingers. "You're very talented. But my grandfather was a pastor—"

"So was mine!" He smiled at her again.

"Then you know what a pastor's life is like. Not much money."

"Money's not everything."

"You get voted in. It depends on how the congregation feels about you. You can be removed, and then you have to find another church."

"That doesn't happen to everybody!"

"If you're a young pastor looking for a church, there's lots of competition, and from older pastors who are looking, too."

"I thought about being a choir leader . . ."

"That's a little better," Erin acknowledged, "but it's still stressful. You still have to please so many people."

"Actually"—a smile played about Dan's lips—"there was something else I wanted to talk about."

"Changing the subject, huh?" Erin couldn't resist smiling back at him.

"Yeah. Uh, I wanted to ask, will you marry me?"

Erin reeled, backing up a few steps as if he'd physically hit her. "Whoa! That is a different subject. But we weren't through with the first one."

He looked at her as if she were crazy.

"Do you promise me that you won't preach if you become a pastor?"

He raised his hand as if taking an oath. "I don't know what to say. If God wants me to, how can I say no?"

There was a pause. "But He hasn't asked you yet, has He?"

"No. He'll let me finish my music degree."

"And you won't go asking Him, will you?"

He hesitated. "No. It would have to be His idea. I want Him to come to me."

"Can you promise me you won't seek this out?"

He sighed. "Yes. That I can do."

She reached out to take his hand. "Then I'll marry you."

During the next months, as they prepared for the wedding, Dan couldn't help but think what a good team he and Erin made. Figuring out how much the wedding would cost. Deciding who to invite. Choosing the church. Erin would be a good pastor's wife, Dan thought . . . if only she was willing to marry a pastor. And he still thought he would be a pastor . . . if only he could be one and still marry Erin.

"There's still one thing," Dan said, taking Erin's hand as they walked out of the caterer's office.

"Your tux," Erin said. "We'll pick it out tomorrow."

"No—it's not that."

She stared up at him.

"My best man. I don't have one."

"Well, that should be easy to fix. Just call somebody."

Dan stopped still. "I can't call the right person."

"Why not? There's still a week and a half."

"I can't find this guy's number . . ."

"I'll help you . . . oh." Erin's face suddenly colored as the realization dawned. "It's Michael . . ."

"Everyone always asks their brother to be the best man. The guy who will be your friend for life, even if you fight half the time."

"I wish we could find him."

"We could try . . . I remember one time my dad said the police told him Michael's mother had a house in Jefferson. It would be the world's biggest long shot if she were still there. Let's look in the phone book."

They looked, then called all three Duttons in Jefferson. Nothing. No one knew of a Michael Dutton who was about the right age.

"There's one other guy I could call," Dan said, at the end of the afternoon.

"You mean we looked all this time and there's somebody else?" Erin asked.

"He's the only other guy I can think of."

"Okay."

Erin waited patiently as Dan picked up the phone and dialed. He waited, three rings, until someone answered.

Dan took a breath. "Dad?" he said. "Will you be my best man?"

All through the wedding ceremony, Dan thought of how Michael should be there, smiling and wearing a tux like him and his dad. Had Michael had his own wedding? Was he married a long time with a large family? Or was he alone? The questions always ran through his mind. And the biggest question of all: would they ever find Michael?

Chapter 10

∞

Seeing his new baby brought thoughts of his missing family to Michael's mind. Somewhere out there, Scary Jack didn't know that he had the most exquisite granddaughter on earth. And what about great-grandparents? Were any of them still alive? Who did this tiny girl look like? The baby girl was fair-skinned, with rosebud lips and thin threads of shiny dark hair. Michael felt captured by her beauty.

"Sarah?" Corinne said. "Or did we decide on Allison?"

"What about Megan? Or Cara?"

"I thought Natalie was right up there."

Michael shook his head. "I can't decide right now. Just let me hold her." He took the small bundle in his arms and felt a sure and calming peace settle over him. Had his dad ever felt like this? Did his dad even see him after he was born? Michael's finger touched the girl's tiny cheek. What would it be like to know this feeling—and then lose track of your child forever?

But if his dad was really Scary Jack, maybe he didn't care.

Why did he have this sorry feeling in his heart for all that his father had lost? His father, who had supposedly molested him in the bathroom.

If that was true, why did he get custody? If that was true, why did he and his mother always have to run?

"I take it you've decided on the name? Tessa? Amber?" Corinne looked at him.

"No." He smiled at her.

"What was all that serious thought, then? You had a distinct frown on your face."

"I was thinking about my dad."

Corinne sighed. "Honey, I can imagine how you feel—becoming a father and thinking of your own father, and the type of person your mother says he was."

Michael shook his head. "I just don't know. I think about all the horrible stories my mother told me and I can't imagine a father doing that to his own child. I just don't know if it's true."

Corinne smiled at him lovingly. "The only thing I know is true is that you're going to be a terrific daddy." Michael looked down at his new daughter and smiled, too.

Now that Dan and Erin were married, they would be moving into the married students' dorm at the university. Dan was helping Erin pack up her belongings when the doorbell rang.

"Mom?" Dan was surprised to see her. "Is something wrong?"

Mary smiled, but it was obviously forced. "I just had to tell you something . . . before you left."

Dan felt Erin step up beside him.

"Is everything okay?" Dan felt a concerned frown creep onto his face, but Mom didn't look upset.

"Everything's fine . . . I just had to let you know that I found her address."

"Whose address?"

"Amanda's. I'm pretty sure it's hers. Actually, it was Stephanie who found it. It's in Sebastian—Florida—and since you're going to live within fifty miles of there . . ."

"Actually, I think Sebastian's only about twenty miles from where we'll be."

"Anyway, since you're going to be down there . . . I thought you might want to drive by the house. You might even see Michael . . . mowing the lawn . . ."

Dan felt chills. "Are you sure it's her?"

"I went back over some old papers. Phone bills from way back. I didn't think there would be anything listed under her real name. And there isn't now. But at one time there was a phone registered to an A. Scott at this address in Sebastian. Maybe she took the name Amanda Scott. And Scott is Michael's middle name."

Dan tried to shrug, to show unconcern, but this was the only time he'd ever felt like he might be coming close to tracking down his brother, and he felt an involuntary surge of excitement. Now he reached out to take the slip of paper Mom handed him.

"I'll give it a go, if I'm down that way sometime."

"You don't have to." Mom smiled at him. "Maybe you're not that interested."

"I'll probably head over that way tomorrow."

Dan saw the sign: SEBASTIAN—NEXT RIGHT.

He felt tension and excitement surge inside him. Never before, in his whole life, had he been this close to his brother. He worked the wrinkled paper with the address out of his wallet.

Seventy-five Honeygrove Avenue. Michael's address. He hoped.

Did Michael think about him the way he thought about Michael? Dan wondered. Could Michael imagine him the way he was at this moment, a blond-haired twenty-five-year-old man surging down the street in a shiny red car with new tires, moving soundlessly toward his unknown fate and hoping against hope to see the face he'd longed to see for nearly half his life?

Could Michael guess? Could he somehow feel the intensity of Dan's hope?

Was there any chance Michael's mother had ever told him he had a brother? How would you bring up a subject like that, twenty years too late?

Oh—by the way—you have a brother you never met. And maybe you never will.

Dan drove on. Almost there. Maybe almost to Michael. What would he say to Michael the first time they spoke?

Let's be brothers. Maybe it's not too late if we start now. Just the thought made his heart thud.

Dan easily found Honeygrove Avenue and pulled the car up to number 75. There it was—white clapboard, black shutters, set well back from the road with a long curving driveway. Michael's house.

Dan squared his shoulders, sucked in his breath, and climbed out of the car. He continued to stare at the house as he stepped closer. It sat strong and silent as a mountain as he approached.

He stood on the doorstep and breathed slowly a couple of times before he rang the bell. What were the right words to say?

Hi, Michael. I'm the brother you never knew about until this moment.

He heard footsteps behind the door, sensed someone might be looking out the front window at him, and nearly turned and ran.

A woman threw open the door. Was this Amanda, the crazy woman who caused his father—his whole family—so much pain? "Yes?" She bit off the word, and his voice suddenly locked inside his throat.

Why did he ever think he should do this? He put on his "hoping to become a pastor someday" voice. "Ma'am,

I was wondering if I might speak to Michael."

"You think he's here?" The woman spat out the accusation. Dan sensed she was challenging him, and he wasn't sure what the right answer was supposed to be. He shuffled his feet and tried to look calm. "I'm hoping he's here."

"And who might you be?" The woman took a step closer. A curled rope of long red hair fell across her shoulder.

Dan's heart pounded. "A friend . . . from a long time back."

"Some friend." She grimaced. "What kind of friend doesn't know Michael moved out eight years ago?"

"Oh." He tried to sound nonchalant even as his heart sank.

The woman paused and narrowed her eyes. "I don't think you even know Michael."

Dan swallowed. "It's been a while," he said awkwardly. "Like five or six years."

"Like never."

"Sorry." He stepped back and lifted his hands in a gesture of surrender. "Made a mistake, I guess. Didn't mean to bother—"

"Who sent you?" she called out as he backed down the step. "Who are you really looking for?"

"Nobody," he said.

"You don't ask for Michael if you're looking for nobody."

"I got the wrong house."

"No, you didn't. This was where Michael lived."

"I can see he's not here now." He tried to back away, step-by-step, as her voice rose and her words raked down his spine. "Who sent you?"

He shook his head as his mind floundered for words.

"Was it Scary Jack?" she yelled at him.

He stopped abruptly, looked up, and caught the fury in her gaze. Was she calling his kind, gentle, wonderful dad Scary Jack?

Seeing his hesitation, she rushed at him, and stopped with her angered face only an inch away from his. Her finger poked his shoulder angrily. "You tell Scary Jack I know he sent you. And he's not getting within miles of Michael, do you hear me?"

He didn't dare answer—it seemed as if responding to her accusations would be like admitting who he was. Instead, he imagined himself as a future pastor, drawing away from wrath and not letting his own anger ignite when someone got mad at him. He eased away, stepping back, but not fast enough to keep her from grabbing his arm.

"Not now and not ever!" she yelled, flinging his hand away.

He didn't speak, but strode purposefully down the curving sidewalk. He waited a few moments in the car before putting it in gear. She still stood on the porch, her hands on her hips, when he uttered the only response he had. Under his breath, he murmured, "He's my brother." But his words were lost in the roar of his engine as he hurriedly sped away, sure that Amanda stood there on the porch, watching until he was gone.

What was he doing here? Michael groaned inwardly. It had been a stupid fight with his supervisor, but Michael had quit in a fit of rage. Dumb move. Now he was out of work and sitting here, in the green room at a TV station, waiting for a job interview. This was crazy! Who did he think he was, anyway, Sean Connery? Charlie Chaplin? Probably more like one of the Three Stooges. Maybe if he got up and walked out of here right now—

"Michael Parker?"

A young blond woman in a short skirt burst through the studio door and looked around eagerly. When he didn't answer, her eyes dipped to her clipboard, then back to him. "Are you Michael?"

He held his breath and nodded. What was he doing

here? Just because one of his best Nordstrom customers, Keith, worked for a TV station and told him he'd be great on the air, didn't mean he could actually do it.

The young woman half smiled at him. "Come with me."

They walked through a door into a room with banks of dials, buttons, lights, and TV screens, then through another door onto a soundstage.

What was it Keith had said? *Just be yourself and have fun, man.* He could do that, Michael decided, if his heart wasn't pounding and his hands weren't so sweaty and he didn't have this feeling that his brains had totally abandoned him.

Too late to back out now.

The soundstage seemed empty with the exception of a man sitting in an easy chair next to a coffee table as if this were someone's living room. Then Michael caught sight of two other men with cameras. The man in the easy chair stood and Michael felt a fresh wave of nervousness flood over him.

"Michael Parker? Ted Carpenter . . ." said the station anchor.

"Good to meet you, Ted," said Michael. Keith said you should call the TV personalities by their first names, as if you'd known them two years instead of two seconds.

"Tell me about your interests, Michael."

"Photography." Michael smiled. "I take pictures. And I sell clothes."

"What kind of pictures? Are they rated X or just PG-13?"

"Rated G for sure." Michael laughed. "Scenes, actually. A train curving around the bend with a puff of smoke bursting out of the smokestack. A country house just at the time the sun outlines each brick. Stuff like that."

"Interesting," said Ted Carpenter, in a tone that suggested photography was about as boring as it could get.

"It's actually, fun, too." What was he supposed to say? "Make lots of money at it?"

"Millions—in my dreams," said Michael.

"What about awards? Got a wall full of certificates?"

"Well, I did win the . . ."

Ted looked as if he couldn't care less. Michael knew he must be failing miserably. Now Ted actually looked at his watch. "How did you get into the business? College major?"

"No, actually, I went to the movies a lot as a kid. I kept noticing scenes in the films and wondering how they were photographed. Finally I got brave enough to pick up a camera myself."

"Really."

"Yeah." Now Michael managed to grin. "I was in movie theaters a long time. My mom used to dump me." He laughed, even though it wasn't remotely funny and was actually one of the bleakest and scariest memories of his life. He still recalled his deep fear that his mom might not come back, and the way minutes stretched into unbelievable hours as he waited on the curb outside the theater.

"You know, Michael, that could be called neglect," Ted Carpenter said. "Leaving a little kid alone at the movies."

"What can I say—she gave me money for Red Hots," said Michael. He sensed his grin wasn't quite as wide this time.

"Still, would anyone do that now? Would you?" Ted asked him.

"No," Michael said, suddenly serious. "I have two little girls. Megan and Melissa. I wouldn't leave them alone for a minute."

"Lucky you made it through with nothing bad happening."

Michael sensed the other man's interest awakening. "Every time she left me, I told myself maybe this was the last time. That's how I got through."

"Were you ever scared?"

"I was lucky. Chester the Molester never found me."

"Were you angry with her, Michael?"

Was he? "I didn't know enough to be angry. She said my father was trying to kidnap me and we had to stay out of sight."

"Did your father try to steal you away?"

How should he answer? "I don't know. If he tried, he didn't succeed."

"Did you ever see him?"

"Never." A shudder of fear filled him suddenly, and a new thought crossed his mind. What if he did go on TV and Scary Jack saw him? What would happen? Was there still someone out there to be scared of?

"Never seen your father?" Ted tilted his head. "Do you want to?"

"I don't know. I don't know the man." His words came out harsh. He was thinking, I'm still scared.

"Interesting story." Ted Carpenter held out his hand. "We appreciate you coming here today."

Even though he thought he had failed the interview miserably, he shook Ted Carpenter's hand and gave him a smile. "Thanks for talking to me." He rose to leave, thinking this was probably a wasted day.

"Michael?"

He looked back to see Ted's puzzled smile. "That was one of the best interviews I've ever done."

"Thanks." Michael smiled again and turned to head for the door, but Ted's words continued and drew Michael back. "You looked at the camera at the right time. Your answers were the right length so I could get into the conversation. And you gave good answers. Ever been on TV before?"

"In my dreams I always win the *Jeopardy!* Daily Double." The two men laughed together.

"College training?"

"Closest I got to college was selling students suits in the Nordstrom's men's department."

Ted Carpenter paused and studied him. "On the morning show—do you think you could talk to our guests the same way you interviewed with me?"

"Sure," said Michael.

Ted Carpenter gave him another look. "You might hear from us," he said.

Chapter 11

∞

First, Erin found the papers. Scraps, they looked like, the paper on which Dan sometimes wrote down their budget for the week. Or the shopping lists she'd write if she was headed to the store.

But these weren't lists. There were words like *work, faithfulness,* and *prayer.* Phrases, too. Like *Trust in God. Have faith. Seek knowledge.*

What was Dan doing? She didn't dare even think. She didn't say anything that day. But then, about a week later, she found more scraps of paper. On the edge of the coffee table. Near the shelf where he kept his Bible. On the nightstand, where Dan sometimes emptied out his pockets and left a receipt or two.

Erin didn't say anything about them until the morning when she awoke and caught him preaching to the bathroom mirror. She was just waking up when she heard his voice. Opening her eyes, she watched him from the bed.

"And with faith in God . . . and a pure heart . . ." Dan pointed at the mirror.

She wanted to laugh, but nothing had ever seemed less funny.

"I know what you're doing," Erin said from the bed, struggling to sit up.

"I was going to tell you about this," Dan stammered.

"We talked about it before we got married." Erin felt her voice rise. "Remember? I said I'd marry you if—"

Dan blurted, "I've been waking up in the middle of the night—"

"You know what it's like to be a pastor's family? You have a glass house. You can't even be yourself. And what about our son Kyle? He's just a baby . . ."

"God's been working on me," Dan said.

"We have a good life, Dan. Two good jobs. A son. If you think—"

"Money's not the most important thing."

"Not the most important—but try to live without it sometime. Pastors have a hard time, Dan. No home of your own. Moving from place to place. And it's not like there's much salary."

"Do you think I haven't thought of all this?"

She was silent. "The stress . . ."

"Do you think I can say no to God?"

"You promised me."

Neither of them spoke. She heard the whipping sound as he tied his tie, then watched as he combed his hair then left the house. She numbly climbed out of bed, showered, and prepared to go to work, filled with dread that somehow their life would never be the same. What was Dan thinking?

Technical director. That was his title now. Michael was surprised that he missed Nordstrom's. He was surprised that he had time to miss anything, now that he directed four live shows a day. There were the news shows, the wrestling shows, the religious show, and the kids' show—*Romper Room*. His head swam as he tried to picture all the people he'd met and talked to.

With a sigh, he walked toward Ted Carpenter's office.

"Michael," Ted said. "This isn't really a great time for me to talk right now—"

"I just need five minutes."

"I've probably got two minutes."

"I can say it in that."

Ted looked at him curiously. "Go ahead."

Michael sighed. "I need a change."

"That wrestling show getting a little old?"

"No, it's not that."

"Your morning schedule a little heavy?"

"No." Michael took a breath. "I want to go back to sales."

There was a tense silence. "I'm not quite sure I understand," Ted finally said.

"I need to make a career change." Michael paused, then gathered his courage. "Away from television."

"Now wait a minute. I don't know if you know what you're saying. Do you have any idea how people fight to get in here? This isn't a small market. And you didn't even go to broadcasting school, if I remember right."

Michael felt his heart pound, but he said nothing.

"This totally blows me away, Michael. Is there trouble at home?"

Michael hesitated. He and Corinne were fighting. She said they had no kind of life with him working all the time. "No," he said finally.

"This job isn't one you can get on a whim. Like Sears or wherever you worked—"

"Nordstrom's. I was senior manager of the men's department."

"Still, the salary isn't comparable. Nothing is comparable."

"It's the right work for me. I know it now. I've been here three years and I need to leave. I'm not doing you a favor if I stay."

Ted shook his head. "Maybe you need a vacation. I think you should think this over. I'll never understand—"

Michael put his hand on the other man's shoulder.

"You don't have to. Just draw up the papers and let me know when they're ready."

"If you change your mind." Ted shook his head.

"I won't. I've thought about this for months."

"I can't say we'll have a hard time replacing you. People would kill for a chance at this."

It should have been a thrilling moment, Erin thought as they walked through the door of their new church for the first time. Yet she felt tension the instant she and Dan entered the pastor's office. A feeling of dread hovered even as the pastor and assistant pastor introduced them to the others—people from the parsonage who held positions in the church.

This should be a happy moment, Erin thought. This was the fulfillment of Dan's dream, a dream she decided she could no longer keep him from realizing. What was wrong here?

"I think our new music pastor should now see the budget," said the assistant pastor.

"I don't have it prepared for today." The pastor dismissed the assistant pastor and turned to them. "Are you settled in your new home?"

Erin and Dan nodded.

"You had your tour of the church?"

Another nod.

"They need to see the budget. They need to know what's happening here," the assistant pastor repeated. Erin's hands were sweating.

Dan's voice wavered. "I don't know that I need to see the complete budget right away. I know what my salary is, and you already reimbursed me for long-distance calls for the interviews before I came—"

"What other benefits were promised?" the assistant pastor asked.

"Health insurance," said Erin. We hope to have another baby someday, she thought.

"Did they tell you that the church building is for sale?" asked the assistant pastor.

Erin's heart sank. We moved all this way, she thought. We gave up other plans, other jobs, and our first home.

"It's not," said the pastor's wife. "Why do you keep bringing this up?"

"Because," said the assistant pastor, "now I know for sure. I found out yesterday. You listed it for sale in the multiple listing book."

"I would never do such a thing," said the pastor.

"You should know better," said his wife.

Erin felt a drop of sweat at her side.

The assistant pastor smiled wanly. He opened his planner with a flourish. "Here is a copy of the listing." He held out the yellow paper, then yanked it away just as the pastor reached to grab it. Instead, he handed the paper to Erin and Dan.

There it was. A listing in the multiple listing book. Church for sale.

"This isn't how it looks," the pastor said quickly. "I need to explain—"

Erin's heart sank. How could anyone explain away a listing in a real-estate book? She thought of the hours and dollars she and Dan had spent to move, the time it took to interview, and the two jobs they left behind.

What would happen to them now?

Why was he nervous? Michael rode up the escalator to the third floor, glancing quickly at the men's department as he strode past. The store even smelled the same—like new fabric, leather, and aftershave. Even the Nordstrom's personnel department still looked familiar, although it had been six years.

He had held various sales positions since leaving the television station, but none of them matched Nordstrom's. Michael sat down and waited for an interview. He thumbed through a magazine, and waited some more. His lunch hour was nearly over when a young woman in a gray suit finally said, "Michael Parker?"

He followed her down the hall to her office, then sat across the desk from her. She stared at him. "Could you tell me a little bit more about what you are looking for?"

"A position in the men's department."

"Where you worked at one time."

"Yes. Well, I actually reached management level. I was the manager of the men's department."

"But then you left."

"Yes."

"Why did you leave—and why do you want to come back?"

"I left because I had a disagreement with an upper-level manager."

"Do you think that could happen again?" She tilted her head at him.

"I don't think so."

"Why not?"

"Because I know this is right for me now."

"What do you mean?"

"I've worked in TV. I sold cars. I even sold government uniforms for a while. And I like this the best."

She paused, looked at his application again. "You do have a lot of experience."

"More than ten years in sales. The TV part was really sales, too. I mean, I had to sell myself continually as the right person for the job. TV is very competitive . . . like retail sales."

She looked up at him. "You won't want to go back to TV?"

"Nope." He shook his head. "Got tired of it."

"But didn't you get tired of this, too?"

"Not really. Just got tired of *him*. The store manager."

She stared at him. "Well . . ." She extended her hand. "We're still interviewing. So I'll get back to you."

Michael rose to his feet. "I was number one in sales. Three years running."

"I'll keep that in mind."

"Really sold a lot of suits."

"We'll let you know."

After he left the interview, it amazed Michael how nervous he still was. Why should he worry? He knew exactly what the job entailed. He could do it in his sleep. He finally decided he was worried about what Nordstrom's thought of him, and if they ever forgave him for the argument that had led to his quitting before. It was a long time ago . . . but sometimes burned bridges stayed burned.

Chapter 12

∽

What would you do if your father found us?

Michael had just come home from his job at Nordstrom's. They had called and hired him three days after the interview. Now he and Corinne were sitting at the table alone, long after the girls had left to go play in their rooms.

"I don't know if he's even looking. He never looked hard enough to find me. I don't even know if he's still alive."

"What if he is?"

"I guess I'd tell him not to hurt my kids." He paused. "I'd fight him if I had to."

"What if he stole one of them?"

"The kids? You got that wrong. My mom stole me." Amanda saw his kids sometimes, but not often. He couldn't believe she was still dating. Still looking for the right man, even though she seemed to be the wrong woman for almost everybody.

"But didn't she steal you so he wouldn't take you?"

"Yeah." Michael sat up and pushed his plate back. "And now you got me." He grinned at Corinne. "And no one can steal me away again."

"I just wonder if he's out there someplace."

"He might have ten other kids. He may have forgotten all about me by now."

"Impossible. You're unforgettable," said Corinne. She grinned at him, cocked her head, and then suddenly turned serious. "I just wonder if you ever want to, you know, find out where he is . . . so you won't worry that he'll come after our kids."

"My mom said he was like that, but now I'm sort of wondering."

"What do you mean?"

"She said he molested me, but I think I'd remember if he did." He paused. "I thought if it happened, I'd remember something . . . maybe just how scared I was. But nothing ever came to mind. Ever."

"So . . . maybe it never happened?"

"Maybe it's still buried."

Corinne looked up him. "Don't you ever want to find out? For your own sanity?"

Michael thought. "Yes . . . and no. I wish I could somehow find out in advance if what I was about to find out was good . . . or bad. What if I find out something that changes my life?"

Corinne frowned. "Like what? What could that be?"

Michael paused. "What if I was only the first kid he hurt? What if he hurt a ton of others, and he's in prison now?"

Corinne stared. "I can tell you've been thinking about this. But look . . . if that was what happened, don't you think you'd know?"

He frowned back.

"If he was some kind of child molester or something, you'd probably see him on the news and know that was him. Or the police would find you and ask you."

"He never found us," Michael said slowly.

"Or wait—" Corinne sat up straighter on her chair. "I know how you'd know."

Michael stared at her.

"Your mother would tell you," she said firmly. "She'd say you were finally safe from Scary Jack. That he wouldn't get within miles of you from now on."

"You think—"

"I *know* she couldn't resist a chance to tell you she was right."

"Maybe—"

"Because she's got to feel bad about all that stuff— making you dye your hair and change your name. She couldn't resist telling you it was all for a reason and all necessary and she was right all along."

Michael shook his head. "I can't argue with you. Mama's always right."

"Except maybe she's really wrong. Maybe he never hurt anybody. Not even you."

Michael's mind reeled. "I'd be willing to find out if I knew it was safe."

"You ought to find out either way."

Lying in bed one morning, Erin decided that resting when she wasn't tired was the hardest thing she'd ever done. She could read—for about half an hour. She could sew—for about an hour. But thoughts of what she could be doing constantly tortured her mind. She thought of casseroles she could make, the floor she should wash, and laundry that must be piling up in the basement. She also spent too much time thinking about the church. Although it hadn't been sold, she felt the pastor was never fully honest with them. She felt that people were keeping secrets and she worried about the church's finances. Spending all these hours lying in bed gave her too much time to worry. But at least she was finally pregnant and if the doctor ordered bed rest, that's what she'd do—lie in bed.

When the phone rang, she was grateful, sure that it must be Dan.

"Hello?"

"Is Dan there?"

"No, he's at the church."

"I'll call him there."

"Is this Margaret?" Erin pictured the bookkeeper's blond hair and glasses.

The woman on the phone hesitated. "Yes."

"This is Erin. You can leave a message with me."

"Actually it's about you, Erin."

"Really?"

"We had a meeting and set a policy. You are no longer allowed to enter the church building."

"What do you mean?" Erin sat up in bed.

"Your job is bed rest. You are to stay home in bed."

"Did you talk to Dan about this?"

"I was calling to tell him now."

"But I'm the pastor's wife. How can you say I can't go to church?"

"Your doctor says you can't leave your bed."

"But . . ." A sour, sick feeling filled Erin. "I don't think this has anything to do with my baby." She swallowed. "I think you don't want me to look at the ledgers."

"That's ridiculous. You have no call to look at them anyway."

"But I might—and somebody can't take that chance."

"You have no right to make an accusation like that. You have no idea what takes place in church business."

"And someone doesn't want me to find out. The board has my résumé. They know I was a bookkeeper by trade."

"I'm going to tell the board about this conversation."

"And I'm going to tell Dan."

"You know that the board oversees him. You're threatening his job by accusing the board."

"If there's something wrong at the church, someone needs to know. It will only get worse if nothing is done."

Margaret hung up on her then, and Erin sat in the bed,

holding the phone in her hand and wondering what she'd just said. The dial tone droned in her ear, but her mind was numb. Her job as a pastor's wife was to support her husband. And now maybe Margaret was right—maybe she had threatened his lifelong dream with a few angry words.

Dan stared down the length of the conference table, feeling an almost palpable tension in the air.

"After much consideration . . . and prayer . . . Erin and I are here to tender our resignations as pastors of this parsonage."

"Your first church? You can't resign."

"We're feeling deep regret, yet we also feel that until the financial situation—and other problems—are resolved, we cannot serve the Lord here."

"No one else will take you if you quit your first church. They won't want to take a chance."

"We'll have to leave that to God."

"No parsonage will want to take a chance with you. They won't want to pay the expense of moving you if they know you are a quitter who won't see it through."

"We don't see another option."

"Good luck." The bookkeeper's voice was bitter. "Do you know how many other pastors are out there, looking for churches? Do you know what the competition will be?"

Dan felt Erin's eyes on him. She had never wanted him to be a pastor. But now she was silent, letting him do the talking.

He squared his shoulders and bore himself up. "If God wants us to have a church, we'll have one. We have to trust in Him. That's all that I can say."

Dan's last day in his office was a bitter experience. It was maybe the last day in his life that he would ever be a pastor. Dan's emotions warred with one another as he sat by the phone. He had hardly slept the night before.

As a pastor, he'd never planned to lie to somebody before. Yet he promised himself he'd make the call today, while he was still here, before he allowed himself to get depressed over leaving his first church. He didn't even have to look up the phone number that his mother had given him. From the moment she told him the number that might belong to Amanda, the number sequence was burned into his brain.

Still, he was torn. What if Michael really was in a bad situation? What if he was in prison? What if he was dead?

I have to know, Dan realized, his heart pounding.

Shaking, his hand found the numbers, one by one.

As the phone rang, he was tempted to hang up. Two rings. Three. Four. He sighed with relief that maybe Amanda wasn't home now.

"Hello?" It was the same raspy voice he had heard when he was a teenager. He would never forget that first angry phone call when he discovered he had a brother. Now years later, thoughts of it still left him shaking.

He forced himself to speak. "I'm looking for Amanda Dutton."

"Who is this?"

"Amanda, this is Grant Olsen, from Sunset Lawn Mortuary."

Silence.

"We selected several numbers in your community and we're prepared to offer you—"

"What are you selling?" He heard suspicion in her voice, and fought the temptation to hang the phone up.

"Not selling anything," he said quickly. "We're just calling to let you know that it is possible to preplan your funeral service."

"Funerals cost money."

"They do—I won't deny that. But you can set up part of the paperwork ahead of time before you make any other arrangements. You can give us your information—names, dates, religious preference—and then we'll have all of the details ready when the time comes—"

"I don't wanna give out my personal stuff. Don't know who you are."

You sure don't, he thought, holding his breath. It was all he could do not to hang up the phone right now, quick, before she got mad, like all the other times. He was about to give up when something within him forced his voice onward.

"It looks like someone has already sent in part of your information."

"Not me. Do you think I'd be dumb enough to give out stuff like that?"

He cleared his throat. "Let's see here. Your name is Amanda Dutton."

"Huh, you coulda got that out of the phone book."

"You live in Lake Worth, Florida."

"Phone book again. You a bill collector?"

He ignored his rising anxiety. It was time to go for broke. "I see here . . . that you have a son named Michael Dutton."

There was a second of heavy silence before her scream pierced Dan's brain. Then he heard heavy thuds of shattering glass amid Amanda's curses and screams. She's breaking things, he thought. I made her so mad she's trashing her house. Fear and worry kept him glued to the phone. What would Michael be like after spending a lifetime with this woman? Was he safe? Was he even alive?

Silence. He fought the urge to hang up. If there was a chance—any small chance—that he might hear something that would give him any kind of clue, he had to wait.

The silence stretched. Then Amanda picked up the phone and breathed—harsh, ragged gasps that gave him chills.

"I know you're there. You've been after me for years. Well, you can just sit there. And I'll leave this phone off the hook for hours—"

"I—I didn't—"

"Yes, you did. Been after me for years. Well, I'll just leave this phone here all night and you can pay the bill—"

Dan hung up. He was shuddering. Why was he so afraid of this woman he'd probably never meet again? Because she stole his brother, and if she'd do that, what else would she do? And would she somehow hurt Michael now, now that he'd called? And how did she know he wasn't who he said he was?

You make one lousy private detective, Dan said to himself. Better stick to being a pastor. But now he didn't have a church. He dropped back into his office chair and felt his heart pounding away.

And I still didn't find Michael, he thought. I'm no closer. And time could be running out.

Chapter 13

∽

They sat there, the two of them, on the couch, with their son Kyle between them, and baby Cassie in Erin's arms. Both Dan and Erin were silent. They had nowhere to go today. They knew the phone wouldn't ring. No one would call and want to talk to the pastor, now that he had a different phone number and wasn't a pastor anymore. Their work at their first church was over . . . had been over for three months now. Dan felt relief and sadness all at once. No one could believe he had quit. But how could they stay there, where someone had obviously mishandled the funds, and there were rumors that the pastor was having an affair with the bookkeeper? There was no way, Dan thought, that he could remain in that hornet's nest and be the kind of pastor he wanted to be.

But what was awaiting him now? He glanced at Erin beside him, relieved and grateful that she wasn't telling him this all happened because he had decided to be a pastor. Erin was watching some TV show—*Jerry Springer*.

Dan said, "I've heard of him, but I've never watched before."

"It's lost loves," said Erin.

Dan watched as two people hugged. He glanced at Erin, the only woman he ever fell in love with. A white phone number flashed onto the screen.

"I'm going to call these people," Erin said suddenly. She stood up to get a pencil and paper.

"What for?" Dan asked.

"I want to get the information about how they find people."

He gave her a puzzled look.

"Wouldn't it be wonderful if they could find Michael?"

A feeling of dread filled Dan. "Oh . . . I don't know about that."

Now Erin looked at him.

"I don't want to hurt my dad in any way. I mean, he's made it this far. He's up in age—and . . ." Dan looked down as Erin started scribbling speedily.

"We can call," Erin said quickly. "We don't have to tell him. I'm just calling to see what the deal is."

What was Erin doing? Dan thought. She held the receiver to her ear, then said her name and her phone number. She put the phone down and looked at him. "They said that due to the overwhelming popularity of the show, they're not able to take our call right now. They said it could take from four to six weeks . . ."

Dan sighed. He wasn't sure whether it was relief or disappointment that he felt.

Erin was sitting in the garden before dinner when the phone rang. Maybe, she thought, it will be someone about a new church. An interview for Dan, she hoped, crossing the lawn, entering the kitchen and picking up the phone.

"Erin Dutton?" A woman's voice, friendly and bright.

"This is Erin."

"Erin, this is Arliene Dunn of BigHugs.com. I have to tell you, Erin, we think your story is very interesting . . ."

"It's been quite an experience," Erin said. "Knowing Dan has a brother but having no idea where he is."

"Tell me why he's not with you," the woman said, and Erin told her everything. The courthouse. The moves. The long years with no idea where Michael was. She finished and waited. What did Arliene Dunn think?

"I'm just getting this information down," Arliene said.

Erin had a sudden thought. "What would something like this cost? I would need to ask my husband."

"Could *I* speak to your husband?" Arliene asked.

Erin paused. What would happen now?

"Phone for you, Dan," she said, handing him the phone. She'd always loved to listen to him on the phone, ever since he had become a pastor. The empathy in his voice. The soothing tones of his words. His hearty laugh that lasted just long enough. Now Erin waited.

"My brother. Right," Dan was saying. "I don't know," he said. "You see, we haven't talked to my dad yet. But if we agree to this, what would it cost?"

Erin watched as Dan listened.

"Let me talk to my sister," he said finally. His eyes met Erin's as he hung up the phone.

"I don't know," he said. "I don't know if this is the right thing to do."

"Wait!" Erin suddenly raised a hand. "I have an idea. We don't need to tell your dad."

"What?"

"He doesn't have to find out."

Now Dan stared at Erin. "What do you mean?"

"I'll call BigHugs.com. If they find Michael, I'll go and meet him. Just me. My mom will watch Cassie. We don't even need to tell your dad if it's bad news. If it's bad, we won't tell Michael where your dad is."

Dan frowned. "You're not going alone to meet some

stranger. We don't know anything about him. He could be—"

"Then you come with me."

"It's not cheap, Erin. It's two thousand dollars."

"But what is your dad's peace of mind worth?"

"He's gone along this far, and . . . you know, Erin, they have a kit. A kit that costs less."

"Stephanie!" Erin said suddenly. "She might want to go in on this with us."

Dan shrugged. "I guess you can call her."

Erin dialed.

"I got her machine," she said.

They sat at the table. "What do you think about telling your dad?" Erin asked.

Dan shook his head. "I just hate to stir all this up with him again. We haven't talked about it for a long time."

"But if something is going to happen, maybe we need to let him know. Maybe telling him is actually the right thing, so he can help us decide."

"I just don't want to see him hurt . . ."

The phone rang again. 'That's gotta be Stephanie." Erin reached for the phone.

"Erin, this is Arliene Dunn again."

"I'm waiting to hear back from my husband's sister— she might help contribute to the search."

"Erin, I want to tell you that I'm drawn to your story and I would like to help you . . . how would you feel about that?"

Erin sat quietly on the couch and told Arliene Dunn everything she'd ever known about Michael, the brother-in-law she had never seen.

"Did you hear anything today?" Dan said.

Erin knew that his words had a double meaning. He was asking if she heard from a church, but he also wondered if she heard from BigHugs.com.

Erin shook her head. "The phone was quiet today." After being a pastor's wife, she never dreamed she'd dread a quiet phone.

Dan said, "Maybe Amanda hid Michael away so well that no one can find him."

"I still won't be sorry I looked," Erin insisted. "Even if we never hear back."

But they both wanted to hear back. She could hear the longing in Dan's voice and feel it in her heart. Maybe if one of the things they worried about—a church or BigHugs.com—came through, they could forget about the other . . . for a while. But even as her mind danced around possibilities, Erin knew she could never forget . . . either the church or Michael. She really wanted to find them both. A new job and a new brother. It was hard not to want both of them right now.

They were in the middle of dinner when the phone call came.

"I'll be there," Dan said, with a springiness in his voice that Erin hadn't heard for a long time. "With my wife?" He paused. "Okay, I'll let her know." He hung up the phone and turned to where Erin and Kyle sat at the dinner table.

"We have an interview."

Erin felt a tingling inside. "At a church?"

Dan smiled at her. "Mountain View Assembly of God."

Now Erin was filled with nervous excitement. Mountain View was a large congregation. "How did you get the interview?"

Dan still smiled. "I'm hoping this is where God is sending me. But if it's not, we're still going there for a reason. Maybe I just need to see what an interview at an untroubled church is like."

"And what did they say about your wife?"

"They want to talk to you, too."

Erin felt a solid knot of fear in the pit of her stomach. *I know what an interview is like,* she thought. *I heard my grandparents talk about waiting to get a church. The thing is, being chosen to lead a parsonage is nothing like qual-*

ifying for a job in business. You can be the smartest or
the most qualified or the most experienced and still not
be chosen as pastor. It all depends on the parsonage's
vote.

The butterflies in her stomach wouldn't hold still. She
thought about the interview constantly as days passed.
Why would they want to talk to her? What would be the
right thing to say?

The two of them were talking about the interview over
dinner a week later when the phone rang.

"We must be about to get that church." Dan smiled at
her. "The pastor's phone always rings during dinner."

Erin smiled at him and picked up the phone.

"Erin Dutton?"

"This is she."

"This is Arliene Dunn at BigHugs.com."

Erin felt her heart pound. "Yes," she said. "Have you
found Michael?"

"We feel like we will find him. We just need to ask a
quick favor from you."

"Oh—anything," said Erin. "Anything I can do."

"Could you fly to New York next Friday?"

Erin caught her breath.

"We're feeling like a nationwide plea might help. We'd
like to take you on *The Carnie Wilson Show*. You would
be able to ask the audience . . . millions of people . . . if
any of them have seen Michael."

"What if his mother hears? She's the one who kidnapped him and she's never approved of the idea of them
meeting. She can get violent."

"It's a chance we'll have to take."

Erin swallowed. "My husband is between jobs," she
said. "The airfare would—"

"We'll take care of that." Arliene's voice was reassuring. "If you can just clear your schedule so you'll be able
to go."

Erin glanced at Dan. "I think that can be arranged," she said.

Everything was happening so quickly. Two days after the phone call from Arliene Dunn, Dan and Erin were in the church boardroom. The faces of the six board members were a blur in Erin's mind as she and Dan sat at the head of a long table. What could she say to these people she never met before in her life? She didn't have time to think before a barrage of questions hit them.

"Tell us about your background in pastoring," said a balding man on the left.

"My background is not traditional . . ." Dan began slowly. "I started out in music and then later went into the pastoral ministry."

"What caused you to make the change?" asked a blond woman wearing glasses.

Dan paused. Erin saw his Adam's apple move. "I felt that this is what the Lord was leading me to do—"

"What is your philosophy of pastoring?" Another man, dignified, with dark hair, asked.

"To be available to the people in my care."

"By that, you mean—" the blond woman again.

"To love and support them . . ." Dan paused. "And to teach them and minister to them."

"What about your role?" The question suddenly hit Erin. "Your role as pastor's wife?"

Erin felt her heart beat. She knew her hands were clammy. What could she say now? Dan was so talented— he could preach, sing, and play the piano. What could she say about herself? All of the board members' stares seemed to bore into her brain. Her heart beat faster now. The board members smiled at her. She breathed, then sighed. Suddenly a calmness clutched her heart and she knew there was only one answer.

"My duties are exactly as the job description says. I am the pastor's wife. I'm there to support him and to care for my family. As far as my position in the church goes, I'll do anything I'm capable of doing. I've worked with the children at several churches."

There was a long silence. Now her heart was in her throat. She had time to take one breath before more questions assailed them.

"You mentioned children, what about the senior citizens?"

"What is your experience in writing sermons?"

"Do you incorporate music within your messages?"

The questions went on for nearly an hour before the bald man turned to Dan. "Is there anything you would like to say to us?"

Erin watched Dan square his shoulders. Then he spoke with the same calming tone that soothed her whenever she was worried. "The only thing I want to say is, if this is the church where the Lord wants me to be, He'll lay it on your heart to hire me." Erin watched the board members shuffle in their seats. "You, as board members, may feel free to take your time. Interview as many people as you can. Don't rush."

There was a silence. Erin watched the board members stare at the two of them, then write on yellow notepads. What were they thinking?

"Do you have anything else to say?" one of the board members asked.

What could they possibly want to know? Erin wondered. She stared at Dan, and a warm feeling of love coursed through her.

Dan cleared his throat. "We don't have a lot of things to offer as far as experience." He paused. "But if you want a couple that will be here for you and love you, we are the couple for you."

Her heart kept pounding, but Erin tried to smile at the board members.

"If you'll excuse us," a man with shiny black hair and glasses was saying, "the board would like to confer for a few moments."

What did this mean?

Dan walked over to Erin's chair and held out his hand to her. When he squeezed her fingers, she felt his palms were as sweaty as hers. Hand in hand, they walked out of the church.

"Dan—" Erin's voice quavered.

He tilted his chin and smiled at her. "I want this church," she said firmly. "This feels right to me."

"I thought you didn't want me to be a pastor."

"It's a little late to change our minds about that now. But this feels good—here in this place."

Dan shook his head. "Gotta wait and see. We can't get too excited yet."

"I felt good about it the moment I laid eyes on it." Erin sighed. "I love the people already."

He looked away, and she watched him swallow.

He wants to be here, too, she thought.

As minutes passed and the two of them eventually sat on the church steps, Erin almost wondered if they should leave and come back another day. What could those board members find to say about the two of them? Did the word *yes* come to mind? And if they were going to say no, why did it take so long?

The door burst open abruptly.

"Please return to the boardroom for a moment," said a man in a gray suit.

Dan took her hand again. Her heart thudded. *It's probably wrong to want this,* she thought. *Dan's right. We need to wait and see. If it's supposed to happen, it will.*

"Please be seated," said the black-haired board member.

Erin and Dan sat.

"We want you to come back another day—to try out for the congregation. Present a sermon to them. Let them see your style of preaching—whatever gifts you have to offer."

Dan nodded.

"Then they will cast the final vote. In two weeks or so."

I want it now, Erin thought.

Chapter 14

∞

Dan and Erin's eyes met as they stood on his parents' porch and rang the doorbell.

"This is it," Erin whispered.

"You started it," he whispered back. Let's hope Dad's okay with this, Dan thought. Please don't let me hurt my dad, he prayed, wanting to turn and run as his father opened the door. Dan stared with compassion into his dad's calm, familiar face. He stepped into the living room and recognized the smell of his mother's meat loaf. He caught sight of his baseball trophies on the hearth next to the wedding picture of him and Erin. This was home, the place where he'd always felt safe, every night and every day since he was a little boy.

Did Michael ever feel safe at home? Dan wondered.

Stepping through the doorway, Erin ventured, "We need to tell you something."

Jack gestured, and the two of them walked in and sat on the familiar beige couch. Dan glanced up to see curiosity in his father's eyes.

"Don't mean to beat around the bush." Dan paused. "We just don't know how to say this."

"We didn't exactly ask you first," said Erin.

Then they were both silent. What were the right words? Dan's mother came and sat next to her husband. "What's all this about?" she asked.

Dan glanced at Erin, who said, "You tell him."

"We saw a search agency on TV. Erin called them about Michael. I said she could."

Both of his parents sat still as stone.

"The thing is, we think they might find Michael," said Erin. "So we thought we better tell you now. I mean, if you want us to stop them, let us know tonight. I'll call tomorrow morning and cancel."

"Erin can just tell them we changed our minds." Dan reached over and took Erin's hand. What did that look on his father's face mean?

Dad sat back with a sigh. He folded his arms.

Dan leaned closer.

"Listen, Dad. This is the deal. I want to know how you feel about this. If you don't want me to search for him, let me know. I don't want to do anything that will hurt or upset you."

Dan felt his father's hands reach over to clasp his own. Their warm, comforting presence reminded him of the safe feeling he felt when he was little. If his dad ever walked into a room, he felt as secure as if God were standing right beside him. Remembering how his dad made him feel when he was small, Dan felt tears in his eyes. Tears for his dad, and for Michael, and for all the years of wondering and waiting.

"Don't cry, son." Dad's voice was soft. "Michael is your brother. You have the right to meet him. I gave this situation to God forty-some years ago. I'm not about to take it back from Him now."

"But what about the search agency?" Erin's voice broke in. "BigHugs.com?"

"I'll leave that decision up to you. If you want to have them search, I'll support you one hundred percent."

Dan leaned over to hug his dad, whose words fell gently on his ears. "Don't know how it will all turn out," Dad said. "Just know that if God sees fit to see me reunited with my son, then I'll see him."

Their hug lasted a long time, before Erin reached out, and joined them in a tearful embrace.

* * *

Did he even sit down once today? Michael was still numb from the anniversary sale when the phone rang.

"Michael Dutton?"

"You have the wrong number." Michael paused. "Wait." How many years had it been since he heard his old name? His real name, the one Mama made him get rid of all those years ago? "Who are you looking for?"

"Michael Dutton."

How should he say this? "I'm Michael Parker. But I *used* to be Michael Dutton. So I'm probably not the one you're looking for."

Silence on the other end. Michael waited.

The voice sounded cautious. "What do you mean you used to be?"

"My name was changed."

"What state were you living in when this happened?"

Who was this? "Well . . . several actually. About the time we moved from Georgia, my mother told me I had to choose a new name."

"And why did you move?"

"Who is this?"

"This is Arliene Dunn. Of BigHugs.com. I'm representing someone who is looking for a Michael Dutton."

"Who is it?"

Arliene paused. "It's your brother."

"My brother? Now I know you have the wrong person. I don't have a brother."

"Is your father Jack Dutton?"

Michael was stunned. No one had asked him that question in more than forty years. He felt chills. Scary Jack. Mama told him never to tell anyone who his father was. He was never even allowed to say his father's name. "Uh . . . I only saw my father once or twice . . . more than forty years ago . . . but that was his name. Jack Dutton."

"He'd like to see you, too."

"To see me?"

"He lost track of you long ago, but he's never forgotten. He's getting up in years, and—"

"He and my mother were divorced. She stole me—"

"From the courthouse," said Arliene calmly. "After your father won custody."

Michael paused, then took a breath. "I think you might have the right person after all."

The church was airy and high-ceilinged.

"I'm going to tell you something. I have a brother I have never seen," Dan began. "My father hasn't seen him for more than forty years."

Not a rustle among the congregants. All eyes were on Dan, Erin thought as she sat on the hard wooden bench and glanced around unobtrusively. She had never dreamed that Dan would talk about Michael. She was surprised that his voice was so calm.

"The truth is, all of us have brothers we've never seen," Dan continued. "Brothers who are also God's children."

Still no restlessness from the congregants.

"Brothers we will meet as our lives continue on. Brothers that God loves, and He wants us to love, too."

A woman in front of Erin started fanning herself with a fan made of feathers. Erin felt the breeze brush her face. Dan finished his sermon and went to the piano. His voice filled the church. Erin imagined the notes reaching the rafters, and ascending farther up, to the sky.

How could the audience resist that voice? How could they not want to hear it again and again, the way she did?

Even through her nervousness, Dan's voice comforted her, so much that she stopped being aware of each minute passing.

"We would like to thank Dan and his dear wife, Erin, for attending our service," the pastor was saying.

Dan was suddenly at her side, touching her arm.

"They said we can go now," he whispered in her ear.

What did that mean? Were they being dismissed? Had they failed?

Erin scrambled to stand next to him, and the two of

them walked out of the church into the silent and empty hall. A rush of air brushed her face as they walked out into the warm, fall day.

Erin glanced at Dan. "We'll hear from them in two weeks?"

He spoke, almost under his breath, not looking at her. "I hope so."

They were halfway to the car when a voice called out. "They want you back at the church." A woman stood in the doorway. "Come right now."

Erin's heart sank. They're not even taking two weeks to decide. They're saying no now. She reached out and took Dan's hand, noticing that he wasn't looking at her. Each step she took toward the church felt heavier than the last.

They walked through the door and into the chapel where the congregation still sat. Erin held her breath— then gasped as the room dissolved into a sea of applause.

"Congratulations, Pastor." Someone was shaking Dan's hand.

Erin felt a hand on her own shoulder and looked up questioningly.

"As you know . . ." Now someone spoke from the pulpit. "Traditionally, there is a vote of the entire congregation after two weeks, but this time the vote was unanimous immediately. Welcome to Spring Hill Assembly of God, Pastor and Mrs. Dan Dutton."

Erin's heart was pounding. "You did it." She squeezed Dan's hand.

"*We* did it," he said. His hand patted her shoulder.

As they walked out to the car and drove away, Erin felt a warm rush that she belatedly realized was relief coupled with amazement. Dan's dream was not dead. They were no longer homeless, without a parsonage.

And in a few days Dan might finally be on his way to meeting his brother.

* * *

"*And now we have another family story to tell you,*" Carnie Wilson was saying. "Meet Dan," she said. "Dan is a pastor, am I right?"

"Yes, ma'am. Mountain View Assembly of God," he said.

"Don't you love that Southern accent, audience?" Carnie asked. "Dan is here to tell us he'd like to find someone."

"I need to find my brother," Dan said.

"Is this a medical emergency?"

"No. But it is an emergency, in a way. He needs to see my dad and my dad needs to see him."

"Is your father ill?" Carnie tilted her head toward Jack, who sat, calm as ever, in his Sunday suit in front of a nationwide audience of millions.

Dan paused. "No, but he's in pain inside."

"You feel like your father is grieving the loss of his son?" Carnie asked, bending so that she now looked over her glasses at him.

"His heart still hurts. I know it. Every time we have a family gathering, his voice breaks when he says the prayer. I know he's thinking about Michael. I know he thinks of Michael every day." When he stopped talking, Dan felt like he was out of breath.

"How long has your brother been gone?"

Dan chuckled ironically. "This sounds weird, I know, but he was already gone before I was born. My mother is Dad's second wife. And I didn't find out about Michael until I was fourteen."

"Your father didn't tell you about your brother?" Carnie leaned toward his dad again.

"He said he always meant to. But I think it hurt too much. He just didn't want to pass that hurt along to me. He hoped he'd somehow find Michael before he ever had to tell me he was gone."

"Let's ask Dad about that." Carnie reached out and took Jack's hand.

"My son's right," Jack said. "I always hoped we'd find

him so I could spare my son the pain of knowing he was gone."

"So you held that pain inside," said Carnie.

Jack nodded. Dan sensed the lump in his father's throat was as big as the one in his own.

"Well, we're here to help you make a plea," said Carnie. "But I have to say—you know, there's no guarantee."

Dan sighed. "Right now I'd settle for half a chance."

"If anyone can do it, we can."

Again, Dan felt a lump in his throat. "I'd appreciate that. I can't see my dad getting any older without knowing that his son is okay."

"He won't have to wait another day," a man's voice called out.

Erin stared at the slim, handsome, dark-haired man who now crossed the stage in an easy stride.

Dan stood, and she saw that he was trembling. "Michael," Dan breathed.

"That's me," Michael said, and the two men hugged. Erin watched as they held each other.

"Dan, isn't there someone you want to introduce to Michael?" Carnie asked.

"Oh! Yes—" Dan dropped his arms from Michael's sides and said, "Michael. This is our dad. Jack Dutton."

Chills rushed over Michael as he gazed at Jack. Though his father was older, and heavier, and had gray hair, the resemblance was unmistakable. He looks just like me, Michael thought. Why, in all her rantings and ravings about Scary Jack, did his mother never say that he looked just like his father? He couldn't stop staring. He couldn't stop thinking that his father was nothing like he expected him to be. This man, Jack Dutton, looked calm, gentle, kind . . . and not scary in the least. Michael somehow sensed that the Scary Jack his mother had talked about all those years lived only in her mind, and wasn't at all like the man whose eyes met his now.

"Son." Jack managed a smile. "I never thought this moment would be . . . and now I can't be happier that you're here. I have thought of you every day. I missed you so much."

Emotion froze his voice, but Michael held out his arms. His father stepped closer, and Michael enveloped the man he'd thought of so many times but never imagined he'd meet. The two men hugged.

"Michael," Jack said.

After their embrace ended, Carnie said, "I think we need to give these folks some private time to talk. What do you say, audience?"

A roar of applause. Then all five of them—Jack, Erin, Dan, Mary, and Michael—walked off the stage.

In the green room, Jack suddenly paused. He took his wallet out of his pocket and flipped to the worn and tattered photo of Michael.

"This is all I had of you all these years." He held out the picture.

Michael stared at a photo of himself as a young boy. He saw himself wearing flannel pajamas and sitting, smiling, in front of a Christmas tree.

"This is me in another life. I always wondered what my life was like before Mom stole me," he said.

"She couldn't steal my memories," said Jack.

"Every family party—lots of them anyway—Dad cried during the blessing," said Dan. "We knew he was thinking about you."

"He didn't ruin the occasion," Erin said quickly. "But we just knew that something was missing. We knew we had to find you."

"I always wondered about my life—the life Mom never let me know about," said Michael. "Do you know—we moved at least twenty times."

"I sure couldn't catch up with you." Dad shook his head, with a smile this time. "All I had was that picture."

"I can get you a more recent one," Michael joked.

Then, just like a brother who'd known him all his life, Dan asked, "When are you coming to visit? Bring your wife, your daughters. How about sometime next month?"

"I'll see when I can get time off." Michael smiled. "I'll call you. Here's my card."

As simple as that. *I'll call you.*

The Only
Family She Knew

Chapter 1

∞

Nine-year-old Hillary Davis stood firmly on her front porch and called out toward the street filled with neighborhood children who were playing outside on this blissfully warm, late spring day. "Everyone come over here, in our yard!" she yelled. Hearing the sound of her familiar words, the children, in groups of two and three, walked over and sat on the Davises' lawn.

"We're going to have a circus! Right here on our street," Hillary shouted enthusiastically. "There'll be lions and acrobats and a trained bear."

"Where you going to get a bear?" asked Tommy, who was eight.

"It will all be us!"

"How we gonna be bears?" he asked again.

"We'll have costumes!"

"I don't have a costume." Another little girl looked forlorn.

"We'll make you one!" Hillary's smile was infectious.

"I don't know how to sew."

Hillary patted the little girl's head. "I'll help you."

"Can I be a zebra?"

"Yes, we'll make you a costume with black and white stripes . . ."

"Are we going to have another parade? Will this be fun like the play we did last year?" An older, freckled boy looked at her skeptically.

"More fun! Lots of fun!" Hillary's heart beat fast. The kids knew she was always putting together a play or a show. And for Hillary, putting on a production was more exciting than anything else she could imagine. She thought the way her heart pounded was probably the way musical-comedy stars felt when they all sang and danced together. Every time she did it, she wanted to do it again.

Through the sheer living-room drapery, Kate Davis smiled at the group of children gathering on her front lawn. She listened to Hillary at the same time as she anxiously waited for the doorbell to ring. Kate was nervous, not knowing what to expect. What did social workers say when they came to your house? What did they look for? If I'm not what they want, what can I do about it? Kate wondered. It seemed like she sat for an hour before the doorbell finally rang.

Kate stood, fluffed her dark hair quickly in the mirror over the mantel, then opened the door to greet a blond woman in a gray business suit.

"Mrs. Davis?" the woman questioned.

"Yes, I'm Kate." Though she smiled and extended a hand, Kate felt her heart pounding.

"Sandra Allen, from the state division of Child and Family Services," said the woman. "And that girl outside—"

"My daughter, Hillary."

"She's actually starting a . . . a circus, was it?"

"She does that all the time." Kate laughed. "She'll put on plays, start clubs . . . things like that." When the woman didn't smile back, Kate asked, "Did I understand what you said on the phone—that you drove all the way here from two counties away?"

"Yes, the situation is . . . quite urgent."

"Well, please sit down." At least a hundred miles, Kate thought. What did this woman travel here to tell me?

As if sensing her question, Sandra set an attaché case on her lap, opened it, and took out a file that Kate guessed was at least three inches thick. She opened the file and leaned back against the wing chair in the corner of the Davises' living room.

Kate's curiosity forced her to speak. "Is that a child's file?"

The woman waved a hand to brush aside Kate's question. "I see here that you heard about the foster-care program from your minister."

"Yes." Kate nodded. "They said there are many children who need homes."

Sandra glanced at her. "Why did you decide to consider becoming a foster parent?"

Kate felt a sad smile creep onto her face. "I lost five babies before I had two. I always wanted a larger family, and I thought this might be a way to—"

"Foster care is not a permanent home."

"I know that."

"The children stay in your home an average of one year."

"Why is that?" Kate couldn't help asking.

"The goal is to return them to their parents as soon as possible."

Kate nodded. "I can understand that. I guess I just thought that we have a happy family life and could share it with a child who needs a home." It was the only answer in her mind—the true answer. But she couldn't read the social worker's mysterious nod.

Opening the folder again, Sandra flipped through a sheaf of papers, then stopped. "It says here that you requested to help a child who is very needy."

"Yes, I told my minister that. I'd like to help a child who truly needs my help."

Sandra stared at her. "Mrs. Davis." She paused, glanced through the sheer curtain at Hillary, then firmly met Kate's gaze. "From the home study I have here—and from watching your daughter on the porch for less than five minutes—I can tell that you have a very well-adjusted daughter. Probably two such children."

"Yes." Why did Kate sense that this fact worked against her?

"And your home here. Again, the study and my observation show that it is spotlessly clean."

"Thank you," said Kate, leaning back and crossing her legs. "I try to keep it that way."

"Then I must ask, how do you think a very needy, maladjusted child would feel at home here? With two well-adjusted children and such a clean house?"

Kate was taken aback. She shifted silently on the couch. "I guess I hoped that our kindness would be a factor. The fact that we are willing to help."

The woman shook her head.

Kate suddenly leaned forward. "Is there a child you have in mind for our home?"

Sandra was silent. "I couldn't release that information until the decision was made."

"There is a child. I can tell by the look on your face," Kate said suddenly. "And you wouldn't drive this far unless you thought . . ."

The other woman sighed. "There is a highly needy child. She is seriously troubled. I'm just not sure that given the circumstances—"

"Tell me," Kate said, suddenly anxious about this unknown girl. "Tell me more about her."

Again, a silence.

"Please, you drove all this way. You must think—"

The woman abruptly flipped open the binder. Her fingers riffled through the pages. "She is five years old." More pages flipped. Kate's instincts told her the woman was measuring how much of the child's past she dared reveal.

"In kindergarten?" Kate asked lightly. "Or maybe nursery school?"

More pages flipping. "No school yet. She doesn't talk much," the social worker said, finally looking up. "She experienced significant trauma in her early childhood."

Kate realized her heart was already going out to this

little girl. "How long has she been in foster care?"

"Most of her life. Let me see . . ." Again, Sandra looked through the folder. "Her health-care needs have been neglected. Particularly dental work."

"I could help with that. We know a good dentist."

More pages flipped. "She suffered abuse in a previous foster home . . . in more than one, actually."

"That won't happen here." Kate was surprised at the firmness in her own voice. Looking at the woman across from her, she sensed dark secrets being weighed.

"Actually—I probably should tell you this—the abuse reached the point that she is now considered emotionally retarded."

"Then she needs a good home."

"I think her problems may be more serious than you perceive."

"Do you feel that her parents will eventually care for her?"

"They are both alcoholic. They have been declared unfit. At the same time they've declined to release her for adoption placement."

"So that's why she is in foster care?"

"It was an emergency placement. Someone called the police. The children were placed in state custody."

"The police? An emergency—"

"Yes." Sandra focused her purposeful green-eyed gaze on Kate's kind, blue eyes. "Addie and her brother were found locked in a closet. It was obvious they were in there for quite some time."

Kate winced in horror. "Locked in? Where was their mother?"

Now the social worker shook her head. "Disappeared. The eleven-year-old son was in charge of the home for at least two weeks. He had no idea how to care for a two-year-old and a three-year-old."

"But . . . Addie is five now?"

"Yes." The social worker's look grew grave. "Unfortunately, after being removed from her custodial parents,

she was placed in several foster homes. At least two of
them were equally, if not more, abusive than her original
environment." The social worker paused.

"That poor little thing," Kate said. "And what about her
brothers?"

"In foster care as well." Again, the social worker
paused. "The children were not placed together in the
same foster homes."

Kate inhaled. "So she was separated from her family . . .
and abused in foster care."

"Yes."

"And now she doesn't have a home."

"Not presently. She hardly knew her father. He abandoned the family when Addie was an infant."

Kate breathed. "Addie—that's her name? How could
such a little child cope with all that? Why don't you just
bring her here to us? We could take her tonight." Kate
pictured the little girl playing outside with the other children, in their calm and friendly neighborhood.

Sandra pressed her lips together. "Before you make
such an offer, I should probably mention that she is still
recovering from the effects of the emotional and sexual
abuse." The social worker paused. "And she's had seven
placements."

"Seven different homes—and she's five years old?"
Kate was amazed.

"I want to let you know what you could be taking on."

"We'd do the best we could."

Sandra sat back against the Davises's easy chair. "I
wouldn't consider you the best match—the girl is so troubled—Your backgrounds are worlds apart."

"We would just try to take care of her, to let her heal
in a safe place. My girls would help." Kate gestured toward the porch. "You can see how Hillary loves younger
children."

"I don't know if healing is possible in this case."

"I'm willing to take a chance." Kate wondered what
was the right thing to say. "The rest of my family is too."

"We've found that placement works best if the 'match' is considered good."

"So you have better matches than we would be? She will go to one of them?" Kate asked, already feeling sadness for this child.

There was a pause so long that both Kate and Sandra heard Hillary on the front porch, still planning her neighborhood circus.

In a voice that was nearly inaudible, Sandra said, "There is no other match."

"You have no one else to take her to?"

Kate's heart ached for this homeless little girl, who'd already been shuffled around so many times in so few years. That's why this woman came, Kate realized. That's why she drove from so far away.

"Then bring her here."

"It isn't that simple. She would visit the home in the beginning—probably more than once; possibly several times—to see if an eventual placement would be feasible."

"Then bring her to visit now. Have her spend some time with us."

Sandra hesitated. "Do you feel like I've provided sufficient information so that you would be comfortable having her stay in your home?"

"I know that she needs us. That's all I need." Kate smiled hopefully.

"If she arrives, and you feel the visit is inappropriate, you would be welcome to call."

"I'll tell my family she's coming."

The social worker held up a hand. "It's not definite yet. I will call you by the end of the week. If you change your mind after thinking about it, let me know. Once the placement is made, you will meet with the child's caseworker rather than me." Sandra closed the file, dropped it in her briefcase, and shook hands with Kate.

Kate watched Sandra stop on the porch and speak briefly with Hillary before she purposefully walked down

the steps and climbed into her car. Kate found herself
anxiously looking out the window and thinking of the
little girl long after the car drove away. Where was Addie
right now? What was she doing on this summer afternoon
while Kate's two girls were outside playing—tanned,
laughing, and carefree?

What sad thoughts were in her pained, little heart, and
how could she and her family make her feel better? Where
was Addie now?

I feel like a mother to her already, Kate thought. I'm
worried about a child I've never seen.

That night, before she fell asleep, Kate thought again
of the little girl, and wondered where she was sleeping
now, maybe a hundred miles away. What would it be like
to live in seven homes before you ever stepped across the
threshold of a school?

Addie froze in fear. The two women in the front room
were talking about her. She knew it. This had happened
to her more times than she could count. The two of
them—her foster mother and another lady—talking about
her. Though she couldn't understand what they were saying, she felt the impact of their words as she sat motion-
less on the bedroom floor. Fear hovered inside her. This
had happened before, lots of times. First a man or woman
came to talk to her foster mother. Then someone drove
up in a car and took her away to a new place. Sometimes
to visit. Sometimes to stay.

She never knew where she would land next. Someone
who looked friendly during the visit would hit her—or
worse—later, when she lived at their house. Fear held her
paralyzed. There was nothing scarier than a new place,
where you didn't know what to do. The people were
strangers. It was a long time before she could sleep in the
new bed, or on the floor, if that was where they told her
to sleep.

Addie glanced around her. She knew the rules at this

house. The main rule was, stay away from everybody. The second rule was, always be quiet. She wasn't allowed to play with the other children, who were big and mean anyway. She couldn't eat at the table with the family. That was a big rule. She had to sit under the table and wait for them to give her scraps from their plates. Lots of times, Addie was still hungry when the family finished eating. Sometimes she lay awake long into the dark night, her stomach growling as she listened to the family snore around her. The family never asked how she felt or what she thought. They knew that Addie didn't talk. So they didn't talk to her. They yelled at her or left her alone. Addie sighed. There was going to be a new house—she knew it. Alone on the floor, Addie waited and trembled with fear.

Chapter 2

∞

Hillary felt the rush of happiness that always filled her when Daddy got home from a business trip. She always thought that Daddy smelled like a city when he walked in the house—his aftershave combined with the odors of smoke and stale air that were nothing like the wide-open freshness of their own front yard. Daddy always gave her a hug and sometimes there was a piece of candy or another treat from Chicago or New York or wherever he traveled for his work at a major oil company. Hillary always held a warm feeling inside when they sat down for their first dinner together after Daddy got back. It was like he had been gone months or years—even though she knew it was only a week.

But this time something seemed different about Mama and Daddy. Hillary noticed the two of them whispering, or talking in soft tones when she was in the next room. If she came into the room where they were, their conversation abruptly stopped. What was going on?

They sat down to dinner, and after everyone had passed around the fried chicken, green beans, and mashed potatoes, Hillary looked up to see that Daddy was looking at her.

"We have something special to tell you tonight," Daddy said as he unfolded his napkin and set it on his lap. Hillary immediately heard something different about Daddy's voice. She could tell that whatever he was about to say was something big. Worry hovered over Hillary. Were they going to move away? Sometimes Daddy got transferred. Or did Daddy lose his job? Did someone die?

"What's wrong?" she asked, a frown knitting her brow.

"Nothing's wrong," Daddy said. He reached out and wrapped his hand around her fingers. "We just need to let you know about something."

"Is someone hurt?" Hillary asked.

"No." Daddy smiled, and if Hillary wasn't mistaken, that might have been a tear on his cheek. "You know how we always said we would like to help a little child that needs help?"

"A poor child?" Kris, Hillary's sister, asked.

"A child who needs a home," Mama said. "Daddy wants to tell you that there's a little girl who needs a home now."

Hillary and Kris stared.

"Where is she?" Kris asked.

"Let's go get her," said Hillary.

"She lives in a foster home right now, but she needs a new home," Daddy said. "She hasn't lived with her real family for a long time."

"Why not?" Kris looked puzzled.

Hillary felt a sadness inside. How would it be to live far away from your family? Wouldn't you miss them?

"Her mommy and daddy had problems and couldn't take care of her."

Another wave of sadness washed over Hillary. What kind of problems would a mom and dad have so that they couldn't take care of their own child? And how would it be to not have your own home? What would you do after school if you couldn't come home and put your books in your room and your shoes in your closet? Where would you eat dinner and where would you sleep at night?

"What does she look like?" Hillary asked. She wondered how a girl would dress who didn't have a home. Would she be hungry?

There was a pause. Mom and Daddy looked at each other. "We don't know now, but we are all going to meet her." Now both Mama and Daddy smiled.

"We are?" Kris asked.

"Yes, she's coming here for a visit. And if everything goes okay—after she visits a few times—we might let this little girl live in our home with us. We would be her foster family."

"Can she sleep in my room?" Kris asked.

"We'll see," said Mama.

"Is she my age?" Kris asked.

"Five years old."

"Oh, a little girl," said Kris, who was seven.

"Will we go pick her up?" Hillary asked.

Mama cleared her throat. "A social worker will bring her."

"When is she coming?" Hillary asked.

"Saturday," said Daddy.

"What is her name?"

"Addie." Hillary's mother smiled at her. "Addie Randall."

"Can she be in my new circus?"

Mama hesitated. "If she's here with us . . . and if she wants to be in the circus."

Addie Randall. The warm feeling stayed in Hillary's heart. What would it be like for this little girl to come to

a house where she didn't know anybody? Would she miss
the bed where she used to sleep? Would she miss the
foster family who used to take care of her? And if she
was five, would she leave her kindergarten class and go
to school with Kris and Hillary? As the rest of the week
passed, Hillary kept thinking of the girl, and wondering
how it would feel to be only five and coming to a new
home.

Hillary thought of ways to make the foster girl's visit
absolutely perfect. "We need to have Mountain Dew," she
said to her mother. "And let's make those cookies that
taste like lemonade."

The day Addie was scheduled to arrive, Hillary helped
Mama clean the house. They baked the lemonade-flavored
cookies and prepared for a celebration dinner. As the
morning and early afternoon wore on, Hillary went to sit
on the living-room couch. She wanted the little girl to
come to her house that very minute.

Riding in the backseat of her social worker's car, five-
year-old Addie Randall felt a familiar fear and confusion
in the pit of her stomach. She shifted her stick-thin body
against the rough, upholstered seat. A near-empty suitcase
sat beside her. There was no way her clothes would fill
any sort of closet. The denim sundress and red-and-white
polka-dot bloomers she wore were the most presentable
of her three flimsy outfits. Her walnut-sized brown eyes
stared out at the scenery around her with fearful curiosity.

Where were they taking her this time? Who would
make her cry at this house? How much would they hurt
her before they said they had enough and she had to move
on? Addie remembered the house before the one she had
just left. At that house, there was a dip in the mattress
that somehow helped her fall asleep when she lay on it.
She remembered how the family ate late at night, long
after she was hungry. She recalled her tennis shoes that
fit just right, and how they somehow didn't get packed in

the small suitcase that lay beside her on the backseat.

The afternoon was still sunny as the social worker's car pulled to a stop in front of a gray-and-white two-story house. Addie stared out, trying to picture what her future might be here.

She caught sight of a sympathetic glance from the social worker. Grasping the handle on the suitcase, Addie waited anxiously.

Looking out the window, Hillary gasped at the sight of Addie. "She's so little. And skinny. But her stomach sticks out like a soccer ball."

"Malnutrition." Hillary's mom placed a hand on her shoulder. "She hasn't been getting enough good food."

"We have lots to eat here," Hillary said hopefully, thinking of the dinner they spent all afternoon preparing. "Look how scared she looks."

Hillary and Kate watched as the social worker grasped the girl's hand and led her up the front walk, past the spring tulips and daffodils. Hillary opened the door and stepped out onto the porch to greet them.

"Wait a minute, Hillary," Kate said gently.

Hillary stood and wrapped her arm around the metal pole where she often spun around. She couldn't take her eyes off the little girl.

Addie couldn't decide about this place. You couldn't tell much when you just walked through a house. She knew that already. The redbrick house where the man and his son both hurt her looked safe. And the home where they said they didn't want her because they already had a girl was a pretty yellow house. Addie held her breath and sighed. She couldn't stop being scared yet.

Before the social worker could ring the doorbell, a tall girl with dark hair opened the door and stepped outside. She and an older woman both smiled at them. "Come in," said the mother. "We've been waiting for you."

The tall girl bent over and looked into Addie's brown eyes. "What's your name?" she asked. "You can be in my circus if you want."

The social worker's hand found Addie's shoulder. "She doesn't talk much," she said.

That didn't stop the tall girl from taking Addie's hand and leading her through the living room to the family room.

The first sight of Addie caught at Kate's heart. Look at that poor little thing, she thought. Those are the biggest dark brown eyes I ever saw. But Hillary is right—her stomach is distended, and her back is swayed.

What caused all this, and what can I do about it? she wondered. Then the thought came to her: This is my first foster-child visit, and I'm already acting like a mom.

Would this family decide to let her stay here? What would she do wrong this time? How long would it take for them to finally send her away? The tenseness in Addie's chest still hovered. She fought not to flinch as Hillary's warm, gentle hand reached out to take hers. She accepted the cookie and glass of Mountain Dew Hillary handed her.

An hour or so later Hillary led her to the Davises' kitchen, where a table was set with gleaming dinner dishes. A warm, welcoming smell filled Addie's nostrils.

Suddenly Addie's heart started thudding in her chest. She felt sweaty. There was a feeling like she'd like to jump out of her skin. Where could she run? Would these people hurt her if she ran away? Confused thoughts filled her mind. What were the rules in this place? As seconds passed, the little girl fought to calm her heart. Her heart thudded faster as Hillary held a chair out for her. No, no, she couldn't sit there. Chairs were for the family, and she wasn't here to stay. Her hands started shaking and a humming filled her head. Addie dropped to the floor and slid under the tablecloth, where she huddled as if she were inside a tent. Her breath came in ragged gasps. For a moment she thought she might wet her pants. She felt her heart beat in her chest and closed her eyes in panic. Yet no one came after her as she sat and listened to herself breathe. Now she wouldn't get whipped for sitting at the table. Her eyes closed and she thought she heard her heart, still pounding.

Yet, moments later, light spilled onto her face as a corner of the tablecloth lifted. Addie frantically covered her eyes with her hands. What did she do wrong now? Now someone was moving closer to her. Help, she thought, terrified, as someone sat beside her. A warm leg touching hers. Her breath came in gasps, waiting for the whip, or the slap, or whatever was coming.

"Addie?" It was the girl's voice.

What did I do? Addie wondered. She shrank in a tight curl, a turtle inside its shell.

The girl spoke again. "Here's your dinner," she said, pressing a plate against Addie's arm. Addie shrank even more.

It seemed like an eternity before the girl spoke. "Better eat it now. It's getting cold."

Addie's stomach growled. The smell was heavenly. Shifting on the floor, she cautiously blinked, then ventured a look beyond her curled fingers. There it was. A dinner plate heaped with potatoes and gravy, roast beef, and butter-topped carrots. Her stomach growled.

"Go ahead," the girl said now. "Eat it all up."

Could she actually eat the food from the plate? Only starvation made Addie brave enough to drop her hands from her eyes. Slowly and cautiously, she eased upward into a sitting position. She saw that the girl held a second dinner plate on her own lap and was chewing with enthusiasm. The girl swallowed as Addie watched.

"Brought you a fork," Hillary said, moments later. She held out napkin-wrapped silverware.

Addie gingerly reached out, took the fork, spoon, and knife. When she saw the girl look down, she eagerly jabbed a piece of meat with her fork. Her stomach growled as she lifted the fork to her lips. But then the meat touched her tongue. So delicious. Addie closed her eyes in ecstasy. When she opened them a moment later, the girl was staring at her.

"Good, isn't it?" the girl said. "Mom's a good cook."

Still staring into Hillary's brown eyes, Addie cautiously dipped her fork again. The meat was gone in three bites. The mashed potatoes were soft, buttery, and comforting. Her stomach felt gloriously full. But not too full for the carrots—sweet, buttery, and delicious lumps. She fought to savor each one, but they were gone before she knew it. She was startled when the girl took her plate from her and placed it on top of her own.

Seconds later the girl came back and sat beside her again. She handed Addie a cookie.

"It's fun under here, isn't it?" The girl smiled at her. Their eyes caught, and they held each other's gaze. Addie felt her heart beat. She couldn't stop looking at the girl. *I want to stay here. I want to live with these people.* The thoughts took Addie by surprise. She usually didn't even dare wish for anything. Wishing usually led to even more pain. Why even think that something happy might happen when it almost never did?

Her stomach wasn't accustomed to being filled and she wasn't used to being smiled at. It felt almost too wonderful for words. She fought to trust these good feelings. But they filled her and she wanted to bask in them.

Yet suddenly the tablecloth lifted again. It was the woman—the girl's mother.

"You two about ready to come up here and join the rest of us? There's some of those cookies left . . . and I made a cake."

At first the woman's voice sounded scolding, but Addie

saw she was smiling. Cookies? Cake? The stomach Addie thought was full suddenly began to growl again. "I'll get some for us," the girl said. She stood, and Addie waited under the table.

Moments later she bit into the cookie the girl had handed to her.

As good as the cookie tasted, she still kept wondering how long it would take these people to decide they didn't like her. When she had wet her pants in a moment of anxious worry, that single incident clinched the Sorensons' opinion that she was brain-damaged. Without stopping to discover the reason, they just sent her to the next home before the end of that week.

At the Stewarts' house, Addie lived with her natural brother Davey. Only a few months passed before Mrs. Stewart told her they planned to adopt Davey. Addie still recalled the helpless pain when Mrs. Stewart told her, "We already have daughters, so we don't want you. But we're adopting your brother. You understand?"

Addie only understood that her heart hurt. The memory made the hurt still fresh. How could she stop being a girl? And couldn't they take one more girl? Didn't they want her to be with her brother? Addie remembered frantic nights of sleepless desperation before the social worker came to get her. And that scary feeling of being in the car, not knowing where it would turn off and where she would be left, with nothing from her life before. No photos, no old friends, no one from the old family coming with her to the new.

As if she were dropped onto a new planet where scary people looked like everybody else and you couldn't tell they were dangerous until after they hurt you.

Chapter 3

∞

Addie visited four more times at the Davises' house. After the first night, she ate dinner sitting at the table with the family. Each time she felt like her stomach would never be filled. All of the food tasted so good. It was as if she could never get enough. And the Davis family kept passing the plates to her, telling her to take more, to keep eating.

It was as if she were in heaven. And after the fourth visit, when she began to spend the night, Addie knew she wanted to stay here forever. The sleep that descended over her each night was the most peaceful bliss she'd ever felt in her five-year-old life. No one woke her abruptly in the middle of the night to slap her, or hurt her in other ways that made her scream inside. She didn't have to sleep on the floor or share the bed with two other children, so that she would lie awake at night, unable to move or relax. The sleep felt like a calming medicine to her. The Davises let her sleep until she woke on her own—the first time that had happened in her entire life. Addie slept late, as if she were somehow resting from all the trauma of years before, and could now finally enjoy healing, relaxing sleep.

Then, one morning, someone woke her.

Addie felt a hand on her arm. It didn't hurt, although the person shook her arm quickly to wake her.

"Addie?"

Addie opened her eyes and saw that it was Hillary.

"Hurry, Addie, it's time to get up . . ."

Addie saw that the girl was wearing a dress. She sat up slightly in bed, and saw the woman in back of the girl, wearing a dress, too.

Panic seized Addie. What did she do wrong here already? Why were they taking her away? Was it because she ate too much? Slept too long? Addie racked her five-year-old brain to try to figure out why someone here would want her to leave. She thought she had done everything right. There were no screams or slaps. No warning.

"Come on, Addie." The girl's hand was on her arm again.

No, Addie thought to herself. I won't leave here. I can't! Her heart pounded.

"Addie, you need to get up, dear." It was the woman's voice. Why did they all want her to go away? What did she do? Addie sat up quickly. Panic seized her again as she saw that both the girl and the woman were looking at her, waiting. She rolled over on the bed, then let her body drop behind it, where she crouched against the wall, rolling her small body as tight and compact as possible. Her heartbeat roared in her ears.

I'm not leaving here!

"Dear, we're just going to church. We'll come back home right after." The woman leaned over and spoke softly.

Addie squeezed herself even tighter, her knees tucked up under her chin.

"Come on, dear," the woman said, reaching down. Addie caught her breath as the woman's arms reached and lifted her out. She began to struggle, lashing out with her arms and legs.

"The poor thing," the woman said, before she wrapped Addie in a hug. Tears drenched Addie's pajamas and the woman's shoulder. Her thoughts raced although she didn't speak. Why are you making me leave here?

"Do you think we should leave her home today?" The woman spoke to the man, who now stood in the bedroom doorway.

Yes! Yes! Leave me home forever.

"Why don't we try to put on her dress?" the girl asked.

Why do you hate me? Why don't you want me? Addie fought until the woman's arms comforted her again.

The girl brought the same dress Addie hated, the only dress she owned, the denim one. She slid off Addie's pajama top and gently pulled the dress over her head. The woman hugged her again afterward. More tears began flowing so fast she couldn't see the woman's face.

Now the woman lifted her up.

No, no, no! Leave me here.

The woman carried her down the stairs.

Addie caught her breath.

The woman carried her to the front door. The girl opened it, and all of them went outside.

Not the car! Not the car! The car always takes me away!

Addie closed her eyes tight and squeezed in a tight ball on the woman's lap as they sat in the backseat of the car. She willed them not to take her, holding her breath and clenching every muscle in her body. She felt the car turn, stop, then turn again. How long would it be before they left her somewhere else, where someone else didn't want her?

The car stopped and Addie grabbed the woman's dress.

"It's all right, dear. We're here now."

"Can you just hold her hand?" the girl asked.

"I'd best carry her."

Addie kept her eyes shut in the woman's arms. She felt the woman walk, go up steps, and then sit, with her still in her arms.

Suddenly there were people singing all around her. Curious, Addie opened her eyes. What was this place? She slid off the woman's lap so she could look behind her. There were rows of people, all singing. The woman was singing, too. She kept her arm around Addie's shoulder as Addie finally turned back, comforted by the music.

Inside, her heart gradually slowed. They hadn't left her yet.

After the singing, a man talked.

Then it was the car again.

Please, please take me back home with you. This time Addie kept her eyes open. She watched the car drive down streets, turning, stopping, finally turning again. The car drove back to their house.

Addie let out a calming breath. You brought me back. You didn't leave me yet.

"I think she kind of liked church, once we got there," the woman said.

"I think she's just glad to be back home," said the girl.

Addie's heart was pounding again. She smiled back at the girl and the woman.

Thank you for keeping me one more day.

Addie couldn't let go of her fear, although lots more peaceful days followed. After school finished for the year, Hillary was home all day. Hillary and Addie colored together, read books, played dolls, and played house. They went swimming at a neighbor's pool across the street. Then it was time for the summer play.

Hillary took Addie's hand as the two of them walked down the street to another house, where there was a big yard where they could rehearse.

"We're going to do *Winnie-the-Pooh*," a girl who Hillary called Kathy announced.

"Tigger!" a boy yelled. "I want to be Tigger."

"I want to be Eeyore."

"Pooh," said Hillary, squeezing Addie's hand.

Who did Addie want to be? Hillary watched as Kathy came up and stood in front of Addie.

"Can she talk?" Kathy pointed to Addie but asked Hillary.

"She can still be in the play," Hillary insisted.

"But can she say anything? Can she have a part with *lines*?"

"Just give her a part. I'll go over it with her."

"But it will screw up the play if she can't say anything."

An idea struck Hillary. "I'll stand offstage and say her lines. I'll say it for her."

"No, that will look stupid."

"Could she be a flower, or something like that?" Hillary asked.

"There are no flowers in *Winnie-the-Pooh*."

"Could she just stay with me? And be my friend, who-ever I am?"

"There isn't anything like that in the play, either." Kathy started to turn around.

"I want Pooh," Addie said suddenly from beside her. Hillary felt chills pour over her body.

"Addie?" She turned to look at the younger girl. "What did you say?"

"I want Pooh," Addie said again.

"She *can* talk," Hillary quickly assured Kathy, though her heart was pounding in her chest. "She wants Pooh."

"I guess I'll give her a part," Kathy said slowly.

"I want Pooh," Addie said again.

"We'll see," Hillary told her.

"I want Pooh, Hillary," Addie said.

"You said Hillary. You said my name . . ." Hillary couldn't believe it. She wanted to run home right then.

"I was going to cast you as Pooh," said Kathy.

"Give the part to Addie," Hillary insisted.

"Then you'll be Kanga."

Hillary nodded, her eyes brimming. She could hardly wait to go home and tell Mama that Addie could talk.

Within weeks, it seemed to Kate like Addie couldn't stop talking. She told Hillary she had a "heady-ache." She sang "Oh-oh SpagettiOs with meatballs and peddios." Hillary and Kris never figured out what *peddios* were—and never stopped laughing while they tried. And one afternoon, Addie ran dashing into the kitchen after school. Grabbing Kate's pant leg, she called out, "Mom! Mom!"

Kate turned to her, and saw Addie's surprise as she realized that there were tears on Kate's face.

"Are you sad?" Addie asked her.

Kate bent down and took the small girl into her arms. Once stick-thin, Addie was now round, and tan like the other two girls.

"I'm not sad. I'm very happy." Kate smiled. "And how are you, Miss Addie?"

"I'm fine," Addie said with a sigh. "I'm going out to play with Hillary and Kris. When's dinner?"

"In a while," Kate reassured her with another smile. "You go out and play."

Chapter 4

❧

When winter came, Hillary, Kris and Addie skated on the lake, danced to records, and played on a small organ in Hillary's room. And they played school. Hillary was always the teacher.

"Blue," Hillary said to Addie as they shared a tattered copy of *Fun with Dick and Jane*.

Addie looked at the book in front of her. The children in the story seemed happy. There was a red wagon and a dog named Spot. She didn't see anything blue in the picture.

"Blue," Hillary said again. This time she pointed closer to the book. "Blue," she said again.

Addie looked up into Hillary's brown eyes. "Blue," she said.

"Look, Addie. Right here. Blue."

Addie looked again. There was nothing blue in the picture. Maybe their eyes were blue? She looked closer. Hillary's finger wasn't pointing to the picture. It was aimed lower, at a group of four black letters.

"Blue, like your shirt."

Now Addie looked at her shirt, then back at the letters.

"Blue." Hillary pointed to the letters, then to the shirt. Addie's eyes followed Hillary's finger, then looked at Hillary's face.

Blue, like her shirt? The letters were black . . . but were they blue, too? Those black letters on the page . . . did they somehow mean blue?

Hillary turned the page. "Blue," she said again, pointing to another group of letters.

Something caught in Addie's mind, and her heart beat fast. These letters looked just like the ones on the page before. She knew it. They looked like the other letters Hillary pointed to, and they meant blue like her shirt. She looked down on the page. There was another place where the letters said blue. She pointed at that place, then looked up at Hillary.

"Blue," she said.

"Wait," Hillary said, looking closer. Addie watched as Hillary's eyes got big. "You're right, Addie. You read it! You can read! That word says 'blue.' "

"Blue." Addie felt her smile spread across her face. She was filled with a warm feeling, like when Hillary, Mom, or Kris hugged her. Her heart pounded. She looked down at the book. What did all those other letters say?

"What's that?"

"That's Jane—that's the girl."

Addie pointed to the other girl.

"That's Sally."

Her finger touched the boy's picture.

"That's Dick."

This time Addie pointed to the word. "That's blue," she said. To her surprise, Hillary stood and ran out of the room. Seconds later she heard Hillary shout out in the hall.

"Mom—Addie can read—"

Kate waited for Sandra Allen to speak

"The girl's health?" Sandra asked her.

"I'd say she's gained twenty pounds."

"She's eating well?"

"Anything and everything. Every night." Kate laughed, then saw seriousness in the other woman's eyes. A shiver of fear filled her. "Is something wrong?" she asked. As Sandra frowned, Kate felt resistance, as if the other woman were brushing her aside.

"Sleeping well?"

"After the first two weeks . . . she had nightmares at first . . ."

Sandra shook her head, and wrote in her notebook.

"What's going on here?" Kate asked. "Are you thinking of . . ."

Sandra stared at her, her face still as stone.

"I'm probably not supposed to ask this, but what about her family? What is happening with them?"

"I couldn't tell you. You should know that."

"I just—do they ask about her? I heard there might be visitation—"

"I'll let you know if that's a possibility."

"Can you tell me if they've asked about her? If I had a girl who was taken away—" Kate was furious at her own voice for breaking. "I'd want to know where she was."

Sandra sighed and shook her head. "I can tell you that her mother has completed some alcohol rehabilitation, but there are other problems, and—"

"So is she all right?" Kate was surprised at the mixture of emotions that she felt. As much as she wanted Addie to stay with them, she worried about this woman who bore the tiny girl she now loved so much.

"I can't say anything further. Just that her caseworker is still in contact with her and—"

"And will she be getting visitation?"

"All I can say is that placement shall remain with you at this time."

Kate breathed heavily. She nodded, unable to speak.

"And please remember that foster care is temporary care. It may end at any time."

The word struggled to emerge from Kate's throat. "Yes," she said.

"I should say that Addie is not currently available for adoption, and we don't predict that will happen in the near future."

Kate could only nod.

Sandra closed her notebook.

"We'll see you again in six months." Sandra stood, and once again walked out of the Davis living room.

That spring, Hillary made an Easter basket for Addie, choosing candy at the five-and-ten. And when summer came, it was time for plays again. This time Addie was a Munchkin in *The Wizard of Oz* and Hillary played Tiger Lily in *Peter Pan*. Summer passed, and Addie learned to swim and dance.

It was late on an October afternoon, almost time for dinner. The time of day that stretches long and lazy. Addie leaned against Hillary as the two of them and Kris sat on the couch, watching TV. Addie loved the feeling of leaning against Hillary's arm. For just a few moments she felt safe here, thinking that no one could grab her away as long as Hillary sat beside her.

Addie could hear Kate moving pots and pans in the kitchen, and the anticipation of a hot, delicious dinner filled her with peace and contentment. She knew that any minute now, Kate would call her and Hillary to come set the table. Hillary taught her how to place forks and spoons next to the plates. Hillary herself placed the knives.

I could sit here forever, Addie thought.

Orange and brown cartoon leaves fell on the TV screen. Right now the *Peanuts Halloween Special* was almost over. Dressed in his Halloween costume, Snoopy, the World War I flying ace, flew over his doghouse in his Sopwith Camel airplane. Somehow, a ball of black string got wound around Snoopy's airplane. Addie watched as the plane dipped, wove, and landed upside down on the doghouse, with Snoopy's long ears drooping over the side of the roof.

Addie abruptly felt a catch in her throat. Something grabbed her insides, and she felt as if she were about to burst. Suddenly her throat moved, vibrating with a delicious happy, helpless feeling. Her stomach pulsed. A strange sound she never heard before escaped from her mouth, and she could feel her stomach moving up and down, too. What was going on here?

Hillary stared at her, smiled, and then instantly jumped to her feet. "Mom," she shouted. "Addie just laughed."

Addie watched Kate run from the kitchen to the living room. Kate bent close and patted her shoulder. At the same time Addie still felt the strange, bubbling feeling in her insides. More noise surged from her mouth. She looked up to see Kate standing next to Hillary, a wide grin on her face.

"Well, Miss Addie, why don't you tell us what's so funny?"

Addie couldn't stop laughing.

Hillary said, "It was Snoopy, Mom. Snoopy on TV. In his airplane."

Kate came over and sat beside Addie. She put her arm around her and gave her a squeeze. "Well, you just laugh anytime you like, little girl." Kate squeezed her again, and Addie felt her heart beat in her chest.

She'd never felt this happy. She had never made that sound in her throat before. All she knew was that she

wanted to stay here, on this couch, next to Hillary and
Kate forever.

"Why do you think she never laughed before?" Hillary
asked Kate.

"Maybe nothing was ever funny until now," Kate said.

The warm feeling inside Addie lasted for a long time,
spilling over into a sense of relief and peace. She was
home, for the first time in her six-year-old life.

Chapter 5

∞

By now, the social worker's car was a familiar sight. Kate
was relieved that Addie was off at school; she herself
always felt a tremor of worry thinking of what Sandra
might say to her.

"Come in," Kate said, smiling past her nervousness.

She noticed the woman always looked around her living room as if she were studying it—the high ceiling, the
doily-draped coffee table, the long couch in front of the
picture window. Kate half expected her to run a finger
along a wall, then check it for dust.

As usual, the social worker thumbed through her files
before glancing up at Kate.

"This year second grade?"

"Third," Kate clarified.

"Still some problems in school?"

"Yes," Kate admitted reluctantly. "But not serious, considering her background." She couldn't tell whether the
social worker's nod was in agreement.

"And her medical care?"

"The dental work is finally complete."

"Did you say her teeth were"—she flipped through the file—"rotted, I think is the word I wrote here."

"Serious decay," Kate said. "We started the work immediately. She's had eight crowns. But now they're all—"

"Eight? And she's eight years old?"

"Well, almost nine. I don't think she ever went to a dentist before she came here."

Another mysterious nod.

"And the rest of her health is good?"

"Yes." Now Kate nodded, too.

"Eating, and—"

"She eats lots of everything. It wasn't long after she came here that she—"

"She's talking now. But there was a developmental delay. A speech problem?"

"No speech problem. She was just too traumatized to talk."

Now the social worker looked fully at her. "How did she move past that?"

"It started gradually. She said Hillary's name first. Then she would come up to me in the kitchen and tell me if she wanted something. She kind of whispered at first. But now she talks and sings and yells like the other girls."

"I'm noting," said the social worker, who wrote on a notebook.

Now came the point where Kate always wanted to ask what to expect—but was afraid to.

"Do you hear from her birth mother?" she asked.

The social worker stared. "You know that's confidential."

"I'm just worried about her. I know at one time that she had the goal of getting Addie back and—"

"I can tell you there are no plans to transfer her immediately."

"What about visits? Still no word?"

Again flipping through the file. "Apparently, the mother has been in rehabilitation. One brother is being considered for adoption placement and the other is still in foster care."

Kate exhaled. "So . . ."

"For the time being, she's here with you."

"For the time being."

"Right now, yes. I've told you this before. The nature of foster parenting is temporary."

"I just can't help asking."

"Just know that the child's welfare will always be put first."

Kate nodded in silence. She'd reached the point, which she always did, where she didn't dare say anything further. She didn't want to get in trouble, which could mean trouble for Addie. But still, she was glad that Addie was still at their house—for one more day.

Suddenly the social worker frowned. "That photo." She gestured with her head.

"It's my favorite." Kate beamed. The photo depicted her whole family—her husband, Linwood; herself; Hillary; Kris; and Addie.

"You included a foster child in your family photo?"

"Of course. We wanted to." Kate was surprised at the vehemence in her voice. "We feel like she's part of us."

"That isn't customary. Most families don't do that."

Kate took a breath. "It's a way we'll always remember her."

The social worker nodded, took her notebook out, and wrote inside it.

"I'm sorry," Kate said quickly. "I'm sorry if it's against the rules."

The woman shook her head and strode quickly to the door.

"I'll see you in six months."

The woman stopped. "If the child is still placed here," she said as she walked out the door.

* * *

Addie sat silent on Kris's bed, cradling the other girl's
new Barbie in her hands. With hardly a second thought,
she eased loose the elastic that held the doll's hair in a
ponytail. A cascade of blond hair, soft as down, spilled
onto her fingers. She let it drop along the sides of the
doll's face, then studied the effect of Barbie wearing a
long and loose hairstyle. Then she drew it up into a
French twist. She divided the hair into three hanks and
was beginning to braid it when the door slammed open.

"What are you doing? That's mine!" Kris called out.

Stunned, Addie was silent.

"Mom!" Kris screamed.

Seconds later Addie's heart thudded as Kate stepped
into the room. The doll felt hot as a torch in her hand.

"She's ruining my new Barbie! The one I got for my
birthday."

"Kris! I'm sure she's just looking at it."

"She took the hair out of the rubber band. That ruins
it. You can't ever get it back the same way."

"Addie, dear. Remember to ask before you play with
Kris's toys."

"Saying that won't do anything. You never yell at her.
She needs a spanking."

"I don't spank you—and I'm not allowed to spank her."

"She's spoiled rotten, and she's not even ours."

For a painful, sickening second, Kate's eyes met Ad-
die's—and Addie saw pity there. Feeling her throat fill,
Addie ran from the room. She was leaving as she heard
Kate say, "Kris. You could be nicer."

"She could be nice to me."

Addie didn't speak that night at the table . . . or the next
night. It was like her heart couldn't stop pounding. Was
playing with Kris's doll a bad enough thing to have done
that it would cause these people to send her away? She
had her own Barbie, but it wasn't new anymore. She and
Hillary had played with it again and again, and now the
hair hung like a ragged rope from being braided and
brushed and styled repeatedly. She loved playing with

dolls with Hillary. And truth to tell, she really hadn't
thought it would hurt Kris's Barbie if she just played with
it for a minute while Kris was at a friend's house. But
now, thinking about it, she knew deep down that the hair
on Kris's doll would never be the same. Kris was right.
But was playing with one little doll enough for these people to decide to send her back? They'd never, never mentioned anything like that . . . not even once. But the people
before didn't mention such things either.

As days passed, Addie tried not to get in trouble. But
it seemed like Kris always got mad at her, no matter what
she did. And she got mad at Hillary, too. "Girls, get
along," Kate would say. Addie couldn't stop wondering.
If the three of them didn't get along, would she have to
leave? The thought filled her with fear . . . and a feeling
of how much she loved the Davis family. But still she
knew that no matter how long she stayed or no matter
how well behaved she was, she wouldn't be their daughter
like Hillary and Kris. In foster homes, everyone talked
about kids being adopted. But Addie already knew that
could never happen to her. Someone kept saying no. Was
it really her birth mother? Did her birth mother still want
her? If she did, where was she? Why didn't she ever visit
or write or call? The question haunted Addie as months
passed. Would she ever know why she didn't live with
the woman who gave birth to her?

When she arrived in a silent house, Kate thought she
was home alone. She imagined the girls were probably
outside, or down the street. She was shredding lettuce for
a dinner salad when she suddenly smelled smoke.

Was something burning? Kate's hand flew to the stove,
which was reassuringly room temperature. She rushed
downstairs to the fuse box, thinking that maybe . . .

Hurrying past the family room, she caught sight of Addie, standing in her Levi's next to a pile of newspapers
from which wisps of flame were rising.

"Addie!" She rushed to the girl's side.

Addie did not look up. Kate caught sight of a book of matches on the floor, next to the half-burned papers.

"What were you trying to do, burn down the house?" The second she released her anger, Kate wished she could call it back. What was Addie thinking?

"Don't know." The girl's shoulders shifted in an angry shrug.

Kate felt a rush of frustration, both at herself and at the smoking newspapers in front of her on the floor. She reached for Addie's arm, but Addie yanked herself away, running up the stairs.

Kate moved to follow the girl, then saw that feathers of smoke still emanated from the newspaper pile.

Kate stomped the smoldering pile with her shoes, then strode to the bathroom for a laundry bucket. She filled it with an inch or so of water, which she dribbled onto the papers. It looks like tears falling, she thought, thinking that the tears could be her own. Her heart ached for Addie and whatever was tormenting her inside. How can I convince her that even though she's not my own, I love her as if she is? Kate agonized.

Then she ran to look for Addie, and found her lying facedown on her bed.

"Addie . . ." She reached to touch the girl, who instantly shrank away.

Kate stepped back, aching with pain for the sorrow she sensed that Addie felt as much as she did herself.

"Addie, I'm sorry I yelled. I don't like to yell at you." Kate paused, feeling that her voice would break. "But fire is dangerous. You could get hurt."

Silence. The girl on the bed lay still.

Kate sat on the bed beside Addie. She lifted the girl's hand. Addie looked up in surprise, and Kate saw her eyes held tears. "Is there something you need to tell me?"

Addie shook her head fiercely.

"Can you tell me why this happened?"

Addie shrugged. "I don't know."

Kate stayed seated on the bed, wishing she could erase the incident along with Addie's humiliation. After a moment she glanced down and saw that Addie was looking up at her.

"Why did you take me?" the girl asked.

Kate shook her head. "I don't know what you mean."

"Why did you let me live here?"

"Because we wanted you."

"No, you didn't. No one wants me." Now Addie struggled to a sitting position and shook her head.

Kate sighed. "That's not true. We wanted you from the first minute we saw you."

"My real family didn't."

"That's not true. It wasn't that they didn't want you. They just couldn't take care of you right then. So we're helping."

"But they gave me away. You wouldn't give your girls away."

"No." Kate swallowed. "They didn't give you away." She slid closer to Addie. "If they did"—she sifted her fingers through the girl's hair—"we'd try to get you. To adopt you."

"You would?"

Kate nodded as her throat caught.

"Can you ask my mom why she doesn't want me?"

What should she say?

"I can't speak with your birth mother because I don't know where she is. The state doesn't tell me. But I can tell the social worker you want to know." Even as she said this, Kate flinched. Would the social worker see this as a failure on her part?

"Why doesn't she write to me? Why doesn't she call?"

"The state probably hasn't told her where you are."

"If she really wanted me, she'd find me. She'd come here and get me back."

It took all the effort Kate had to force the words out. "Maybe she will . . . someday."

"Next month? Next year? When?"

"I don't know." Kate had to shake her head. "But I hope you'll be here with us until then."

"I hope they don't take me someplace else."

Kate leaned to give Addie a hug. "I hope so, too." She kissed the top of the girl's head, gave her another hug, and went downstairs to fix dinner, her heart filled with pain for a world where a child could feel she wasn't wanted. As days passed, she watched Hillary, Addie, and Kris playing outside together and the pain continued to hover. What could she do to heal Addie's heart? Couldn't Addie tell how much all of them loved her?

Chapter 6

∞

The two girls stood outside during recess. "You can try it on," Michelle said to Addie. Michelle held out her hand, and Addie slid the round band over her finger. The metal felt cool against her skin, and the turquoise stone was bluer than the sky.

I never had a ring like this, Addie thought. No one ever bought a ring for me.

She held her hand out, and sunshine caught the blue of the stone. Her vision blurred.

What would it be like to have a home where someone bought her a ring like that without her even asking?

"Hey, let's go outside," said Michelle, reaching for the ring.

Addie reluctantly slid it off her finger.

The two girls ran. They played hopscotch, rolled down the hill at the top of the playground, and jumped rope.

The recess bell rang. Then it was art—papier-mâché, the smell of fresh glue and newspaper ink.

Addie saw Michelle put the ring in her crayon box. As she draped strips of glue-dampened paper over a balloon, the ring stayed on her mind. She wanted to feel it on her finger again. Should she ask Michelle? But when she looked up, Michelle was at the sink, washing off her hands.

The ring was still in Michelle's desk. Maybe she could look at it once more, Addie thought. She looked up, saw Michelle was still at the sink. With her eyes on the back of Michelle's head, Addie walked slowly to Michelle's desk. She opened the other girl's crayon box and caught sight of the ring. She stared at it for a moment, then seeing Michelle was still at the sink, slid it onto her finger.

She went back to her own desk, the ring weighing heavy on her hand. As Michelle suddenly turned, Addie hid her hand beneath her own desk. Her heart pounded. She held her breath as she watched Michelle fumble with the papers on her desk.

"My ring!" Michelle's voice filled the room and pierced Addie's heart. "Where I did I put it?" She knelt and frantically pawed through the cubbyhole in her own desk.

Addie's hand was stiff and still.

"Where did I put it?" Michelle's voice grew increasingly frantic.

The teacher suddenly stopped talking and turned toward the class.

"Michelle? What is the problem?"

"My ring's gone!"

"Did it fall off your finger?"

"No! I put it in my desk because of the papier-mâché."

The teacher strode back toward Michelle's desk. Addie held her breath. The ring now felt like it burned on her hand. She watched in horror as the teacher picked up each of Michelle's books and all of her papers, then turned to face the class.

"Have any of you seen Michelle's ring?"

The teacher's anxious gaze riveted on Addie.

"Addie? Did you play with her at recess?"

Addie's tongue turned to stone.

"Didn't I see you out there playing hopscotch?"

The teacher stepped closer, frown lines creasing her forehead.

Slowly, Addie nodded.

"Did you see her ring?"

Addie sighed. Her arm felt heavy as iron as she lifted it up onto the desk.

"My ring!" Michelle gasped. "You stole it."

Addie's eyes dropped to the floor.

"Miss Adams! She took my ring!"

"Addie?" The teacher stepped closer.

"I just wanted to try it on."

"No, you didn't. You wanted to steal it!"

Addie's lip quivered. "I'm sorry—"

"Return the ring, Addie." The teacher's voice was firm.

Why wouldn't her lip stop quivering? A flood of tears streamed down Addie's face. She felt the class stare at her. With shaking fingers, she slid the ring off and reached her hand out.

"I'll have to tell your mother, Addie," the teacher said.

"I don't have a mother."

The teacher shook her head. "Everyone has a mother. A parent. And I will have to call yours."

"I don't live with her. She doesn't want me."

"Then who is taking care of you?"

"My foster parents."

"Then I will talk to them."

"They're not my real parents."

"They're in charge of you. They will deal with discipline."

"They're not allowed to hurt me."

"No one will hurt you. But you can't steal."

"I said I was sorry."

"Just don't do it again."

"Don't let Addie see your stuff," Michelle said to the class. "She steals."

The teacher strode to the front of the room. Everyone stared, leaving Addie feeling hot with embarrassment and limp with tears. Later that afternoon, Addie went out to recess, yet quickly rushed into the girls' bathroom, where she sat in a stall where no one could see her. She wept, knowing her eyes would be red when she returned to class, but still unable to help herself. Tears dropped onto the white blouse and plaid jumper that the Davises had bought for her. She looked down and saw the new black school shoes the Davises had also bought her.

The Davises. Were they going to find out about this? How could she explain that even though they loved her very much and made her feel as safe as if she were wrapped in a warm blanket, she couldn't forget her real family? Memories of her birth parents floated in her mind like ragged pieces of a quilt that she couldn't stitch back together or remove.

"Addie Randall, please report to the principal's office," came a voice over the loudspeaker.

Addie gathered herself together after a last sob, then stood. She washed her hands, then wiped her eyes with a stiff brown paper towel. She glanced at her reddened eyes, then smoothed her skirt and walked down to the office. The recess bell rang when she was halfway there. What would her classmates think when she didn't return to class?

"Addie? Go on back to see the principal," the secretary told her when she walked in the office.

Addie's heart thudded. She had never talked to the principal before. She knew what the prinicipal looked like— a tall, imposing man who never smiled.

He stood in the doorway as Addie walked toward his office.

"Adelaide?" He acknowledged her with his huge chin.

"It's just Addie. That's all the name I have."

"Please come in and be seated."

Addie's heart sank when she saw Kate sitting in a chair next to the principal's desk.

"Mom! Why are you here?" Her voice burst out, but then she shrank at the sight of the principal's frown.

"The school called me, honey," Kate said gently, in the warm voice that had soothed Addie to sleep when she first came to live with the Davises.

"I called your mother, Addie," said the principal.

When Kate didn't correct the man, Addie felt forced to say, "She's not really my mom." It hurt to say those words. Who had been more of a mom to her than Kate? If she could somehow choose a mother, Kate would be the first one she'd pick.

Now the principal raised his eyebrows and looked at Kate. "What's the meaning of this?"

"I'm Addie's foster mother. I don't know if it says anything in her file—"

"You're the one who has been charged with her care?"

"Oh yes." Kate smiled at Addie. "We feel that she's part of our family."

"Since you are the one supervising her, we need to discuss a serious matter."

Kate's smile faded as she looked at the principal.

"As you know, Addie confessed to stealing another girl's ring this morning."

"Addie?" Kate turned to her.

Addie's chin drooped as she nodded.

"Where is the ring now?" Kate asked, as if the principal weren't in the room with them.

"I gave it back." Addie wiped her eyes with her hand. "I said I was sorry."

Addie watched Kate look to the principal, who met her eyes with a forceful gaze.

"Although the child returned the ring when confronted, this sort of behavior cannot be tolerated. Stealing, even at such a young age, is illegal and unacceptable behavior."

"She said she was sorry. She gave the ring back."

"Not until she was accused of taking it. We need to be

assured that such an event will not take place again."

"Addie?"

When Kate addressed her, Addie felt forced to look her in the eyes. "I won't do it again," she said. "I said I was sorry."

"May I suggest that, considering the child's background, more than an apology may be necessary?"

"What do you mean?" Kate asked.

"I'm considering the possibility that some sort of therapeutic action needs to be taken, that possibly this behavior is the symptom of some sort of pathology."

"You're saying there's something *wrong* with Addie? She's just a little girl," Kate protested.

"Surely her background suggests there may be psychological scars, or the child would not have been removed from her original home."

Kate sighed. "There were problems. I can't deny that."

"Possibly such problems require treatment."

"What exactly are you referring to?"

"I'm suggesting counseling."

Kate reached out and took Addie's arm. "We'll look into it. I'll do anything if it will help Addie." She reached out and took Addie's hand. "Okay, Addie? We'll try and get some help for you."

Addie couldn't speak. What were they saying was wrong with her now? What were they going to do? Was this it, the final straw that would make the Davises give her back? Would they "help" her by giving her to someone else? Addie's fear didn't subside, even as Kate placed a hand on her shoulder and walked with her all the way back to class.

Kate wondered what Addie was thinking as she and Hillary sat next to each other on the couch and watched the movers load boxes onto the truck. Did the little girl really understand that she was still going to live with them? That she wasn't being taken away again?

"There's the one with our books and stuffed animals," Hillary called out, and pointed as the mover hoisted a box labeled GIRL STUFF onto the truck.

The phone rang. It was probably Linwood, Kate thought, calling to see if the moving van had arrived.

"Hello, Mrs. Davis, it's Sandra." Something about the tone in the normally calm caseworker's voice caused a shiver of fear in Kate.

"How are you?" Kate struggled to keep worry out of her voice. "We're just heading out today." Why was Sandra Allen calling her now?

"I'm fine, but I need to let you know about a possible problem."

Now Kate's worry heightened. "We're leaving today."

"I'm sorry to say this, but you might want to reconsider—"

"The movers are here. The van is half packed. I—"

"I heard from Addie's mother. She has several concerns."

Addie's mother. The thought made Kate's heart thud. "But you said that everything was fine. That we could leave and Addie could go with us." Kate heard rising panic in her own voice.

"She's worried that Addie is getting too close to you."

Kate waited. "I can't deny that. But we just can't help it. Our family has fallen in love with her. I would think her mother would want her foster family to care about her."

"I think her mother's worry is that if you take her, she won't ever come back here."

"Could you please tell her that this is just a work transfer? We aren't trying to run off with her."

"I think she is afraid she'll never see her daughter again."

Kate paused. "Is she ready to see her? Could she take care of Addie?"

"I seriously doubt it," the social worker said. "She's

gone back into rehab. She's still struggling with alcoholism."

"Does she have any of her children with her?"

"No, they're all in foster care, except Addie's brother, who has been adopted."

"This seems really strange to me . . ." Kate struggled to keep her voice even. "If all of her children have been taken away, why is she allowed to make this decision?"

"Her parental rights haven't been taken from her. Legally, she's still Addie's mom. She has to sign a release before you can take her with you."

Suddenly the view outside the living-room window seemed bleak and gray. Kate stared at the profiles of all three girls as they sat giggling on the couch, pointing and laughing at the movers.

"If her mother can't take of her, she'll have to go to another foster home." Kate winced as she spoke. "Has she thought of that?"

"I think so, but I'll ask her again."

Now Kate sighed. "I don't think that it would be good for Addie to leave here now. Please, ask her mother to let her stay."

"I'll talk to her"—Sandra sighed—"but she sounds quite determined."

"Please try to settle this," Kate pleaded. "We've got to head out."

"I can't force her to sign the paper. But I'll get back to you." Sandra's voice didn't sound hopeful. "I'll call you as soon as I can."

Feeling helpless, Kate held the phone and stood in the kitchen long after Sandra hung up. What should she do now?

Minutes, then an hour, passed.

Linwood arrived home, a tense look on his familiar face. Kate was trying to explain when a moving-company worker came to the door.

"You know the clock is ticking, ma'am. We charge you from when we leave the warehouse."

"I know," Kate said, her heart pounding. "I'm sure it will be just a few more minutes."

The man shrugged. "It's your money."

Please, Kate begged inside, anxiously wondering what she would do if Sandra Allen called back and said they couldn't leave the state. Would they stay here, in one of the motels downtown, and anxiously wait for word? Or worse—she didn't dare think—what if a social worker said they couldn't keep Addie? What if they came to take her away?

The phone rang, and before she could tell him it was for her, Linwood rushed to answer it.

Kate watched as he listened for a long time. "Guess we'll go on ahead," he said finally. What did that mean? Who was going to go on ahead? Kate held her breath.

"Sandra Allen," Linwood said as he hung up the phone. "Said she can't promise things will be okay when we get to the new place, but as for now, we should head on out."

"She didn't tell you what happened? How they finally resolved everything?"

"Kate, she's been working until now—eight o'clock at night. She just got us cleared to go. I didn't get the feeling I should ask about anything else."

Linwood was right, Kate decided. They would just go ahead now—and pray that the future would be bright.

Chapter 7

∽

As cold as Sandra Allen had seemed, Kate now longed for the familiar blond hair and official-looking business suits. At least with Sandra, she knew what to expect. Now she watched as a short-haired, serious-looking woman dressed in a navy-blue dress walked up to their house and rang the bell.

She held her breath and opened the door.

"Mrs. Davis?"

"Yes." Kate nodded and welcomed the woman inside her house.

"I received your phone message that you wished to speak with me. How may I help you?" she asked flatly.

"I want to ask for your advice." Kate felt a flood of emotions. What were the right things to say? What words could she use to help change Addie's life? "We are having a wonderful experience as foster parents . . . except . . ."

The counselor sat like a stone. "There is a problem?"

"Our foster daughter . . . Addie Randall . . . well, she's behaving . . . in a way that I think is a cry for help."

"In what way?"

Did she really want to tell this coldhearted woman about Addie's struggles? "She is . . . as you would say . . . acting out . . ."

"Oh? Describe her behavior to me."

Kate hesitated. Was this really the only way to help Addie? "I found her with matches in our family room. It appeared she meant to deliberately start a fire."

The woman nodded. "Go on."

"Later"—Kate paused to look for any crack in the woman's armor—"that same week, she took a ring that a friend showed her."

"She *stole* a ring?"

"Yes, I'd have to say she took it. But she admitted it right away and apologized to the girl . . ."

"So what do you want from our office?" The woman gestured impatiently.

"I'm feeling that this behavior isn't like her, that counseling might help."

The woman's smile was amused. "You're suggesting the state pay for counseling!"

"I'm just trying to help her."

The woman sat back and braced her hands against the

desk. "Mrs. Davis. We don't even have enough foster homes for children who need them. We are trying to find a place for these children to eat and sleep . . . and you want counseling."

"I know she's had a very rough background. There was abuse and neglect."

The woman held up a hand. "Like about ninety percent of the children we see. I would need to look in her file. But there seems to be some confusion. I couldn't find her name in the files before I left the office. I came here to make sure I have the name correct. Addie Randall? That was the name you gave me?"

"Yes."

"There's no Addie Randall in my files. I checked twice. From which office was she placed?"

"The South County office."

The woman cupped her face with her hand. "There's no South County office in this state. She's from out of state, and you expect our office to provide counseling for her?"

"We made arrangements with the South County office when we moved here. They said you were assigned as her counselor."

"I have to tell you. There is no way our office will pay for any sort of treatment for a child from South County."

"Even if she is living here?" Kate knew she was grasping at straws.

"It's this simple. We don't have enough money to pay for our state's evaluation and counseling. There are no funds."

Kate stood slowly. "I guess I have my answer."

"I'm sorry," the woman said firmly. "I wish things were different, but there's just no money."

Kate nodded sadly. "Thank you for your time. Goodbye."

After the woman left, Kate wondered how she could help Addie the most. Without knowing just what secrets were locked in the young girl's past, it was hard to know how to heal Addie's pain. The more she thought, the more she felt convinced that professional help might be the right idea. But how could she get that now?

With her radio blaring, Hillary mouthed the words to song lyrics in the mirror. "Before you break my heart . . ." She tapped her foot while half-thinking of the next line. After the Supreme song ended, the Beach Boys came on. Then the Beatles. The Rolling Stones. When she and Mick Jagger finished their last song, Hillary walked out to the kitchen, where Kate was making Jell-O salad.

"Where's Addie?"

"She waited for you awhile, but then she left." Kate stirred a can of pineapple into the lime-green salad.

"Why didn't she come in and get me?"

Kate looked at her levelly. "You told the girls to stay out of your room. No little kids allowed, remember?"

"But I told her we'd go to the store. She wanted to get some bubble gum."

"I think she got tired of waiting," Kate said calmly.

"So where did she go?"

"She said she was going to Pam's."

"Again? Didn't she go there yesterday and the day before?"

Kate nodded and sighed. "I think our Addie has found a friend. Can you believe it?"

Hillary was surprised at the bittersweet feeling that filled her. "But I was her friend."

"Far as I know, you still are," Kate said. "The two of you living in the same house and all."

"But she left without me."

"She got tired of waiting. You know"—Kate paused— "you've been spending a lot of time alone in that room where she's not allowed."

Hillary swallowed.

"Why didn't she come get me?"

"She waited outside the door. I guess she thought you'd get mad if she disturbed you."

"I wouldn't."

"She thought you might."

Hillary turned to walk back toward her room.

"You know," Kate said, "someday Addie is going to do more than find a friend." She paused. "Someday she's going to leave."

"I hope not." Hillary turned back toward her mother. "I hope not until she's an old, old lady."

"Someday you'll leave, too. And I'll be the old, old lady." Kate laughed.

Hillary shook her head. She was halfway down the hall toward her room when she heard Kate say, "My three girls are growing up."

Her three girls, Hillary thought, Addie is really my sister.

Kate was paralyzed with fright. Just seconds before, she had caught her first glimpse of the tractor that was now heading straight for the car where she sat in the backseat. She stared in terrified disbelief as the tractor crashed against the side of the car with a thunderous roar that jarred her teeth and rattled her bones. Oh my . . . was she going to live though this?

What will happen to Addie? she thought just before she lost consciousness. Addie and my girls.

Where will they go if I die? And what about Linwood?

Chapter 8

∽

Waiting for her appointment with the social worker, Kate struggled to stifle a sudden feeling of panic. She tried to assure herself that the meeting was only routine, but couldn't ignore her gut instinct that something was wrong. She was still recovering from the tractor accident that had put her father in the hospital for a week, and her crutches lay beside her on the front-room couch, next to the new white cast that reached nearly to the knee of her left leg.

Yet there really hadn't been any warning of a new crisis. All three girls were at school, and Linwood was out of state on a business trip. She was still searching her mind for the source of her unease when the doorbell rang, and she hobbled to the door to answer it. Like Sandra Allen, Mary Larson was blond and cool, and her thoughts never showed in her face. Kate held her breath.

"Mrs. Davis." Mary Larson's voice was matter-of-fact as she held out a cool hand to Kate and stepped inside the Davises' living room. It was impossible to read any hidden meaning into those two words. Still, Kate trembled. She tried to formulate answers to possible questions Mrs. Larson might pose. But she didn't get very far because the woman spoke, and what she said struck Kate with the force of a sledgehammer.

"I've been instructed to arrange alternate placement for Addie Randall."

"No!" Kate's whole being felt slapped, and she felt chills and instant tears. Yet she spoke without stopping to consider her words. "We need more time," she breathed.

Mary Larson's cool blue eyes stared back at her as she sat down opposite Kate.

Kate sighed. "You know how well she's doing with us. She's made so much progress, and she'll keep going if . . ." Kate paused.

The woman in the chair across from her sat still as stone.

"If this is because we talked about the possibility of adoption . . ." A single tear slid down her cheek as Addie's smiling face and shining eyes hovered in her thoughts.

"I know you've all become quite attached," Mary Larson said stiffly, her fingers wrapped tightly around a pen.

"Yes," Kate admitted almost inaudibly, her eyes drifting to the shaking hands in her lap. "I've grown to love her too much to let her go. We all have." Kate's last words wavered, and she wiped her eyes quickly. Then she forcefully brought her focus back to the seemingly stone face across the room. "It's too bad all foster children can't fit in their homes the way Addie fits in ours."

When the social worker didn't answer right away, Kate fought an urge to grab the folder from the woman's briefcase and search for reasons for this devastating decision.

"She couldn't even talk when she came to our house. You know that. Now she's been in plays, and has neighborhood friends, and . . ." Kate's words trailed off as the sudden helplessness rose within. What could she say that would stop this stranger's threatening her happy family?

"You've served very well as foster parents. There's no dispute there. We would very probably place another child with you if you so desired." Kate watched Mary Larson's throat move as the younger woman swallowed and she fumbled with her pen and folder. She's fighting what she feels inside, too, Kate thought. She's not completely sold on this bureaucratic decision.

Abruptly, Kate asked, "Is it her mother? I know she feels jealous about how happy Addie is with us." Kate stopped herself before she could say that her instinct was that Addie's mother would never sign the adoption papers, yet would likely not recover from alcoholism to the point where she could be a parent herself. So why couldn't Addie stay in the only real home she'd ever known?

Mary Larson's words came in a rush. "Mrs. Davis, we've talked before. As you know, the average foster-home placement is a year. Addie has been with you far longer." She lifted a file from her briefcase and flipped through its pages. "Five years. Not to mention the violations of other rules—taking the child out of state—"

"We moved for my husband's work."

Larson only shook her head. "Have her things ready on July eleventh. We'll be here to pick her up."

"But that's her birthday!" Kate protested.

There was no response. Kate stood, but the social worker would not look up and meet her eyes. Kate's lip quivered as she again fumbled for the words that would somehow change this pronouncement. "You know she's been abused in other foster homes. And she's been through more moves than any child deserves."

Larson only nodded. "Her two brothers will be in the next home with her. They've been crying for her and asking why she isn't with them. And she's said that she would like to see her real mother."

Kate was silent. Mary Larson had brought up the one thing she could never give Addie—her biological roots. All the sumptuous dinners, good-night kisses, homemade Halloween costumes, and laughing together couldn't change the little girl's genes. And there was no doubt that Addie cried out in confused frustration about why her biological family had been broken apart. Getting into fights at school, starting the fire, wondering why she never had a baby picture. Kate couldn't deny that the scars from her abandonment were still healing "It might be good for Addie to be with her own brothers," she conceded. "And I agree that she's going to need to confront her mother before she can completely heal. You know I've tried to get therapy for her for years. There are never funds for foster children to seek counseling."

"Counseling will be arranged in the new placement." Larson's words were abrupt.

Beneath her deep pain, Kate tried to objectively decide whether counseling and being with her brothers could possibly benefit Addie more than being in a home where she was loved like a sister and daughter. Kate knew she could never decide Addie's fate the way the social workers seemed to be doing. "If she's in a good home in a place with excellent health-care facilities . . . But I still can't see that it's right to move her again. She's so happy. Why can't you just leave her where she is?" It was a meek final protest, but a part of her still wanted to rage, to grab the social worker by the lapels and ask, *How can you take her away from us now?*

The social worker offered no answer to Kate's question. The two women waited in silence until Larson idly looked at her watch. Knowing the verdict had been pronounced, Kate couldn't stop herself from speaking one more time. She began, "I just think—" but then she shook her head. Moments later her eyes met the other woman's again. "We can write to her, can't we? We can phone her."

Mary Larson grimaced. "There's no law against it. I'll give you the number. But we ask you not to make contact. It could interfere with her adjustment to the new placement."

Kate wanted to ask, *What about our adjustment to having her ripped away?*

Larson looked at her watch, then stood. "We appreciate all of the kind care you've given her up until now."

Kate couldn't answer.

"And I need to get to my next appointment."

Words stayed frozen in Kate's throat. A chilling breeze wafted through the front door as Larson said good-bye and left the Davis home. Kate's thoughts came in a rush. How could she numb herself enough against this pain so she could tell the girls what had happened without crying?

Memories of Addie replayed in her mind. The wind-chime sound that was Addie's first laugh at age seven. Addie and Hillary cooking together and saving soup labels to join the Heinz Happy Soup Club. Addie dressed as Snoopy on Halloween, her eyes seemingly as dark and shiny as those of a real beagle pup. Addie dressed in bell-bottoms and a peace-sign T-shirt sitting between Kris and Hillary on the porch swing.

If she went along with this decision, Kate reasoned, there was a hope, however slight, that Addie could some-day come back. And an even slighter hope that her mother would change her mind, and they could adopt her, making her one of them forever. "Please . . ." Kate whispered a plea to the universe.

That night, Kate fixed Addie's favorite spaghetti. She couldn't help noticing how Addie sat comfortably at the table in her place, as if that long-ago night when she felt forced to eat on the floor had never happened. She watched Hillary and Addie laughing together as Addie sang "Uh-oh Spaghettios . . . with meatballs and peddios."

Kate sadly watched her family, eating, talking, and laughing as if the happy night would never end. She thought about saying that they would have Addie's birth-day party early this year—but she already knew that if this was to be the last party, she'd make it the surprise party Addie had always wanted. Finally feeling that she couldn't wait a moment longer, Kate said, "We're going to make Addie's birthday really special this year—be-cause afterward, she's going to live in a home with her two brothers. The social worker feels she will be happier with someone in her own family."

The laughter and informal conversation at the table sud-denly died and Kate found herself facing a heavy silence.

"What?" Hillary's anger was instantaneous. Her face blanched in shock. "They're taking her away from us?" First her angry frown was aimed at her mother, but almost immediately she turned on Kris. "It's your fault, because you always get in fights with her."

"It is not!" Kris looked to her mother for defense.

"It's nobody's fault," Kate started to protest, but Hillary interrupted.

"And it's your fault, too, Mom, because you let her keep getting in trouble at school. You didn't fix her problems."

"Hillary!" Kate cried, and for the first time Hillary sensed her mother's pain and looked away.

"Maybe it's my fault . . ." Hillary's words fell into the room like cold rain. "I haven't played with her as much lately. She has her own friends now."

Moments later Hillary asked Addie, "Why don't you just tell them you want to stay here?"

Addie couldn't speak. The small girl's whole being filled with a frightening ache she hadn't experienced for five years. Even though a full half of her life had passed since she felt this sense of helpless desperation, the wound was now as fresh as it had been when she left the last foster home. There was the same panicked yet numb knowledge that she must have done something wrong to be forced away from here, too. What could it be? She thought of the fires, of getting in trouble at school, but when her ten-year-old mind tried to analyze life at the Davises', her only lasting impressions were of happiness and love. Yet her mind simultaneously registered that it had been like this in a way at the other houses, too. First, she didn't know what went wrong, and then suddenly she was snatched away.

The next day Hillary watched Addie run across the street and dash through a neighbor's sprinkler. To her, Addie looked like a captive horse that had been momentarily set free. Run—run far away as fast as you can, Hillary thought to herself. Then hide—until they stop looking for you. Then come back and stay with us. When Addie walked back home, wet, trembling, and smiling, Hillary reached out and hugged her. She didn't know if the coldness she felt was from Addie's wet shirt or from her own knowledge that this hug might be one of the last.

That night was Addie's surprise party. All her friends from down the street came over, hiding behind tables and chairs in the Davises' upstairs family room. When Kate called Addie away from watching her favorite Charlie Brown cartoon, the children leaped up and yelled "Surprise!" Addie jumped back, and for an instant her eyes looked puzzled and scared. Then she laughed, and her friends surrounded her at a table heaped with presents. Hillary handed her the biggest present first, her smile wavering and her eyes brimming with tears.

"Hmm . . . what could this be?" Kate said in her most mysterious voice.

Addie smiled as if she couldn't imagine. Then she slid the crackly paper off and her mouth opened in genuine surprise. She gasped. "My track! My racetrack!"

"But she's a girl!" said Tommy from the down the street.

Addie hardly heard as she opened the box and began to snap the pieces of track together.

"What about your other presents?" Hillary asked gently.

There were Barbie clothes, a fluffy toy rabbit, doll dishes, a new dress, candy, and a dollar Linwood folded in half in an envelope.

"We love you, Addie," Kate said firmly, hugging the small girl close. Hillary walked over and ruffled Addie's hair.

No one mentioned that it could be the last party for a long time. Hillary wondered if she'd ever feel like having a party again.

All of the girls were playing at the neighbors' two days later when Kate began to pack Addie's belongings. Scanning the closet, she caught sight of the tiny suitcase Addie had brought to their home five years before. It looked no bigger than a cereal box. Now it seemed far more appropriate for a doll than for a lively ten-year-old girl. Covering the small suitcase with a doll blanket, Kate searched for the largest packing container her family owned. She finally settled on Linwood's navy footlocker—larger than a suitcase, yet smaller than a trunk.

Filling the open footlocker with toys and clothes, Kate stopped when she picked up Hillary's and Addie's Barbie dolls. Their ponytailed hair had been brushed hundreds of times as the two girls voiced hours of make-believe conversations. For a moment Kate could hear their Barbie voices, talking about going to the prom or the mall or a make-believe school. She recalled Hillary's motherly tones, suggesting Addie's Barbie should wear the satin dress and the white plastic pumps. She thought of Addie's eager laugh, and the two of them searching for the ideal purse to go with the dress. She suddenly felt it wasn't any more right to separate the two dolls than it was to separate the two little girls. She placed both Barbies gently in the footlocker, along with Addie's clothes. As she folded them, she wondered where Addie would wear them next. In a smaller pocket of the footlocker, she inserted a check for the bicycle they'd planned to buy next Christmas and the savings bond earmarked for Addie's future college education. Then she dropped in a new blue purse they'd bought for Addie to have as a surprise at her new home. Finally she closed the footlocker solemnly, and two tears fell, small splashes against the gray metal surface.

On July 11, Addie's birthday, even before she heard the thud of raindrops on the roof, Kate awoke with a feeling of heartache as she sensed this would be the blackest day of her life. It seemed so ironic that Addie's eleventh birthday would feel like a death to be mourned rather than an event to celebrate.

Kate inched her injured body to the edge of the bed, fully aware that she was fighting tears, not from any residual pain she felt from the accident, but from the knowledge that Addie would be leaving within hours. As she had done over the last week, Kate tried one more time to find a small gleam of light within this senseless loss. She thought of her past efforts to get some therapy for Addie, and how there hadn't been any funds for counseling for foster children. Maybe now, she thought to herself, Addie actually would receive treatment for the emotional wounds that still remained all these years after the abuse.

Sighing to herself, she went to Hillary's bedroom. For a moment she gazed at her beautiful daughter in sleep, her dark hair framing her head like an aura. Then she touched her daughter's shoulder. "Hillary, time to get ready."

Hillary turned over, then mumbled quickly. "I'm not going to my tennis lesson today. I won't even be able to hit the ball."

"We talked about this," Kate said gently. "Don't make it any harder for Addie . . ."

"Can't I please stay home and say good-bye to her?"

Kate couldn't answer. Anything they did this morning would still end with Addie leaving as soon as the social worker arrived.

"I don't know what time she'll be leaving," Kate said finally.

"Can I go give her a hug now?"

Kate paused, then nodded.

Hillary tiptoed into Addie's room. She looked around in the early morning silence. Even with the toys packed and the closet nearly empty, this would always be Addie's room. There were the drawings from school tacked to the bulletin board. And the family picture, with all of them together. And the mirror above the chest of drawers, where Addie's big dark eyes stared as she combed her hair. Hillary remembered coming in the room to surprise Addie while she was fixing her hair, and the way her heart always leaped at Addie's mirror-grin.

"Hillary?" She heard her mother's voice call out softly. Rushing to Addie's bedside, she held the small girl in her arms. When Addie didn't wake up, she kissed her soft, dark hair and touched her cheek.

"You will always be my sister," she said, then looked up to see Kate standing in the bedroom doorway.

As the two of them walked down the hallway to the kitchen, Hillary asked, "What did I do wrong, Mom? Why does she have to go?"

Kate's heart felt heavy as iron. "Nobody did anything wrong, Hillary. You were the best sister you could be. We were her family."

"We can't let her go!" Hillary protested, her heart thudding in her chest. Feeling her own tears well, Kate squeezed Hillary's hand and left the kitchen.

Kate went into Addie's room. Gazing at the sleeping girl, she thought how much Addie looked like one of their family with her dark hair and eyes. Kate looked around the room and was hit by a rush of memories. There was the stereo the girls always played, and the corner of the room where their Barbies lived their make-believe lives.

Kate looked at the clock and knew she couldn't wait any longer. She leaned over and hugged Addie. "Come on," she said gently, hoping to infuse some cheer into her voice. "It's time to get up."

Addie stirred, then her eyes were filled with the apprehensive look Kate remembered from the first night at their house. Kate's tears finally escaped with memories of Addie's past pain and the realization that she could no longer keep her foster daughter safe. As the small girl sat up in bed, Kate hugged her. "Don't worry, honey. We'll be together again." Kissing her cheek, she added, "We'll write and we'll call at night. You're going to be with your two brothers—they've been crying for you, girl."

Addie's silent face looked a million years old. Kate pressed her cheek against the small girl's. She thought that Addie felt like a small, scared bird as she held her in her arms.

"We'll be together again," Kate repeated, leaving the room so the girl could dress.

The sound of the doorbell pierced Hillary's heart moments later. Her knees turned to jelly and there was a pounding in her head. Don't answer, Mom, she silently begged Kate. Maybe if we just hold still, they'll go away and never come back. Maybe they'll forget all about Addie and she can stay here.

Yet even as she agonized, Hillary found herself rushing silently to the door. If there was anything she could do, even now, at the last minute . . .

Hillary caught up with Kate and Kris joined them as the three of them forced themselves to take the last few steps.

Hillary stared at the social worker. Stoic-faced, with icy-blond hair and cold blue eyes. Neither she nor her mother nor Kris spoke.

"I'm here to retrieve Addie Randall," the social worker said.

Retrieve, thought Hillary, as if Addie were a football. That's how they think of her, she realized. As if she is an object.

Kate didn't invite the social worker in. And she didn't call out to Addie.

"Before you take her, I need to know the number where she'll be at tonight. There's something I need to let her know, and I won't have the information until then," Kate said.

What was her mom talking about? Hillary wondered as her questioning glance met Kris's. She hoped it meant they could still somehow talk to Addie.

The social worker shuffled her feet, then said, "Barbara Walker." She opened her file and showed Kate, who quickly wrote the phone number and address.

Hillary stared at the social worker. Go away, she thought. Go away and never come back.

The social worker glanced at her watch. "We need to be going," she said.

Do you have someone else to "retrieve"? Hillary wanted to ask. Someone else that you don't care about in the least? Someone else to whom you are going to cause lifelong pain?

Neither she nor Kris nor Kate went to get Addie.

Go away, Hillary wanted to yell. Go away and never come back.

"I need to take the girl now," the social worker said, her patience obviously wearing thin.

Hillary was filled with a furious electricity. "Leave her with us," she begged.

"Hillary." With a sigh, Kate turned and trudged up the stairs and into Addie's room, where she saw the girl, frozen with fear, sitting on the bed.

Kate saw that Addie looked like a frightened deer caught in a trap. And she's all clenched tight, just like that first night, when she curled up under the dinner table, and Hillary went to sit beside her.

We didn't save her. The thought brought a catch to Kate's throat. We loved her as much as we could, but we lost her.

Kate reached over to hug the small girl. She felt Addie's ribs quivering beneath the sweater, and leaned to brush her cheek against Addie's. "We love you, Addie-girl," she said softly.

"Mrs. Davis?" the social worker called up the stairs. "We need to be going."

Kate forced her voice to be light. "Those brothers of yours will be glad to see you today. Now give me one more hug. We'll all talk to you on the phone tonight."

This time Addie's arms reached out and gripped Kate, as if she would never let go. Kate closed her eyes to blink back tears.

"Do I need to come up there?" the social worker called out. Kate heard the woman step firmly on the first stair.

"No." Kate's voice was softer than she meant it to be. "We'll be right there."

Holding Addie in her arms so that she was nearly carrying her, Kate eased the girl off the bed and down the hall. She caught sight of Hillary and Kris, standing next to the social worker. All three were staring up the stairs. The social worker's eyes blazed with anger, and Kris appeared sad and bewildered, while Hillary's eyes were filled with the same frightened look Addie's held.

Was there anything she could do now, at the last minute?

Hillary watched as her mom half carried Addie down the stairs.

"Addie . . ." she called out.

When Addie's eyes met hers, Hillary called out, "Friends forever . . ." A second later she said, "Members of the Heinz Happy Soup Club."

"Remember Snoopy," said Kris.

For a moment they all stood together at the bottom of the stairs.

"Time to go now, Hillary." Kate's hand patted her daughter's shoulder.

Hillary shook her head fiercely yet stepped through the front doorway and onto the porch. "I love you, Addie," she called out desperately. "I don't want you to go!" They stared into each other's eyes before a flood of tears burst onto Hillary's reddened cheeks.

Addie stared as the images of a crying Hillary and a tearful Kris were imprinted on her brain as firmly as if they were engraved there. They all love me, Addie thought. The realization brought a lump to her throat. For a brief moment her sadness overpowered the terrifying feeling.

"We'll call you tonight. We promise." Now Addie felt Kate's arms hug her shoulders. A sob worked its way up to her throat, and Addie wailed. Now Kate knelt beside her. "We'll be together again." She paused and swallowed.

"We must be going," the social worker said firmly.

"One more hug," said Kate.

Looking over Kate's shoulder, Addie caught sight of Hillary, walking away in the distance, on her way to her tennis lesson.

I love you, too, Hillary, she thought.

The front door seemed to close with a whimper, and Kate rushed to the window to watch Addie climb into the car, her legs tanned and healthy from half a summer of swimming and playing outdoors. After the car drove off and Addie was truly gone, the silence in the house roared around Kate like thunder.

The deep aching sadness within Kate was sorrowfully familiar. It's the same way I felt after my miscarriages, she thought. I have lost a child, as painfully and as truly as the five other times when I lost a baby. She sighed with the thorough understanding that this was a pain that wouldn't go away. At the same time her deepest hurt was for Addie and what she must have been feeling. Does she know how much we love her? Kate wondered. Does she know she'll always be in our hearts? Walking through the house, she felt Addie's presence in every room. She heard Addie's voice reading slowly along with Hillary's encouragement as the two of them played school. She glimpsed the kitchen table and recalled that long-ago first night when Addie took her plate under there to eat dinner. Now the table looked barren and vacant. In the laundry room, she remembered Addie's clothes, and how, at first, she was so painfully thin. Kate's thoughts turned to prayer. Please take care of my little girl, she prayed to God. *Please bring her back to me.*

Chapter 9

∞

Addie hardly breathed in the car. She couldn't look around her as the social worker drove along dips and curves, then turned onto a freeway where Addie heard air whoosh past. She was too afraid to move, too terrified to cry. Could anyone guess how helpless she felt? She thought of her room at the Davises', and how it felt to eat dinner each night. She thought of Hillary, hearing Hillary's voice in her brain and feeling Kate's gentle hand on her shoulder.

None of them could comfort her now. What did she do wrong at this house, where she had been so long? She did lots of things, Addie guessed. The fire. The fighting. But nothing seemed to make the Davises stop wanting her— until now. What happened to bring her to this—a long, exhausting ride in a strange car with a woman she'd never met who now wouldn't even look back at her? Why was she here?

When it seemed like they had driven forever, the woman finally stopped the car. Addie cautiously looked out and saw only a street filled with stores and buildings. Where is this woman taking me? she wondered. Should she get out of the car and run away? Could she find her way back to the Davises'? Would someone else come and get her if she did? Addie's thoughts raced, but before she could open the car door, the woman slipped outside and locked the doors behind her. Addie peered out of the car and saw she was in a shopping-center parking lot. Where am I? she thought. I want to go home. Now her tears flooded. "Mom! Hillary! Kris!" she called inside the stifling stillness of the car. "Come get me!" she yelled.

She was jarred with surprise as the social worker suddenly opened a door to the car and tossed an object over the seat. Something warm landed in Addie's lap. She looked down and saw that it was a hamburger wrapped in paper. At the sight, her stomach growled. She hardly tasted it, wolfing it down in bites.

"Thank you," she murmured, almost inaudibly. The woman didn't look back.

Addie sat stiffly as the afternoon wore on. Sunlight had given way to twilight before the car stopped in front of a yellow house. A current of silent fear shot through Addie. She grabbed a piece of the black plastic racetrack the Davises had given her and held it with one hand, placing the other hand on the metal footlocker.

The two objects that sat on the car seat on either side of her were all that remained of the life she left behind, and she grasped them tightly against her sides as she stared at the yellow house. She didn't move when the woman opened the door beside her.

"Come on." The social worker yawned at her. "Been a long drive."

Addie sat, waiting for some sign, some indication that this was a safer place than the car where she sat. The woman reached for her arm.

Addie stepped out into the vacant, airy twilight.

I want to go home, she thought. Her stomach growled with thoughts of dinner at the Davises' table.

Suddenly a boy ran up beside her and roughly yanked the piece of racetrack out from under her arm; it scraped against her side as he pulled it away.

"Stop!" Addie managed, her lip quivering. "That's mine."

"Oh, shut up, Addie, you're just a dumb girl." The boy started to head toward the house, his eyes on the piece of racetrack.

"Davey!" Addie shouted, stunned with the realization

that this was her brother, and he had no more interest in her than to steal the toy she carried.

"You know him?"

"He's my brother."

"Oh—well, you'll be right at home here, then." Addie heard falseness in the social worker's voice.

Davey went in the back door of the house and slammed it without looking to see if she followed.

"It's your fault she left." As soon as she flung out the words, Hillary saw instant pain in her mother's eyes.

"Hillary . . ." Kate's look was bewildered and sad.

"You could have kept her here. You tried to get counseling for her, and that stirred up trouble . . . so they took her."

Kate shook her head. "Hillary, I had to try to help her. It would be like not taking you to the doctor if you broke your leg."

"You could have taken her to a counselor or something . . . without telling the state or whoever."

"I would have if I could," Kate said. "But she isn't my daughter. As soon as I filled out the form in the doctor's office, and I said she was a foster child, they would tell me I had to go through the state."

"You could lie and say she was your daughter. Give her a different name." Hillary knew this was crazy, and none of them would ever think of doing such a thing, but she said it anyway. Her despair over Addie's leaving seemed to pour over the rest of her life, leaving a bleak sadness. She'd never felt so lonely; it was as if she had been unplugged from reality. Before, if she had an asthma attack or felt out of place at school, she could come home and Addie would be there, waiting and willing to listen, willing to play along with whatever adventure Hillary dreamed up.

Now she was alone. There were times when she didn't care, because in a way, she'd been alone her whole life.

She was the only one who started the neighborhood circuses, led the neighborhood parades. She was the lone leader of a group of followers. No one ever saw and melted her inside loneliness. Until Addie . . . and now Addie was gone.

Inside, Hillary raged at her parents, God, and the universe for taking Addie away. All the time she wondered where Addie was sitting at school, or if she even went to school, or had any friends, or even a bed to sleep on. No matter what is happening to me, it can't be worse than what happened to Addie, she reasoned. Still, it never seemed fair that Addie couldn't stay in the one place where she knew she was loved, the one place where someone would be sure to care about her.

Chapter 10

∞

Why wouldn't the ache inside her go away? As months passed in the new foster home, Addie knew she would never feel at home the way she did at the Davises'. Her brother Davey didn't have the time or the interest in playing with her the way Hillary used to, and Kevin, her older brother, only wanted to be with his teenaged friends. They were supposedly her "real" family, yet they wanted nothing to do with her. Her foster mother, Barbara Walker, fed her on time and washed her clothes. She was a kind woman who was old enough to be Addie's grandmother. But even though Barbara took care of her, it just wasn't the same. Addie didn't feel at home the way she did at the Davises'. Why hadn't the Davises called the way they said they would? Addie felt a sharp ache inside. She thought that probably the social worker never gave them Mrs. Walker's phone number. Or what if they called and Mrs. Walker never told her about the call? Or if they didn't even try to call, going on with their lives and forgetting about her. This last possibility was the most painful, and though Addie didn't know if it could be true, she battled the ache of not knowing. Please God, she prayed. Let me see the Davises again.

I should have run away, Addie thought. I should have gone that first minute, in the parking lot, when the social worker left to get the hamburgers. I should have run away and called the police. As months, and then almost two years, passed, she thought about running away whenever she had a free moment. She mentally chose which clothes she would pack, and guessed which roads she could hitchhike on to somehow find the Davises' house. She imagined ringing their doorbell around dinnertime and stepping inside a house filled with delicious smells. She thought about losing herself in Kate's hug and sitting on Hillary's bed and talking for hours. Sometimes she fell asleep to memories of the Davises' house. I was there half my life—from when I was five until my eleventh birthday, Addie realized.

She was nearly thirteen when the social worker came to call on her foster mother. Addie stood, frozen, in the kitchen, as the two women talked. What were they deciding about her now? What did she do wrong?

"Addie . . ." Barbara's voice flowed questioningly out to where Addie sat at the kitchen table. "Come here, please."

Addie swallowed hard, then stood and went to the living room, where the two women sat. She'd never seen this social worker before, and the dark-haired woman's smile failed to lessen the fear inside her.

There was a vast silence in the room before her foster mother spoke.

"Addie? Come here and sit down," Barbara said. "Mrs. Stanley is here to talk to us about something important."

Addie wanted to scream to them to leave her alone. She wanted to run, far away, as far and as long as it took her to find the Davises again. But fear for her future forced her to sit like a stone on the couch.

Barbara's fingers touched her hair. "Mrs. Stanley has some news for you," she said gently.

"Addie, I'm here to let you know that you're going to be going home."

"To the Davises'?" Addie's eyes flew up.

"No, dear. You probably thought this might never happen, but your mother now feels she is able to care for you, and would like to have you live with her again."

"What did I do now?" The words were out before she could stop them. Barbara's laugh was gentle, yet Addie sensed her patience was wearing thin. "Nothing that you did, dear. It's your mother. She's ready to take you back. You're going to live with her again."

"What?" Addie couldn't sift through the storm of emotions that filled her. There was fear—would her mother now be able to care for her? What would happen if she could not? And she also felt tremulous relief. Maybe if she was home—what the social workers considered her real home—she wouldn't have to leave again. She would have a permanent address at last. She wouldn't be considered a foster child anymore. Yet a tear threatened to escape at the thought that she wouldn't be going to her real home—the Davises'.

"My old family," she said to Barbara. "The Davises. They said they would call me, and they never did. I guess they didn't really care about me."

Barbara paused. "I never told you this when you asked before."

Addie's heart pounded. "What didn't you tell me?"

"They did call—the first night you were here. But I followed the social workers' instructions and didn't give you the phone. She thought it would be too upsetting. Talking to them would have interrupted your getting settled with us."

"Do you have their number?" Addie asked. Was there any way she could go back to the Davises' now, instead of to her mother's house?

"That was years ago when they called." Barbara sighed. "Why on earth would I keep their number?"

"Because I loved them. I wanted to call them. Because they are my family."

"No." Barbara's touch at her back was half a pat, half a push. "You're going back to your family now. You won't have to worry about foster homes ever again. You'll finally be at your real home."

"Why aren't Davey and Kevin going with me?"

"Because"—now the social worker spoke—"your mother has undergone therapy. She has completed rehabilitation, yet her status as a fit mother has yet to be established. She asked for you first. This is on a trial basis. If she proves to the court that she can care for you, at least one more—and possibly all three of you—will live there."

The thought made Addie's head swim. Was there any other way they could test her mother's fitness than by sending her back to this woman she hadn't seen in more than seven years? "Do I have to go?" she asked.

Addie watched as Mrs. Stanley shifted on the couch, then straightened her skirt. "By going to live with your mother now, you can help bring your family back together. You—all by yourself."

Addie felt totally confused. It didn't seem that she should be the one to decide where she and Davey and Kevin should live. It felt like a heap of responsibility— one she wasn't sure she wanted to shoulder.

"Go start packing now," Barbara said, "and tomorrow you'll be home."

Addie felt a torrent of emotions rush through her at the thought of being returned to the place where she had once been taken away. How did anyone know that the mother who was once declared unfit could now care for her? And where were the feelings she should have for this woman?

When she thought of the word *mother,* Kate ... or even Barbara ... came to mind.

Addie placed the last of her clothes in the suitcase, which seemed to close with a moan. Why did this have to happen to her? The next morning, only Barbara was waiting when the social worker's car drove up to take Addie away. Davey and Kevin had left for school without a word to her.

It was another long drive in the back of the social worker's car. As miles of fields and cities passed, Addie realized that during all of these years, her mind had never envisioned what her mother's house might look like. When the social worker drove the car up to a small, beige brick house, Addie found herself filled with the same apprehension she always felt when she was suddenly dropped in a brand-new place.

As soon as the car stopped, a woman with graying hair and brown eyes that Addie recognized as identical to her own ran out to the car. Addie cautiously got out of the car and the woman gripped her in a tight hug. Despite the electricity she felt while encircled within her mother's arms, Addie felt as if she were cloaked with a shroud of dread. Why did she feel like something terrible was about to happen?

Later that night the two of them sat in her mother's small, stuffy living room. Addie was thinking it was time to go to bed when her mother suddenly said, "Tell me about them ..."

"Who?"

"That family ... the one you lived with so long."

Addie's heart warmed. "Oh, the Davises."

"Four years or something, wasn't it?"

"Five ... almost six. I left on my birthday." A sadness filled her. She couldn't read her mother's look.

"Tell me what they were like."

"They were"—Addie hesitated—"my family. There

was the father, who traveled. And the mother, who was an artist. And Hillary, my sister, who taught me how to do the Mash, and Kris, the other sister, who I played with."

"You missed me, didn't you, when you were there with them?"

Addie swallowed hard. "I thought of you."

"But you knew they weren't your real family, didn't you?"

"I asked them where you were."

Her mother tilted her short-haired head. "What did they say?"

"They said that you couldn't take care of me right then, but you would be back later . . . maybe . . . to get me."

"I wasn't going to let anyone adopt you. My sister said, 'That girl, you get her back. Don't let anyone take her.' So if they tried . . ."

This revelation hit Addie like a sledgehammer. "Did they want me? Did the Davises try to adopt me?" She wasn't aware of the loudness of her voice in the small, hot room.

"Someone said they wanted to keep you. But they're not your people."

"But they took good care of me." Addie paused. "I loved them."

"You couldn't love them like you love me. I'm your real mother."

"They were kind to me. They loved me, too."

"But not like real family—with the same blood."

"I was in their family pictures and everything. I called them Mom and Dad."

Her mother stood then and slapped her. "How could you call someone else Mom? Do you know how hard I was trying to get you back?"

"But I never got to talk to you. It was way more than five years. I never knew if you were ever coming back."

"I tried every day. The state wouldn't allow it."

"You'd like the Davises! They were nice people. They

always said nice things about you. I can't help it if I loved them."

"Just don't ever say that to me again."

"What?"

"That you loved them instead of me."

"I never said 'instead of.' I said I loved both of you."

"You were too young, I guess, to know I was your real mother . . . instead of that lady."

"Kate. Her name was Kate."

"You'll never see her again, so you can stop thinking about her now."

"I'll never stop."

"Just remember. I am your mother. I am your family. You have no one else."

Her mother stood and stormed out of the room.

Yes, I do, said a small voice inside Addie's head. *I'll always have the Davises. If I ever find them again, their house will always be a home to me.*

In just days Addie discovered the routine at her mother's house. Mornings were safe. You could say what you wanted and receive a reply that made sense. Near noon, though, and sometimes even sooner, her mother's true personality began to drift away into a bottle of whatever liquor she had hidden around the house. Her mother—who Addie now thought of as Joyce—was no longer herself by early afternoon. Dinner was often a haphazard affair. Her mother might leave a perfectly good soup on the stove and never get to the point of pouring it into bowls. Or raw meat might just as easily burn to a crisp. Addie often went to bed with a growling stomach, and try as she might to avoid it, she couldn't help remembering dinners at the Davises' and the long talks afterward.

One afternoon, Addie smelled fire. Something was burning in this unfamiliar house that still didn't feel like home to her. She rushed down the hall toward the kitchen. A heavy cloud of black smoke hit her face and burned her nostrils before she entered the doorway. As she bent low, the heat hit her eyes. She heard meat crackling sharply in a pan on the stove. She held her breath, closed her eyes, and stepped toward the sputtering noise. Through narrowed eyelids, she caught sight of a billowing, smoke-filled pan. Surging toward it, she grabbed the handle, then leaped back as it burned her fingers. She edged closer then bumped the pan with quick pokes until it moved off the burner. Then she ran to the back door and gulped for air—long, fresh, cooling breaths. She opened the doors and windows. Still the smoke hovered like a low-hanging cloud. She leaned outside to take a final gulp of fresh air, then she went to look for Joyce.

She'd almost decided the house was empty when she caught sight of her mother lying on her bed.

Her breath caught. "Joyce? Are you all right?"

Silence.

Pushing closer, she heard the rustle of sheets and smelled a sickly-sweet scent that brought back black memories of times in other foster homes.

Alcohol.

Her mother was drunk. Her mother, who was supposedly through with rehab and ready to take care of her, was passed out drunk on the bed.

Addie sighed and walked dejectedly back to her bedroom as memories flooded her mind. Life at the Davises'. Life at other foster homes. What was going to happen to her life now? Sitting alone in her room, she began to wonder if her current situation was her own fault. Didn't she ask Kate about her birth family? Didn't she say she wanted to meet them? Didn't she ask where they were? Now I'm there, Addie thought. I'm at the place I was always curious about. Now I'm with my mother, and I wish I wasn't.

The day after the burned dinner, Joyce left all the clothes wet in the wash, so Addie had nothing to wear but the stained dress she'd worn the day before. The next night, Addie needed help with math, but Joyce could hardly focus her attention enough to sit on a kitchen chair, let alone do long division.

Addie stared at her math paper, hoping the sheer force of her will would cause her to understand the problems. She tried to work the first one again and again, guessing at the required steps. She erased her efforts repeatedly, until her pencil erase wore down and its metal edge caught on her paper and tore it.

I can't do this, Addie thought. What will I tell Mrs. Tuckfield tomorrow? She stayed awake until after eleven o'clock that night, waiting and hoping that Joyce would somehow wake up and be her morning self.

By midnight, Addie yawned and her eyes burned with fatigue. She went to bed and lay in the dark, staring at the high, black ceiling. Where are you, Hillary? she asked in her head. Why am I here, and why are you so far away?

It seemed that she had scarcely fallen asleep when Joyce shook her roughly, telling her to wash her face and get ready for school.

"My homework isn't done," Addie ventured.

Joyce frowned sourly at her. "Why didn't you do it?"

"I needed help."

"Why didn't you ask your teacher?"

"Because it was night, and I was here, at home." *Because I need a mom*, she wanted to say, *a real mom, who doesn't get so drunk at night that she forgets who I am.* Now I know what they meant when they said my mother couldn't take care of me, Addie thought. But what could she do about it now?

At school she held her breath when the teacher asked the class how many problems they had gotten right on last night's homework. Her name drew closer. Pearson, Price, Ramsey, Randall.

"Addie?" Mrs. Tuckfield gazed at her with a questioning look.

"Zero," Addie said, the sharp-edged word catching in her throat.

She heard the class gasp around her.

"Do you mean zero wrong?"

"No. Zero right."

"Did you forget the assignment."

"No. I couldn't figure it out."

"Did you ask someone for help?"

"She—Joyce—uh, my mom couldn't help me."

Mrs. Tuckfield stared at her for a fraction of a second, then said, "Please stay after class."

Oh no, thought Addie. What's going to happen to me now?

She pretended to be looking for something in her desk until long after the other students left the classroom. Finally she looked up to find Mrs. Tuckfield staring at her.

"Come up here, Addie. To the front of the room."

Addie obediently walked up and sat in a chair in the front row.

"I need to ask you, what did you mean when you said your mother couldn't help you."

No quick and convincing lie came to Addie's mind. "She was passed out," she said.

"She was asleep?"

"No." Addie sighed. "She was drunk."

"I see. Does this happen often?"

"Well, I've only lived with her three months and—"

"Where were you before?"

"I was in foster homes."

Mrs. Tuckfield sighed and stared at the ceiling. "I feel I should report this—probably to the principal."

"No," Addie cried out. "Don't. Joyce will get mad at me."

"Who is Joyce?"

"My mom."

"Addie, you have to be in a home where you are safe. Where someone is taking care of you."

"She was supposed to be all through getting drunk when I came to live—" Addie clapped a hand over her mouth. "But she's not. She didn't stop drinking like she said. But I don't want to go somewhere else. They hurt me in other places."

Mrs. Tuckfield nodded. "I have to tell someone. I don't have a choice."

"Just tell them to leave me where I am."

"I'll tell them that's what you want."

"I can't move again!" Addie burst into tears. "I've lived in too many houses. Ten or maybe twelve."

"Is there somewhere else you'd like to go."

"Yes. The Davises'. They were my family. But I don't even know how to find them. I can't—"

There was a long pause. Then Mrs. Tuckfield said, "I'll get back to you, Addie. I'll let you know." When Addie didn't move or speak, the teacher said, "You may go home now."

Addie stared at Mrs. Tuckfield for a long time before she gathered her books, slid them inside her book bag, then walked outside the classroom.

Joyce was already drunk when Addie arrived home after school, and soon after, she passed out. She wasn't awake when Addie left for school the next day. When Addie came home, before she even walked into the house, she heard Joyce screaming at her.

"Get in here, young lady."

Familiar fears, like all the times when she was sent away from other houses, filled her. This time she asked the question she'd thought to herself so many other times. "What did I do?"

"Get in here and I'll tell you."

Addie was trembling as she sat on the couch. "I did my homework," she said.

"And you told your teacher that I drink."

"I had to. She asked me."

"Do you know why you had to live in foster homes all those years? Because I drink. Do you want to go to a foster home again?"

Addie shook her head slowly. "No," she said. At the

same time she thought, Yes. If it's the Davises' house, please *do* let me go back.

"Then keep our personal business to yourself!"

"But you were drunk. The social worker told me you didn't drink anymore."

Now Joyce ran up and shoved her mean, angry face into Addie's. "I'll drink if I need to! And you won't tell a soul! Now get to your room and don't come out."

Addie went to her room. She sat on the bed and wished harder than ever that this was the Davises' house. She waited and waited. There was no mention of dinner, but she didn't dare leave her room. She watched the sky darken outside her window and tried to read or find something to do. Finally, with her stomach growling in hunger, she shut off her bedroom light and lay in the dark for hours before she finally fell asleep.

Chapter 11

∽

Hillary walked around the house for the last time, thinking that these rooms were filled with memories. The TV room, where Addie laughed for the first time. The front porch, where she herself directed circuses and plays. The kitchen—here Hillary's throat caught—where the same round table still sat. That night—eight years ago—was fresh in her mind. She still remembered the bewilderment on her mother's face when Addie dived under the table while they were eating dinner. And she still remembered the electric current of feeling that filled her as she took Addie's plate and crawled under the table, too. She remembered the sense of connection that filled her as their eyes met, there in the subdued light under the white linen tablecloth. Friends forever, she thought to herself. Members of the Heinz Happy Soup Club. If they left this house, how would Addie ever find them? She'd have to find Addie herself someday, Hillary thought as she ran upstairs to put on her cap and gown. Graduation. What was going to happen in her life now?

Two months later, getting ready to leave for college, Hillary ran across the long-ago photo of Addie in a yellow dotted-swiss dress. She packed it with her college things, and on Addie's birthday, she took the photo out and wished on it. "Where are you, Addie?" Hillary asked, staring at the brown-eyed, round-cheeked girl in the photo. "Please come back to us. Please have a happy birthday." She ran her finger across Addie's brown hair in the photo and wondered where Addie was now.

In another month, she remembered her mother's words when she and Dad had decided they would be foster parents. *We want to help a child who really needs us,* Kate had said.

Her mother's words echoed in her mind as Hillary sat, poised with a pencil, in the registration office. She paused, then filled in the blank. *Special education,* Hillary wrote, thinking, I hope I can help just one student, and be as close to that student as Addie was to us. Months later she changed her major to handicapped education, just because the course offerings were broader. But her feeling inside of wanting to help was still the same.

Hillary never pictured herself dating Jeff. He was Kris's old boyfriend, for Pete's sake. Was she jealous of the fun Kris used to have? Did she think she needed someone to keep her from taking herself too seriously? All she knew was that she found herself waiting by the phone, imagining what they'd do each weekend. Jeff laughed easily, but Hillary wasn't able to do that. There were just too many important things in this world for her to let her intensity dissolve into laughter.

Now Jeff started the phone call with a laugh. "Hey, I have an idea."

"Okay." Hillary pictured a drive-in movie or a picnic in a park.

"Should we get married in September?" Now he really laughed.

Married? The idea had never crossed her mind. Her thoughts were more on graduate school, internships, and foreign countries, where she could travel to work with her new degree.

"I didn't hear anything. Is that a yes?" Another laugh from him.

"Married ... hmm ..." said Hillary.

"You know ... duh-*duh*-duh-duh. Here comes the bride."

"Well ..." What would he do if she said no? Hillary wondered. Would they continue to date, carefree and fun? Or was this fish-or-cut-bait time?

"I'm waiting. I'm drumming my fingers on the countertop here ..." More laughter.

"Well ..."

"Is that a yes?"

"Well, I'm thinking."

"Saying yes usually doesn't require a lot of thought. Your tongue sort of starts near your bottom teeth to form the *y* sound and then—"

"Yes."

"Wait! Did I hear something? That sounded like a yes to me."

"It was." Hillary had surprised herself by saying yes. Did she really mean it? she wondered. What was she thinking?

"You said yes. Now don't think about that too long—just come over here to the place and celebrate. I'll cook you dinner."

The place. The apartment she helped him pick out when he needed somewhere to live.

"Okay," she said lightly, "but I have to work at the

station at eight. And I really should study."

"I proposed marriage to you. And you accepted. Isn't that worth a celebration?"

Hillary didn't answer. A grin was sneaking onto her face.

"Be here in half an hour. I'll toss something on the barbecue."

"I'll be there," she said. Hillary hurried to dress. At the same time she thought she heard a voice inside her telling her to run the other way as fast as she could. This was just new to her, Hillary decided as she drove to his apartment. She was used to work assignments at the radio station, school projects, and volunteering at the ecology center. This just wasn't like her. She didn't know how to be herself in this new arena of life.

She and Jeff were standing out on his deck when he said, "How about this for a view? How about we get married out here? Just the two of us and a justice of the peace or whoever?"

"I can't get married here," Hillary protested.

"Why not?"

"We need to go home. Where my parents are. My mom would never forgive me."

"You mean we have to do the church thing, and—"

"Yeah. We do."

He sighed.

They were standing in his kitchen when Hillary caught sight of a tin. Through the open lid, she saw that it held some sort of black powder. Beside the tin, there were piles on the black substance on the table.

She frowned. "What's that stuff?"

"Oh, just a little gunpowder."

"Gunpowder? Like in cap guns?"

"Well, I'm a man of many talents."

"With gunpowder?" Hillary stared at him in disbelief.

"I built a black powder pistol from a kit. I still have the powder."

"Well, I'd appreciate it if you'd get rid of it before I

come to live here. I can't live in a house with gunpowder."

"Fussy, aren't you?"

"I just don't want to blow up someday."

Two months later Hillary was admiring her wedding
dress in the mirror, flanked by Kate and Kris. Two more
hours and she would be Mrs. Jeff McBride.

Married. She had never thought it would happen to her.
But at least this way, all the guests who counted would
be at her wedding. All except one. Addie, where are you?
Hillary wondered inside her head. Are you somewhere
close, or thousands of miles away? Do you like school,
and do you remember how the first word you ever read
was *blue*? Addie—

Hillary's thoughts were interrupted by the phone ringing.

Kate answered. "Yes. She's here." She shrugged before
handing the phone to Hillary.

"Hello?" Who would be calling her today?

"Is this Hillary Davis?"

"Yes."

"This is Dr. Curtis's nurse. At St. James Hospital. I've
been asked to notify you that there's been an accident."

Hillary's heart sank. "An accident? What happened?"

"Jeff McBride was injured when—"

The sinking feeling dipped even lower. "He's my husband—I mean, this is our wedding day."

"You may want to consider postponing the wedding.
He's suffering severe burns and will need to be hospital-
ized."

"Oh—" Severe burns! Hillary's eyes closed in horror.

"I'll let you talk to him."

"Wait—"

"Is this my bride-to-be?"

"What happened, Jeff?" She felt her heart pounding in
her ears.

"Oh, just a little incident with a lighter and some gunpowder."

"You started a fire?"

"You said to get rid of it, didn't you? Believe me, it's gone . . ."

Hillary fought to contain her composure amid a sea of emotion. Tears pricked the corners of her eyes. "But what are we going to do about today? I better call the minister. There's no way—"

"Just come down here."

Hillary felt a sick feeling inside. "I've got to go to the church. Everyone's already waiting—"

"Just phone the church and let them know what happened. I've already talked to the nurses. The ceremony could be performed here with just immediate family. Then you could go to the reception hall."

"I don't know." Another wave of emotion washed over Hillary. This wasn't how it was supposed to be. But could she blame Jeff for the accident? Was it possible to ignite gunpowder and burn it safely? Couldn't he just put it in the garbage? Hillary's head swam. There wasn't time to stop and consider all of this logically—not with everyone waiting at the church.

"I'll have to see," she said finally.

"Your bridegroom awaits . . ."

Hillary couldn't decide whether the misgivings she felt were a result of the accident, or of the thought of canceling the wedding she and her family had planned, or if they had to do with the idea of getting married in the first place. Despite her tears and worry, she numbly moved ahead. Jeff was in a private room because of the serious burns; he was right in stating that no one but immediate family was allowed in. The crowd at the church transferred to the reception hall. Even though Hillary braved a smile when a nurse cut a hole in her surgical glove so that everyone could see the ring, her heavy sadness never lifted.

*   *   *

Addie froze as she caught sight of the officer sitting in a parked car in front of her house after school. She stood still on the sidewalk, grateful that he faced away from her. What was wrong now? This wasn't a social worker, but Addie couldn't help wondering what she had done. Where was Joyce? What was happening here?

Taking a breath, she started to walk around to the back of the house, hoping the officer wasn't there for her, or if he was, that he wouldn't see her.

"Miss?" The officer's voice barked loud in the placid afternoon sunshine.

Addie turned.

"Addie Randall?"

Addie's nod was fearful.

"There's been an emergency. I've been instructed to take you with me."

"No!" Addie said, the sharp, thin word scraping her throat.

"I have my orders. I'm sorry."

"What happened?"

"They'll tell you about that at Child Protection Services. Please get in the car." The man must have caught the terror in Addie's eyes. What did she do this time?

"Where's Joyce?"

"She's in the hospital. They'll tell you more about it when—"

"Did she fall and get hurt?" Addie pictured her mother stumbling around the house late at night.

"I don't think so. They'll tell you when you get there."

Addie reluctantly climbed into the back of the car, and again felt the uncertainty she'd felt so many times about where her life was headed, and wondered what on earth she had possibly done wrong to have someone disrupt her life.

This time the ride to Child Protection Services was short—just downtown. By now, Addie wasn't the terrified little girl who didn't know who a social worker was or why some such person would want to talk to her. But her curiosity blended with her anxiousness over why she was once again in this unknown place.

At the office, a gray-haired social worker stared at her before speaking. "I need to let you know that we will need to place you in a new foster home."

"But Joyce—my mom. She just got me back."

"An event took place earlier today that makes it necessary to arrange another placement."

"What's the matter?"

"How has your mother behaved while you've been living there?"

"I don't know what you mean."

"A neighbor found her unconscious this morning."

Addie hesitated. "She sometimes passes out at night."

The social worker flipped through her file. "In my notes, it states that she had completed alcoholism rehab, but today—"

"She still drinks. But I'm used to it, and I take care of her. The grocery store even gave me a charge account so that I can—"

"Your mother's home has been deemed unfit."

"But I live there. I'm all right. Let me go back."

"I can't do that. You need supervision."

"I can take care of myself."

"You're not of legal age. And I'm afraid I must tell you, we believe that your mother made a suicide attempt this morning. She apparently ingested alcohol and a sedative."

"She wouldn't do that—not now that she'd got me back." Addie proclaimed her thoughts firmly, but inside, her head swam with emotion. Was Mom that depressed? What was going on here? "I'll watch her," Addie said finally.

"I'm sorry. The state will not allow you to live with her now."

"What if she goes through treatment?"

"We couldn't make another decision until then."

Chapter 12

∞

Hillary felt a familiar feeling of dread as she approached the door to her and Jeff's apartment. What was she worried about? What was this sinking feeling inside? Though it was hard to determine the reason for her apprehension, Hillary only knew that she felt this unease often since she and Jeff had gotten married. She felt a sadness that the home she lived in now was so different from the one where she grew up. Why didn't she realize then, Hillary wondered, that her home was rare and precious, rather than something to take for granted. With a sigh, she opened the door.

"Were you home again today?" Hillary stared at Jeff, still in his boxer shorts at noon, watching TV.

"Yeah." He tried to give her a grin.

Hillary was home on her lunch hour and thought Jeff would be at work, too. "Why didn't you go in to the office?"

Another forced grin. "I just didn't feel like it. Isn't that terrible?" A bitter laugh.

"What about your class this morning?"

"Couldn't go in dressed like this."

Hillary worked all night at the radio station and had gone straight to the office after her shift. This was her first time home since last night. She felt her heart beat in her chest. "Look, I've gotta get out of this situation. I can't stay here."

A stricken look came over his face. "Hey, it's no big deal."

"It's a big deal to me. You're not doing anything you're supposed to do. No studying. No work and no going to class."

"It won't happen again, okay? Last night was the last time."

"You're right. It was." Hillary rushed into the bedroom and threw her suitcase on the bed. Jeff was right behind her. "Look, I didn't know it was bugging you so much. I'll stop right now."

"I've waited two years for things to change. I'm not waiting any longer. You can have the place. I'll get my stuff out tonight."

"But you're my wife!"

"I never should have been. It was my big mistake. I'm sorry."

"Come on, Hillary."

"You'll still have your friends. Your apartment. And I won't be here getting mad at you all the time."

"I love you, Hillary."

She took a deep breath. "You should have thought of that sooner."

Jeff walked out of the room and then Hillary heard the outside door slam. Good, she thought. It's better this way. Something inside her realized that her marriage had been an agreement more than a partnership based on love. She agreed to help him, to be the strong one, in hopes that he would somehow acquire strength. But now she knew he wasn't going to change. It was time to end this now.

What would happen, Hillary wondered, if I ever need someone to be the strong one for me?

Addie sat in the social worker's office, no longer afraid of this woman now that she was a young woman herself.

The woman paused and looked at Addie. "We've agreed to tell you. Your mother is suffering from cancer. She's asked that you go back with her now."

"Does she still drink?"

The social worker stared at Addie. "It's my understanding that she's very ill. She needs you."

"I don't mean to sound cold, but where was she when I needed her? When I needed a mother?"

"I think that she could use your compassion."

Addie sighed. She knew what compassion felt like. She thought of the Davises, and how they took in a little girl who couldn't even read or speak.

"I'll try," she said.

The social worker sighed with relief. "I think you'd be sorry if you didn't."

This time, from the beginning, there was no pretense that Joyce was looking out for Addie rather than the other way around. Addie prepared the food, cleaned the house, and spent long hours at Joyce's bedside. Joyce's illness made her cranky, discontented, weak, and critical.

"Those people weren't your family. You were just staying there until I could come get you back."

"Who?" asked Addie, though she knew full well what Joyce meant.

"The caseworker just left you at their house until the state said I could have you."

"They took good care of me. The way things were going, I might have ended up in an institution."

"Not while you still had a mother."

"The Davises knew you were my mother. They said nice things about you."

"But you called her Mom . . . how could you do that?"

"She was my mom then, when I needed a mom and you weren't there."

"I thought of you every day. I promised myself I would get you back. Those people tried to hang on to you."

"They let me go when the social worker came."

"Remember that. They let you go."

Addie fought within herself. She recalled the last day, how all of them had cried. She thought of the surprise party, the check for college that her new foster mother cashed and kept. She remembered Davey and Kevin and how they never had time for her, while Hillary always did.

Did the Davises love her? She would give anything to find out. And she and Joyce continued to fight about it clear up to the day that Joyce died, lying in her bed with her head in Addie's lap.

I was here for you, Addie said to her mother's lifeless body. We fought, but I was here.

Now Addie went to boarding school, then to a foster home on weekends. The boardinghouse she lived in wasn't a real home—even though the bed was comfortable, the meals were good, and she went to school. Addie still missed the Davises and Barbara Walker . . . and Joyce, too. When she met with the boarding-school counselor, she was surprised to find herself talking about the families she would never forget. But would she ever see the Davises again?

She was lost in thoughts of her days with Hillary, Kate, Kris, and Linwood when she heard a voice.

"Don't stay like that—your face will freeze that way."

Startled, Addie looked up, into a pair of friendly brown eyes.

"Didn't mean to scare you," the young man said, pulling up a chair and sitting beside her. "I just know how that school lunch tastes."

"Pretty bad," Addie agreed.

"How long you been here?"

"Six months," Addie said. "What about you?"

The boy rolled his eyes at the ceiling, making her laugh. "Too long," he said. "Way too long."

That was how she met Mark. For the next two years, until she was seventeen, they talked, made fun of the school, and talked about escaping someday. He was the only thing that held her together when she thought she couldn't take another day.

It was on a warm spring afternoon when he said, "We

really could get out of here, you know. We could live on our own."

"Sure." Addie laughed. She'd thought about living on her own someday, but it always seemed like that might happen far away in the distant future. She knew she would need a job, money, and her own place before she could live alone, and that didn't seem like it would happen anytime soon. "How would we leave here?"

She saw Mark's face turn serious. "We'll get married," he said.

"Married?" Addie had been so worried about what would happen to her from one day to the next that she really never thought about getting married someday. "They don't let married people go to school here," she said, laughing.

"We won't *be* here, silly."

"Where will we be?" The idea was foreign and intriguing to her.

"We'll be somewhere else."

"Where?"

He shrugged and smiled. "Away from here."

"They don't take married people in foster homes."

Suddenly his voice turned serious. "We'll have our own home."

Their own home. A place that would belong to her and Mark, where she would never have to leave. No social worker would drive up to the door and tell her to pack her things. It wouldn't matter if her foster mother didn't care about her, because she and Mark would care about each other. The prospect was so heady that she couldn't speak.

"Guess I blew you away, huh?" he said, laughing at her again.

"I just never thought about it before."

"So, will you marry me?"

Tingles erupted from her shoulders to her toes. "Yes," she said, feeling like she was taking hold of her destiny for the first time in her life. "I will marry you."

Chapter 13

∞

Holding a clipboard so her serious thoughts wouldn't get wet, Hillary sat in the bathtub, planning her campaign to one day become a state representative. She thought of services for the poor and advancement opportunities for women and minorities. Pages flipped on the yellow pad. Was this her need to be heard, Hillary wondered, or was she avoiding thinking about the staleness of her second marriage, now three years old? Hillary flipped to a new page and began to write. Below her campaign promises, she listed reasons why her second husband, Paul, was as different from her first husband, Jeff, as he could possibly be. Older. More settled. Already had a career. They were both going back to school—he for a Ph.D. and she for a master's. Everything should have been all right, except . . .

It was a month later, after dinner, when she was in the front room reading the paper while he watched TV on the couch beside her that she finally voiced her concerns. She waited until she heard a commercial interrupt the show.

"I need to talk to you," she said.

Paul looked up, eyes wary. "What do you need?"

Hillary felt her annoyance rise. "I don't need anything."

"Then I'll just get back to my show." He turned toward the TV.

"No, I need . . . I mean I want to talk to you."

"What about?"

"Can't we just talk . . . not about anything . . . but just talk? Do you know how long it's been since—"

He waved her away. "Not right now."

"How long it's been since we've been intimate?"

He paused. Then his head jerked back and his blue eyes met her own. "I didn't think you'd even noticed. Much less cared."

"And we don't talk, either."

He shrugged, then linked his hands behind his head and turned back to the TV.

"You pulled away from me," Hillary accused. "Our relationship is functional . . . but that's all. It's not a marriage."

Again he waved her off. "I don't know what you're all upset about."

"We don't even talk . . . or anything else!" She hesitated. "When you lost your job, you left me, too."

"You have no idea what it was like," he accused. "Just because it wasn't about causes and the poor and society . . . it still meant something to me."

"But it shouldn't have come between us!"

He turned to her, his face filled with fury. "Listen— you want to change something, then *you* do it. You're the one who knows what everyone in the world should do. *You* do it!"

Hillary felt slapped. "I just thought we could both—"

"No." He shook his head in anger. "This isn't going to be one of those times where you say we're both doing something . . . and it's really you telling me what to do. I can't handle it right now. You do what you need to do."

Hillary stared at him a long time, yet he didn't look up again. She left his side and went to sit alone in the silence of the deck. She sat still and sensed that the icy pain inside her had been there for a long time.

Kate realized that this was the first time her meeting with a social worker had nothing to do with her children. This was the first time that she herself was the person under consideration. Now the social worker, whose name was Mrs. Bennett, stared at her.

"It's rare that people actually approach us in this way." Her stare continued, before she dropped her eyes to Kate's résumé. "I'd have to say, your credentials are excellent," the woman said. "You are presently a fashion artist for a department store?" She looked up at Kate.

"Yes. When my children grew up, I went back to work at that."

"You know that the atmosphere here would be drastically different?"

Kate stared back at the woman. She said slowly, "I can understand that."

"I probably should mention . . . your students would all be those serving long sentences—for crimes such as murder, rape, and armed robbery. You would work with the prison psychologist to blend therapy with art. Does this sound like—" The woman paused.

"I'll take the job. It is a volunteer position?"

"Yes. Even with your credentials, there is no money available."

"When would you like me to start?"

"There's a problem. You need to obtain a clearance to enter the prison."

"I'll be happy to do that."

"It requires fingerprinting and a background check."

"I've had a background check before."

"You have?" The woman stared closer at her.

"Yes. When I was a foster mother."

"You know what to expect, then."

"I do. Let's get going."

Now Mrs. Bennett sighed. "I'm sorry. I don't think you would be approved for the position."

"Why is that? You just said I have good credentials."

"That doesn't matter."

Now Kate frowned. "I know I'm perfectly well qualified to teach art."

"That fact is, the board has never given a woman clearance to enter the prison."

"Why would that be?"

"They considered the possibility of—endangerment."

"Do you think I'd be in danger? Wouldn't the psychologist be there with me?"

"The rules state that women are not allowed. I don't think they'd make an exception."

"Who could I ask about that?"

"The warden initiated this policy and the board agreed. I don't know who else you could ask."

"What about the governor?"

"You're certainly welcome to write to him. I can't promise that he'd respond."

"Why not? Education for prisoners is critical if they are to return to society." Kate felt as if she were Hillary, fighting for the rights of the less fortunate.

"You're free to write to him." Mrs. Bennett sighed again. "I couldn't begin to predict what he'll say. Or if he'll answer at all."

"I'll let you know," said Kate. Shaking with fury, she gathered her purse and portfolio and hurried out of the social worker's office, filled with the same feeling of bitter rejection she'd felt when she'd been told that Addie had to go live somewhere else.

It was Addie's day off. Walking into the apartment after grocery shopping, she was stunned to see Mark sitting on the couch, still dressed in his pajamas. "Thought you were leaving for work this morning . . ."

"Forgot to tell you—I quit." Mark's laugh was thin. He picked up the remote and aimed it at the TV.

"What?" Addie held Jessica's hand and balanced tiny Alyssa against her shoulder and stared at Mark. "How are we going to pay the bills?"

"Just tell the bill collectors they'll have to wait."

"But they won't wait, Mark."

"They don't have a choice."

Addie gestured at the apartment around her. "We can't live here if we can't pay the rent."

He shrugged and flipped the channel to a football game. "We got a while before they try to throw us out."

A cloak of exhausted frustration draped itself around Addie, and she fought tears by pressing her face against her baby's warm cheek. Never in a million years had she dreamed that she'd want to leave a marriage the way she wanted to leave all those foster homes. She thought that once she had her own home, everything would be all right. But now worry nagged at her like a persistent fly, and she lay awake night after sleepless night.

Weeks later, after Mark finally moved out, reality hit Addie square in the face. She was alone with her children. Now it was up to her to take care of her girls the way her own mother had never been able to take care of her.

"It'll be okay," she whispered softly to Alyssa, who lay asleep in her arms. "Don't worry. I'll be here for you. I'll never let you go."

Placing the baby in her crib, Addie paced the room, worried. Could she be the kind of mother she wanted to be? There was no way to move but onward. If she was going to give her children a good home, she'd have to get a full-time job instead of working twenty hours a week. And maybe she'd have to give up night school. Addie sighed.

Did anyone else feel like this? Whenever she looked for work, Addie felt as if she were five years old again. Applying for a job felt like being considered for a foster home. Would anyone want her? What would be their reason for not choosing her? An unexpected rush of feelings of inadequacy filled her as she donned her one red suit. What would be their reason for saying no? Was she too dumb, not pretty enough, not quite as articulate as she needed to be? Her heart pounded.

She combed Jessica's hair and quietly dressed Alyssa, fingers trembling as she fastened the tiny buttons, then leaned close to smell the sweet scent of her baby's hair. She kissed the baby's cheek, then pressed her own cheek against the tiny round one. If I could, baby, she thought silently, I'd stay with you every minute of your life.

I know how it is to have someone not stay, she thought. People didn't stay with me the whole time I was growing up. I never knew when someone would leave. There was a feeling of not wanting to get close to anyone in order to avoid the feeling of abandonment when they suddenly left.

Lifting the baby against her shoulder, she fought against admitting that Alyssa and Jessica were the real reasons why she wanted a full-time job. U.S. Stores was rumored to have an on-site day-care center.

She sighed, wrapped Alyssa in a blanket and took Jessica's hand as she walked to her friend Andrea's house.

"Good luck," said Andrea, taking the baby's infant carrier.

"I'll be back in an hour," Addie said, still feeling her heart beat.

Were all these people in the waiting room applying for the same job? There was a gray-haired man in his fifties, a girl in her late teens who had probably just graduated from high school, and another woman in her twenties like Addie.

Who would they rather have than me? Addie wondered. She waited, wondering how long her suit would look crisp and fresh, and how long it would be before she herself as well as the suit drooped in despair.

"Addie Larsen?"

Addie ventured a smile, then followed the thin, red-haired woman, who also wore a suit. Good, she thought, maybe I dressed right. Maybe there's one point in my favor.

"You will speak with Sherill Shaw," said the young woman.

Addie couldn't read the gray-haired woman's face as she studied her résumé. Abruptly, the woman looked up.

"Your high-school education?"

"It's in there." Addie cursed her voice for trembling.

The woman frowned. "Your diploma?"

"No—" Addie shook her head quickly, reached for the folder, then with trembling fingers, searched for the right paper. She handed it to the woman.

"Oh, a GED," said the woman, as if the high-school equivalency diploma were worthless.

"I've taken computer courses at the community college."

The woman waved her away and continued to study the folder.

"You have a GED and you have not finished community college. Am I correct?"

"I'm finishing at night. I'll be through in December."

"You're continuing with computer science?"

"Yes."

"This position requires a degree."

"I didn't know that. I have experience working in computers . . . in my last position."

"You were dismissed from there? Fired? Laid off?"

"No, I still work there. It's a twenty-hour position." One right answer.

"Then why are you seeking another job?"

"I noticed that the pay was higher and I need to work full-time." Don't mention the day-care center, Addie told herself. Don't let her know that appeals to you. She'll think that's the only reason you want to work here.

The woman sighed. "I don't make the final decision, of course." Addie watched her flip through the papers one more time, as if trying to find a single redeeming fact.

Why don't you just tell me no now? Addie wondered. Please don't be like all those foster homes who have kids come to visit once . . . then twice . . . then say they can't live there.

The woman folded her hands on her desk. "I'll get back to you."

No, you won't, Addie thought. "Thank you," she said.

"Did you wish to tour the facility?"

To see where I won't be working? Addie wondered. "Sure," she said.

The offices looked much like the one where she worked now, only the building was three times the size. The last stop was the on-site day-care center. The facility was brightly lit, clean, and filled with children's art projects.

What would it be like to be able to work, and go visit your child when you took a break? To drop in and give your child a hug to sustain both of you through the day. Addie felt her heart beat. What were Alyssa and Jessica doing now?

"The tour is complete," said Sherill Shaw. "The exit door is right there."

"Thank you," Addie said again. "Thank you for your time."

"Certainly."

Without looking back, Addie walked outside. Pausing in the fresh air, she realized that she was shaking. If not here, somewhere else. Somewhere, I'll get a job where I can be close to my daughters. Where someone wants me, and thinks I have talent and a brain.

She promised herself that she'd find someone who'd give her a chance, like the Davises did all those years ago.

If Hillary were hiring, Addie thought, she'd give me a job.

A sweet sadness filled her as she remembered those early days at the Davises'. I couldn't even talk when I got there, but it didn't matter. My teeth were rotted. I was skinny as a stick . . . but they didn't care.

"Someone called for you," Andrea said when Addie returned to her friend's house, and handed her Alyssa's infant carrier.

"For me? Who would have the number here?"

"I don't know. They asked for Addie Larsen."

Addie thought. There was only one possibility. She'd listed Andrea as a reference on the résumé she turned in this morning. And now they'd already called. They couldn't even wait until she got home to reject her.

"I know who it was," she said wearily. "I'll call them

back. Thanks for taking my girls. I owe you one."

"You're welcome. Alyssa's a good baby."

A good baby. What kind of baby was I? Addie wondered. Did anyone besides the Davises think I was good?

The message light was flashing when she arrived home. Get it over with, she thought. She braced herself, then hit the button.

"Sherill Shaw calling, Addie. Please call me when you get in."

Couldn't they just tell her no on the machine?

She held Alyssa in her arms, picked up her cordless phone, and dialed.

"Sherill Shaw, please." More waiting.

"May I tell her who is calling?"

"Addie Larsen. I'm returning her call."

"Oh. Yes. Just a moment."

Still more waiting.

"Addie? Sherill Shaw here. Our pay period begins on the first of the month. Would that be okay for you? Your start date would be October first."

Silence. She couldn't speak. Finally Addie swallowed and said, "You're giving me the job?"

"Will that date work for you? If so, let me know and I'll process your—"

"You're hiring me?"

"Is there some problem?" Sherill paused. "Do you have a question?"

"No." Addie let herself drop gently on the couch, the baby still in her arms. "That will be fine. October first."

"That's great, Addie. We'll see you then."

The tears came long after Sherill Shaw hung up as Addie still sat on the couch with the cordless phone in her hand. Warm, sweet tears of relief that she let fall on the jacket and skirt of her red suit, leaving her feeling limp and soggy but at peace.

She had the job. Someone wanted her. And she could see Alyssa and Jessica at work—on her lunch and on break, anytime she wanted.

Addie blinked. There was a safe feeling about her now, as if she were wrapped in a blanket. There was nothing like the feeling of finding out you were wanted when you didn't think you would be.

*Addie stared at the ornate script on the graduation an-*nouncement.

Ms. Addie Larsen.

She'd never seen her name written in such a classy way. Graduation from college was an accomplishment she never thought she'd possess. Now there was this box of thirty announcements. Who would she invite besides Jessica and Alyssa while she herself marched past in her cap and gown.

Mark? Not when she'd achieved this milestone on her own, in spite of his leaving her.

Her brothers? Years and miles away.

Her mother? She felt a momentary rush of sorrow that Joyce could not see that her child who was raised in foster homes was graduating from college.

When she asked herself who would be truly happy for her, who would know what this milestone meant, she thought of Hillary, who taught her to read. Kate, who fed and loved her. The Davises. She called directory assistance in the city where they had lived. When there was no number listed, she asked for a statewide search. Still nothing. Where was it that Hillary's father worked? Her mind searched frantically until the answer came to her. A fuel company. Gas stations. Major Oil Company. She looked in the phone book and dialed.

"Linwood Davis, please." Addie held her breath.

"What division?"

Addie racked her brain. All she could remember was that Dad was out of town for one to two weeks at a time. "He travels," she said.

"He travels from division to division?" The voice dripped sarcasm.

"He travels for the company," Addie said quickly.

"In what capacity?"

She took a deep breath. "I'm sorry. I don't know."

"Do you know his extension by any chance?"

"No."

"His supervisor's name?"

"No. He is—was—my foster father. I was with their family a long time. I called him Dad." She could hear her own desperation.

"Do you have any idea how big this company is? It's an international multibillion-dollar conglomerate. There's more to Major Oil than a gas station on every corner." The woman sighed. "I'll put you through to personnel."

Addie barely had time to breathe before a woman answered.

"May I please speak to Linwood Davis?"

"There's no one by that name in this department."

"I'm not sure where he works."

"Is this to verify employment?"

The question threw Addie off. "No," she said calmly. "I just want to talk to him."

"What is this regarding?"

"He was my foster father. I wanted to call him."

"I can't give out his number for personal reasons."

"Can you connect me to him?"

A long pause. "He isn't in this territory. I'd have to know where he worked to connect you."

Addie remembered. The Davises had lived in three states. And they could be anywhere by now. What should she say? Addie was surprised to feel tears welling up as memories of her sadness when she left the Davises filled her mind.

"You just don't want to help me," she accused, surprised at herself.

The woman sighed. "This has nothing to do with personal feelings. I can't locate him for you without—"

Addie hung up. She didn't know anything else. The foster-care system had made sure of that. But where would she be without that system? Addie wondered. She wouldn't have found the Davises on her own—and she never would have left them, either. Addie sat still on her couch, filled with hopeless disappointment.

The feelings of being displaced so long ago were still fresh in her mind.

Chapter 14

∞

Division of Family Services. As soon as she opened the heavy, glass door, Addie felt chills. The building looked sterile and cold—as vacant and vulnerable as she felt inside.

I was here once, she thought. Back when I was too traumatized to talk and almost too scared to breathe. My mother was here, too, she thought. How did Mama feel the day she discovered her children would be taken away? Angry? Guilty? A touch relieved? What was Mama like before the liquor took over her personality? Was she like any other young mom who could imagine no worse tragedy than losing her child?

Finally stepping inside, Addie realized she still remembered the smell of this office. The scent was a combination of stale air, old files and papers, furniture polish and floor wax. Breathing the air brought back memories of the most frightening days of her life, the days when she was taken from one foster home and placed in another. She reminded herself that she was no longer the little girl whose voice was afraid to emerge from her throat. No one could get the best of her today.

A young woman with black hair smoothed into a ponytail sat at the reception desk.

"May I help you?" Addie saw that the woman's gaze took in her charcoal-gray suit and white blouse. Her best clothes. The clothes she wore for job interviews, staff meetings at U.S. Stores, and night classes.

"I'd like to speak to a social worker."

"Have you an appointment?"

"I'm in from out of town—"

The woman wrinkled her forehead. "Is there something I can help you with?"

No, Addie thought instinctively. The powers that be wouldn't trust a receptionist sitting at the front desk with the hidden secrets in people's lives.

"I'd best wait for a social worker."

"I can't guarantee anyone will see you. Their schedules are often booked weeks in advance—"

"I won't need more than ten minutes of anyone's time."

"I can't promise you even one minute."

"Ask someone for me." Addie handed the woman her card, her computer programmer card, although it had nothing to do with why she was here today.

The young woman, whose name Addie saw was Carol Dayton, sighed.

"I'll call somebody, but—"

"Thank you." Addie sat on the edge of a waiting-room chair. Line after line rang on the switchboard. Suddenly the woman didn't even have time to take a breath, let alone call someone. Maybe this is a wild-goose chase, Addie thought. Like looking at a star and wishing every night. Like calling oil companies. Like waiting for the Davises to somehow come and find her. She'd nearly dozed off when the receptionist said, "Florrie Lamb will see you now."

Addie pulled herself together and stood. "Thank you," she said.

"To your right. Room 351."

A gray-haired woman who sat at a desk looked at her questioningly, then gestured at a chair. "They said you've been waiting an hour. I think that anyone who has waited that long deserves to be heard."

"I was placed in ten foster homes from this office. I'd like to see my records," said Addie, in a tone she hoped sounded determined.

The woman paused. "I was wrong in what I said. The fact that you've waited doesn't give you the right to something like that."

"I just want to find one family."

"A foster family?"

Addie nodded. "I just want to find out what the records say about me . . ."

"Most of them burned in a fire—"

"Can you check and be sure that mine did?"

"And the rest are confidential."

Surprisingly, Addie felt tears at the back of her eyes. "I only want to thank them. I don't want to interfere in anyone's life. Can you just see if my records are there?"

The woman stared at her.

Addie stared back.

Moments later the social worker moved to a row of filing cabinets. Addie held her breath. She watched as the woman pulled open a long drawer, then flipped through a seemingly endless series of files. Addie finally exhaled as the woman lifted a file and slammed the drawer shut.

"That's mine?" Addie asked.

A nod.

"Look, I'm thirty years old. I have four children and a job. I think I should be able to know what happened to me. Please let me see that file."

The woman shook her head, then opened the file and began looking inside it, holding it back from where Addie could see. Suddenly she stopped. "This is completely against policy. And if you tell anyone I told you this, I will deny it. But I thought you might want to know. In my notes, it indicates the family expressed interest in adoption."

"Adoption?"

The social worker's voice calmed to a whisper. "In adopting you into their family."

"Really?" Addie felt her heart beat fast while a wave of relief, warmth, and love filled her. "The family I was looking for talked about adopting me?"

The social worker nodded.

"But I was taken away."

Again, the woman flipped through the file, talking under her breath. "I shouldn't be discussing this with you. But permanency is so important, and I thought you might want to know that if someone was interested in adopting permanently—"

"If they wanted to adopt me . . . how come they didn't? Did they change their mind?"

"Oh no. Someone blocked the adoption."

"Who would do that?"

The social worker shook her head. "This all happened so many years ago."

"But it's important to me now."

The woman stared at Addie a moment, then looked back into the file. "The name it lists is Joyce Tyler."

"My mother?"

"It says that mother and an aunt desired to delay the adoption, in hopes that permanency with the mother would someday be established."

"It never happened." Addie realized her hands were shaking. "I was never permanent."

The social worker sighed. "I'm sorry to hear that. But I thought you might want to know that this family wanted you. They wanted you to stay with them."

"I wanted that, too."

The woman looked helpless. "I'm sorry. I don't know what more I can do."

"You could let me see the rest of the file."

"I've already gone way too far. Again, I'm sorry."

Suddenly a lump filled Addie's throat. She stood, and with a quick nod to the woman, rushed out of the room, down the hall, and through the heavy door.

The Davises wanted to adopt her. Again, the thought filled her with exhilaration. *Someone wanted me. The family I loved most wanted me, too,* she thought.

I have to find them, she decided, rushing back to her car. *I want to tell them I wanted to be adopted and I never stopped thinking of them. I have to tell them thanks.*

That night, sitting at the table with her four children— Jessica, Jeremy, Lindsay, and Alyssa—Addie said suddenly, "Do you remember when I told you about my real family?"

Alyssa abruptly looked up from the pasta salad and corn bread. "You mean Grandma? Or your foster family?"

"The Davises. One of my foster families."

Jessica looked at her. "Was that the place where you played Barbies?"

"And you never laughed before you got there."

Addie swallowed. "And they taught me how to read. And how to dance."

"Why don't we ever go see those people?" Alyssa's round blue eyes looked earnest, then she grinned. "Don't you ever want them to meet your wonderful children?"

"Are you ashamed of us?" Jessica asked, in a voice that was only half kidding.

"No," Addie said quickly. "It's not what you think. I've wanted to see them forever. I've looked and looked."

"I've heard that name before lots of times," Alyssa said. "Davis. What kind of a name is that?"

Addie shook her head. "I don't know. Probably English."

"I think it's really common, Mom. But maybe we can still find them." She looked at Addie questioningly.

Hillary opened the phone book. There it was. Randall. Could she call every Randall until she found the right one? She'd give it a try. She picked up the phone and dialed the first number.

"I'm looking for an Addie Randall?"

"No one by that name here."

"Do you know how to reach her?"

"Never heard of her."

Another number. "I'm trying to reach Addie Randall."

"You have the wrong number."

"Do you know her number by any chance?"

"I've never heard that name before."

Another number. "Could I speak to Addie Randall, please?"

"No Addie here."

"Do you know how I could find her?"

"I'm the only one here. Name's Angela."

For another hour Hillary plowed through the phone book. She wouldn't stop until she heard Addie's familiar voice.

She phoned until someone asked her, "Do you know what time it is?"

Chapter 15

∽

Thirty-four years old. Addie sat up in bed. She couldn't believe it . . . another birthday was here. And she was alone again . . . but not really. Although her marriage to Mark's friend Steve was over, at least she had their two children, Lindsay and Jeremy. It seemed like she was only twenty-five a couple of months ago. But, she reminded herself, she wouldn't have her four children if she was still twenty-five.

There was a timid knock on her bedroom door.

"Come in," she said, standing and wrapping her bathrobe around her.

She saw Alyssa's and Jessica's eager smiling faces—which quickly fell at the sight of her. "Mom, get back in bed! This is supposed to be breakfast in bed!"

"What are you guys doing?"

"It's your birthday. We made you something to eat."

Addie looked closer. Alyssa held a plate of pancakes and Jessica held a smaller plate with a candle-topped cupcake. Lindsay and Jeremy stood behind them, anxiously waiting.

"Happy birthday to you . . ." her children started singing.

Addie felt tears moisten the corners of her eyes.

My kids, she thought. I'm so glad we've shared so many special times.

Jeremy held out a card.

Addie took the envelope and felt that it was thick. A funny card, she thought. One of those funny cards where there's a clown on a spring. Or a flap that opens to show a big picture of a woman with frazzled hair. A mom.

She slid her finger under the flap. The card dropped open and a pile of money fell into her hands.

"What's this?" What did you kids do, rob a bank?"

She saw that Alyssa's eyes shimmered with tears, too. "It's just your present, Mom. We wanted to give you what you want the very most."

"I don't want your money," Addie said, suddenly serious.

"It's not just money. It's to buy you a present," said Lindsay.

"I can buy myself a present for five dollars. This is too much." She picked up several bills and tried to hand them to Alyssa, who conveniently leaned out of the way. The money dropped on the floor.

"Pick that up," Jessica said to Lindsay.

"And put it back in your bank," said Addie with mock ferocity.

"No," Jessica and Alyssa replied in unison.

Jeremy said, "It's yours. We want you to find your family."

"My family?" Addie was puzzled before it hit her. "Oh, you mean the Davises."

"Yes, your real family."

"So what's this for?" Addie lifted the bills and dropped them in a pile on her bedspread.

"For whatever it takes," said Lindsay.

"For as long as it lasts," said Alyssa.

"I still think this should be put in the bank for your college—" Addie called out as her four kids rushed from the room before she could give them their money back again.

Addie dialed. The phone rang at least three times. When the woman answered, it sounded as though she were far away. "Bauer Publishing."

"May I speak to *Woman's World* magazine?" Why did she feel so nervous? Addie wondered. These people were hundreds of miles away and didn't know her.

"What is this regarding, ma'am?"

"I thought they might be interested in a story about—"

"One moment."

The phone rang. She was already connected somewhere.

"Editorial."

"Yes. I'm calling to tell you my story about looking for my family—"

"You were separated from your family?"

"Yes."

"By adoption? We often run adoption reunion stories."

"I was a foster child."

"And you were adopted?"

"No. They wanted to adopt me, but the state took me back."

"And then you found them later?"

Addie hesitated. "No. Not yet. I wondered if you would be interested in the story of how I'm looking for them."

"We might consider running the story after you find them. And incidentally, we prefer query letters submitted in writing. Or you can fax—"

"I thought a story might help me find them."

A long pause. "I'm sorry. But our readers would want to know the ending. When you have the ending, please do contact us."

"Oh. Thank you."

It was the same with the other magazines she called. *Family Circle. Ladies' Home Journal. Guideposts.* People want to know how the story ends. They need closure. I need closure, too, Addie thought.

It was weeks later, long after she called the magazines, that Addie saw a reunion show on television.

"Is there someone missing from your life? Someone you'd like to find? Contact these folks." Sally Jessy Raphael gestured and a sign appeared at the bottom of the screen. BigHugs.com.

Should she call? Addie felt her heart beat. She felt like she had nowhere else to look. She dialed the number on her TV screen.

"You have reached BigHugs," said a voice. "Please listen to the options."

I want to talk to someone, thought Addie. She pressed "0," hoping she would get an operator.

"BigHugs.com," said a friendly female voice.

"Are you the ones on Sally?"

"Yes, we host reunions on many national talk shows."

"Family reunions?"

"Yes."

"What about someone who I think is my real family . . . but isn't my biological family."

"All the time. We find families like that all the time."

Addie sighed with relief. Then another worry cropped up. "How much does this cost?"

"That depends. It varies, depending on the complexity of the search."

"My kids—my son and daughters—gave me their savings." Her throat closed at the thought.

"Why don't I have someone call you back?" said the woman from BigHugs.com. "You could tell them about your search and then they could tell you about any expenses."

"Okay." Addie felt as if she'd suddenly landed after a long flight. She sat on the couch and basked in the peace of being alone at home on a day off.

It was four or five days later when the phone rang during her lunch hour.

"Addie? This is Arliene Dunn from BigHugs.com."

Addie wondered if she'd heard right.

"Joan says you have a story to tell us."

Addie sighed. "I do. I want to find the people who were my family—my only real family—when I was growing up."

"Why do you want to find them?"

"I want to thank them." Addie paused. "I want to let them know that I never had a happy memory until I lived with them. My happy memories began at their house."

"They were your adoptive family?"

"My foster family. I lived with them for five years."

"A long time."

"They taught me to laugh. To dance. To read. I want to let them know that what they did for this little girl really made a difference. They gave me a life."

"It sounds like you still miss them."

"Every day."

"Can you give me their names?" Arliene asked.

"The mother's name was Kate. I'll never forget that," Addie began, "and the dad was Linwood."

"Were there other children?"

"Yes . . . Hillary was like a second mom to me . . . and there was her sister, Kris."

"And when did you live with them?"

"I was with them for five years."

"What years were they?"

"Let's see . . ." Addie thought back. "About 1965 to 1970."

A pause. "I'll call you back, Addie. Your story is very interesting."

Sure, Addie thought. You'll call me back.

A calm sunset bathed the room in a warm, golden light. Hillary leisurely packed her clothes, feeling mixed emotions about saying good-bye to this country that she loved. She'd come back to Australia, Hillary promised herself. She couldn't stay away for good. This place was home now, too. Folding her last blouse, she began to open a box of items that had been in storage. As she lifted the first flap, her eyes caught on Addie's photo, which she had placed carefully atop a pile of important papers. Hillary sighed. For a moment Addie's brown-eyed gaze seemed to be actually leveled on her, and the thought caught at her heart.

"Addie?" she asked, as if Addie were actually in the next room, only a few feet away. When there was only silence, Hillary continued. "Addie, will I ever see you again?"

More silence. Hillary felt her heart thud. Could Addie be dead, as she sometimes feared? Or was she out there somewhere? And was she safe? Hillary touched Addie's hair in the photo and remembered how it felt to touch Addie's soft, fine hair in real life, all those years ago. She ran her finger along the line of Addie's chin and recalled the little girl's heart-stopping, crooked grin. Hillary thought of the yellow dotted-swiss dress Addie wore in the photo. She saw that the edge of the photo was frayed and gray. For the first time she noticed that the photo itself was faded from where sun rays caught at the edge of her shelf at home.

"This picture would have to fade to pure white before I'd give it up," she said aloud. "It's all I have left of you, Addie."

The silence in the room suddenly roared at her. Where was Addie? Was she alive? What was she thinking now?

Chapter 16

∽

Kate heard thunder outside as she smoothed the sheet neatly on the bed. The phone rang, interrupting her thoughts about Linwood's cancer treatments. She admired his determination and upbeat spirit so much.

"Hello?"

There was the sound of air rushing, as if it was a long distance call. Suddenly a voice, speaking with what Kate recognized as a New York accent.

"Have I reached the Davis household?"

"Yes," Kate replied, curiosity growing inside her. Who would be calling from New York on this gray winter day?

"I'm calling on behalf of Addie Larsen." The woman paused. Kate felt her heart skip a beat. She'd thought of Addie's name thousands of times in her mind, yet no one outside the family had said it aloud in years. Who on earth would connect her with Addie?

"Addie?" Had she heard that name right? Kate fell awkwardly on the bed, yet gripped the phone with determination. "Do you know Addie? Where is she?"

"Actually, I'm looking for her foster mother."

Kate was momentarily puzzled. Her breath caught. In her mind, she'd silently hoped and prayed that Addie was somewhere safe and happy and all grown up, long past the vulnerable years of needing a foster mother. Wait a minute, Kate thought, her pulse quickening.

"Maybe I'm the person you're looking for," she said, trying to sound calm, although she suddenly felt chills. Could this really be happening? Someone calling after all these years of silence and closed records?

"Are you Kate Davis?" the voice asked.

"Yes," Kate said emphatically. "That's me." She couldn't believe this. She sat up straight on the edge of the bed and continued to clutch the phone. "Where is Addie? Who is this?"

"This is Arliene Dunn. I'm from BigHugs.com. We are an international search agency."

"Did you talk to Addie?" That someone might know if Addie was all right still seemed like a miracle. Kate hardly dared breathe.

"I talked to her yesterday," Arliene said brightly. "And I'm calling to tell you she's looking for you."

"She's looking for *us*?" A picture flashed in Kate's mind, of tiny, scared Addie, her brown eyes as huge as walnuts. Now, after all the years of waiting and wondering . . . Addie was looking for them.

"I think of her every day," Kate said slowly. "And now you're saying she's thought of us, too?" Relief washed over her in waves. Addie was alive. She was safe.

"She said she's thought about you all the time over the years," said Arliene. "You should be proud. She said you were the only stable influence in her youth."

Kate's throat caught, and for a moment she couldn't speak. "She was our little girl. Our daughter." Now her voice broke. "Please tell me where she is."

"That's why I'm calling. Sally Jessy Raphael is planning a show on long-lost loved ones. Would you be willing to come on the show to see Addie?"

"Oh—" Kate's heart leaped at the thought. A tear pricked at the corner of her eye. "I'm already crying. I just know I'd bawl on TV. Could I meet her some other way?"

"Well . . ." Arliene Dunn paused. "We planned the show as a surprise for Addie. We want to surprise her by having you meet again."

Kate thought of the surprise party Addie had wanted all those years ago. Addie loved surprises. There was no way she could keep her from having this long-awaited surprise. "If I could see Addie, I'd probably do anything. Or go anywhere."

"We'd like to bring the whole family on the show."

"My husband is going through cancer treatments. He'd love to come, but he is too weak. And one of our daughters is in Australia."

"But the rest of you?"

"Yes," Kate managed. "My daughter Kris and I—"

"You'll be able to be there?"

Again, Kate pictured Addie, the little girl with stick-thin legs and big brown eyes. "We wouldn't miss it," she said. Not for the world.

"Good," said Arliene Dunn. "I'll be getting back to you soon."

"Thank you," Kate said. "For doing this for Addie."

"My pleasure," said Arliene. "We'll talk soon. Good-bye."

With the click of the phone, Kate realized that she was in shock. Addie. After all these years. They were going to see her and she wanted to see them. More tears flowed then, what seemed like buckets of them. Kate reached for the photo, the one with all of them sitting together. The one with Addie in the dotted-swiss dress. She held the picture in her hands and tried to look at it through a waterfall of tears. She'd probably never cried so hard. And she knew that tears had never, ever felt so good. The tears were followed by a sweet, peaceful calm, as warm and soothing as a down blanket. Somehow, she knew this happy news would lift Linwood's spirits, too.

*   *   *

"Hillary?"

Jeff's voice, calling from half a world away. It was weeks ago that they last spoke, yet scars from the breakup were still painful. Will I ever find the right man for me? Hillary wondered. At least Jeff had finally learned to phone without waking her in the middle of the night. Now she'd just eaten dinner and was sitting on the patio. Sunset bathed the wooden deck a dusty rose.

"How are you?" she asked, keeping her voice even. "How are things there?"

"Fine." He paused. "I'm calling to tell you something important. It's about your mom."

"Why didn't she call me herself?" Hillary felt the first twinges of annoyance.

"I just happened to call your house, looking for you, and your mom said I could tell you about this . . ."

Hillary sensed urgency behind his words. "Is everybody okay? Is Dad all right?" That was the thing about being so far from home. You held your breath and prayed that everyone would be safe until you could return to them.

"Everybody's fine," Jeff said.

What could he be calling about? And why wasn't he telling her? "Then why are you calling?" Hillary asked. "I sure hope nothing's wrong. You know, I'm coming back in four weeks."

"You'll want to come back tomorrow." She thought she heard a smirk in his voice.

"I can't think what would make me what to rush back when I don't have very much time left here. If everyone's okay—"

"Your mom found something of yours," Jeff broke in. "You'll never believe it."

"Something of mine?" She couldn't think of anything she lost at her mom's house. And couldn't Mom just keep whatever it was for another month?

"Yes." The smile in his voice stayed. "Something you really wanted . . . since you were a little girl."

"Really?"

"Yes, you were angry with her about it for a long time."

"Angry with her? I can't remember anything like that." Hillary racked her brain. "And I was mad because I left something at her house?" She was confused.

"Well, not exactly. You didn't really leave it. Your mom gave it away."

"What do you mean?"

"She found your Barbie doll."

"My doll . . . I haven't had a Barbie since . . ." Chills draped her body. Suddenly she was fifteen again, and her Barbie doll was missing from the shelf.

"You mean . . ." She sensed he enjoyed keeping her in suspense and making her reason through this puzzle on her own.

"I never wanted another Barbie after I lost my last one. I was too old—already fifteen. But the real reason was that losing my last one tore me apart," she remembered. "I lost my Barbie when I lost Addie. Mom put both Barbies together because Addie and I couldn't stay together . . ."

Suddenly Hillary's heart started beating fast. How could anyone find her Barbie, unless . . . "Addie had my doll. If Mom found the doll, it means she found Addie."

Dead silence from Jeff.

"You have to tell me," she ordered him. "I can't wait another second."

"I said they found the doll—"

"So they found Addie?"

"You got it!" Jeff said suddenly.

"Where is she? Is she okay? Do we get to see her?" Hillary paused amid her frantic questions. "You're right," she admitted. "I do want to come home now." She felt her heart pound inside her chest. Suddenly a month sounded way too long and the United States seemed too far away.

* * *

Where were the people who were supposed to pick her up? Kate fidgeted on the couch, then stood and looked out the window. She adjusted her pearl necklace then sat down again.

Addie. They were going to see Addie. How many times had she dreamed about seeing Addie again? She thought of her every day, Kate realized. Every day since that painful day when Addie walked out their front door with the social worker. *I knew since then,* Kate realized, *that nothing would take away the pain until Addie came back. There was a hole in my heart that wouldn't heal and the hurt wouldn't go away. Maybe now—*

A car horn suddenly honked outside.

Still sitting on the couch, Kate looked outside and saw nothing. The winter day outside stayed gray and hushed.

Seconds later a man yelled.

Kate rushed to the door. She opened it and gasped. Before her was a sea of heavy fog that had moved in during the night. She inhaled misty, stale wetness. Twin yellow beams from a car at the bottom of her driveway caught her eye.

She glimpsed a faint outline of the car through patches in the fog. It was a limousine. She heard footsteps and the man called out to her again. Kate stepped out into the frosty, mist-thick morning. Cold instantly penetrated her fingers as she gripped the slippery porch railing. She saw that ice decorated the front lawn and porch railing and delicate tree branches in a lacy filigree.

"Everything's frozen, lady. I can't get up the slope." The man waved his arms, hoping she could somehow catch sight of him.

"I didn't know it froze last night," Kate said truthfully. At least she was wearing low heels. She inched across the frozen porch—then slid helplessly into the porch rail. She clung to the cold iron banister and moved slowly down the steps, one by one, clinging to both hope and the rail.

I'm coming, Addie, she thought to herself. *I won't let this weather stop me.*

Her breath caught in a gasp as she slipped and nearly fell. Seconds later she lost her balance and slid against the frozen stiffness of the front hedge. Ice particles grazed her cheek.

"We got a plane to catch," the man yelled up at her.

"I'm coming," she shouted back. How many times did I want to go get Addie? How many times did I want to bring her back to our home? A million. At least a million. Nothing could stop her now.

She slipped again and caught herself, feeling jarred and nervous. One baby step followed another. She fell once, climbed to her knees, then brushed off her coat.

"I'll help you, lady," the driver said finally when she slipped again. He pulled her to her feet and the two of them inched toward the limousine. Kate's breath flowed out in a mist. She was nearly to the limousine when she slipped, then caught herself one more time.

I'm coming, Addie. Wait for me.

The limousine slid down their street, shimmying on the glassy surface as the driver fought to steer it straight.

"Sorry, lady," he called over his shoulder as they reached the end of the street.

"We'll get there," Kate said as she braced herself with one hand against the front seat and found herself holding her breath. The fog around them was as thick as a blanket. Though the windshield wipers cleared away the intermittent sleet, the view ahead was endless gray.

When they reached the airport, the runway was as icy as her driveway at home. Could the plane drive straight to take off? Kate wondered. How would they get into the air if it didn't? What would the Sally show do if she didn't arrive on time?

All the lights, conversations, and people rushing around her heightened Addie's nervousness. Was it really possible that the Davises—the only family she ever knew as her own—knew she was here? She'd seen other shows where they didn't find the person that the guest on the show was looking for. Did the Davises know they would soon see her? Addie sat in the green room until a young woman with clicking high heels hurried into the room.

The young woman smiled at Addie. "I'm Paige," she said simply, holding out her hand to shake Addie's. "Now, if you'll come with me?"

Addie stood and could feel that her knees had turned to mush. She felt her heart beat in her throat as she struggled to keep up with Paige. They walked to the edge of the soundstage, where Addie glimpsed a sea of lights, technicians, and a waiting audience.

I'm nervous, she thought. Please help me say the right things. Please help someone find the Davises. They are my family.

Kate and Kris waited anxiously offstage.

"I'm going to let you in on a secret." Sally Jessy Raphael's voice was a near whisper as she sat alone on the soundstage. "The people who are here today think that they are coming to make a plea to find their families. The truth is, we've already found these people. Let's watch what happens. Keep watching. This is 'Surprise Reunions'—"

Kate felt her heart beat fast throughout the first reunion. Her heart went out to the girl who wanted to find her family.

"Now meet Addie. Addie wants more than anything to find the foster family that changed her life . . ."

The camera shifted and Kate's heart thudded as she caught sight of Addie. She's really here. Look how beautiful she is, all grown up. I'd know her anywhere, Kate thought as she felt tears on her face. Those same brown eyes . . .

"You were in several foster homes," Sally began.

"I was five years old and I'd been in ten of them."

"Ten in five years," Sally breathed. "They work the

system so you won't get attached, but that makes it very hard emotionally."

"They didn't even tell me why I was in a foster home. I didn't know it was something my mom did. I thought there was something wrong with me. The foster family assumed that because I wasn't talking, I was brain-damaged. They were told that all three of us children were brain-damaged and that was how they treated us."

"You were considered handicapped while you were in foster care? Because of the circumstances?"

"Yes, well, we were found in a closet. My younger brother and me. My mom left, and left us with my eleven-year-old brother for two weeks. He didn't have any idea how to take care of us."

"So you ended up in foster care. Did you ever get back together with your mother?"

"I did, but she wasn't capable—couldn't take care of me. Now that I'm a mom, I understand that—"

"So you have a child yourself?"

"I have four kids."

Four children. Kate dabbed at her eyes. Now Addie was a mother herself. When she had come to their home, Addie didn't talk at all. Now she was talking to millions of people on TV, Kate thought. Kate patted Kris's shoulder as Addie told the TV audience about how her previous foster family wouldn't let her eat at the table with them—and how she immediately crawled under the table her first night at the Davises'. "The oldest daughter, Hillary," Addie was saying. "She didn't bat an eye. She just crawled right under the table with me."

"And that was the beginning of—how long did you stay with the Davises?"

"Five years—very unusual. Foster children usually didn't stay more than two."

"And they wanted to adopt you?"

"Yes. I found out about that much later. It was in my records."

"So why didn't that happen?"

Addie sighed and wiped her eyes. "Ironically, the person who was ruled an unfit mother was allowed to make the decision. My mother let my younger brother be adopted. But her sister—my aunt—said to my mom, 'You're going to get her back. Don't let her be adopted.'"

"But your mom never got you back for good."

"No." Addie wiped her eyes and shook her head. "The cycle never got stopped. Not for my mom. It stopped for me when I went to the Davises."

"What were they like?" Sally leaned her head thoughtfully. "Were they warm and loving?"

Addie smiled through her tears. "My oldest foster sister—she taught me to sing. And to read. That was a lifetime gift in itself. She taught me to do the Mash."

Kate and Kris smiled as Addie pantomimed the dance step from so long ago.

"And I remember when I laughed there—for the first time."

"The first time?"

"The first time ever in my whole life. The older daughter put Snoopy on the TV, and he was flying in his airplane and it cracked me up."

"What was her name?"

"Hillary." Addie smiled. "The other sister was Kris. And there was the dad, who worked at an oil company. And the mom, who was an artist. And a little dog named Jake."

"And these people were always kind to you?"

Addie sat a little straighter. "They gave me a life. They planted a seed." She paused thoughtfully. "I wasn't a person until I lived with them. I was treated as an object before. They planted a seed of love and self-confidence. And you know—it's really funny. The mom was an artist, and now my daughter, Alyssa, is really talented in art. The mom also loved acting, and one of my other daughters, Jessica, wants to be an actress."

"Do you remember the day you had to leave them?"

"It was my birthday—July eleventh—and I was eleven

years old." Kate watched as a flood of tears flowed down Addie's cheeks. "I watched Hillary go off to her tennis lesson, crying because she didn't want to go—" Addie's throat caught. Tears pricked the corners of her eyes. "I always wanted to be with them, but I didn't know how to find them." She paused. "Then I saw your show."

"An earlier reunion show?" Sally asked gently.

"Yes." Addie snifffed. "With BigHugs.com."

"You saw them reuniting other families."

"Yes . . . and it was the first time I thought I might have a chance to see them. If it wasn't for that show, I would just still be waiting."

"You don't have to wait any longer," Sally called out.

That was their cue. Kate's heart thudded. She followed Kris out onto the stage and watched the two of them— the two girls, her two girls—hugging each other, trembling and crying as if they would never stop. Seconds later Kris gathered her in, and she hugged Addie, too. Addie, who she wondered about every day of her life—who she now knew was safe, and all grown up, and beautiful.

"You remember that day, too—don't you, Kate?" Sally asked, moments later.

"It was a gray dreary day. Do you remember what I said to you as you left?" Kate turned to Addie.

"I remember watching Hillary cry. I heard you say that we'd be together again—"

"And now you are," Sally said.

"I really wasn't a person before I met you," Addie was saying.

"And this girl." Sally pointed to Kris. "Is this the girl you were so close to all those years ago."

"She was really close to my older sister, Hillary," said Kris.

"Hillary—are you there?" Sally called out. "Are you on the phone?"

"Where is she?" Addie asked, smiling through her tears.

"In Australia," said Kate.

"That figures," said Addie. They laughed together, each

remembering the girl who could put together a play, a circus, or a club, on the spur of the moment.

"Are you on the phone?" Sally asked again.

"I sure am." Hillary's voice filled the soundstage. "I'm looking forward to coming back on Monday, when I will call Addie. I love her so much and I've missed her—and we're going to get together."

Sally turned to Kris. "And did you think about Addie?"

"Of course." Kris handed Sally a small photo of a little girl in a yellow dotted-swiss dress.

"I keep this on my desk—in a box with my letters."

"That was first grade." Addie brushed aside fresh tears.

"That hard teacher," said Kris, and the two of them laughed together.

"I think you have a lot to talk to about," Sally said. "Shall we let them go off to talk, folks? We're all so happy for you."

Kate's thoughts were heady as she felt the grief she'd carried all these years begin to lift. I still want to adopt her, she thought, walking through the assortment of lights, cords, and machines. She's still my little girl.

"We need to beat the system." Hillary's words emerged with firm determination.

Her family looked at her curiously.

"What do you mean?" Kris asked. "We got her back. We know where she is now."

"But she's not ours for good."

"She's all grown up—she doesn't need a mom and dad anymore," Kris protested.

"She still needs a family."

"She'll always have us," Kate's voice was gentle. "We'll be here for her . . . forever."

Hillary shook her head. "That isn't the same thing."

Her father gave her a bewildered smile. "I don't know what else we could do."

"We could adopt her . . . now . . . legally."

Her family stared.

"She's thirty-five," Kris said finally.

"No one's ever too old to be part of a family," Hillary said. "We always wanted her to be Addie Davis."

"Can we really do that?" Kris asked.

"I would like to provide for her ... I mean, help her financially ... if she needed me," their dad said.

"We'd have to ask her if it's what she really wants," Kate said.

"She wouldn't have looked for us all those years if she didn't want this."

"Let's ask her," said Kris. "Let's call her right now."

"I think we should surprise her," Kate said suddenly. "The next time she comes to visit."

Hillary could hardly wait.

Chapter 17

∞

Addie gazed at the snow-frosted roof, railings, and porch of the Davises' house. Who would I be if I grew up in this home? she asked herself. A second later the thought came rushing to her: I am who I am because of my five years with these people. Her heart fluttered, she blinked back a tear and walked up the front steps.

Her mind couldn't help flashing back to the first time she'd met this family. My heart was pounding that day, too, she recalled. Only it shouldn't have been. If I had known that this was where I would first find a family who loved me, I would have run up the steps and hugged them with all my strength.

She felt like doing that now. But instead, Addie, twice

as tall as she'd been when she first approached the Davis home, stepped neatly in her high heels to the front door and raised the knocker. She knocked three times, imagining that the beats against the door were in sync with the pounding of her heart.

She was home. It was a feeling she'd experienced so rarely in her life that it was a battle to fight off tears. She wanted to be dignified, and all grown up, but inside she was still that little girl who wondered what her fate would be.

Now I know, she thought.

Hillary opened the door to Addie's knock, her own smile brimming. "I hope you're hungry," she said.

"Are we having Heinz happy soup?" Addie asked, remembering the soup club the two girls had joined fifteen years before.

"With Mountain Dew," Hillary said, and the two of them laughed together.

Really, though, dinner was fried chicken, potatoes with gravy, green beans, warm dinner rolls, salad, and chocolate cake for dessert.

Addie thought it was the best food she'd ever tasted. "Thank you," she said, trying to be dignified again. "It was delicious."

"Our pleasure." Kate's smile was warm. "You don't know how many nights I wished you were sitting at this table."

"We all did." Hillary smiled at her.

"I did, too," Addie said. "Lots and lots of nights."

"And now," Dad said, "we need to talk to you in the living room."

What could this be about? Despite the warm, peaceful feeling inside, Addie felt a shiver of fear. Somewhere, deep within her, was hidden the scared little girl who didn't know what life would hand her next. Dad's voice was serious. Could something be wrong?

Addie followed the Davises into the living room. She

thought she caught sight of a quick smile between Hillary and Kris, but she couldn't be sure.

Her heart pounded. She was thirty-five years old, but she felt about seven. Vulnerable was a word she knew too well.

Dad sat in the leather chair and drew a pile of papers from his briefcase.

His voice sounded stern and businesslike. "We need to make you aware of a decision we made."

What was this?

His voice warmed slightly. "The truth is, Addie, we want to make you aware of how much we want you in our family—how much we've always wanted you in our family."

"Since the first moment we saw you." Kate's smile brought tears to Addie's eyes. There was no more pretending that she was all grown up. Inside, her feelings felt raw and new. She had always longed to be wanted, to be loved. She had always wanted a home, where she knew she could stay. But what did all this mean?

"We want to beat the system," Hillary said with a firm nod and a determined smile.

Thinking of all the years that were now past, Addie found her voice. "How could we do that?"

"We want to adopt you," Dad said.

"Now," Hillary added. "This year."

"We'll go to court and complete the legal transaction," said Dad.

"And you'll be our sister forever," said Kris.

"No one can take you away ever again," said Hillary, in a tone that sounded suspiciously like the voice Addie carried in her memory all these years.

Addie was speechless. Her heart—and eyes—filled. "What can I say?" She wiped a tear away with shaking fingers. "I feel like I'm ten years old again—and my dream is finally coming true this time. After all these years. I can't believe it."

"Believe it," Hillary said, reaching out to touch her shoulder.

Addie couldn't look at Hillary. She knew she'd sob if she did. But—like always—like every time something good seemed about to be happening as she was growing up, there had to be a catch. There had to be something standing in her way.

"You guys . . ." Addie felt her throat catch. "There's nothing else that you could say that would make me this happy, but . . ."

They all looked at her questioningly. "What's wrong?" Hillary asked.

Addie hesitated. "Did everybody forget? I'm thirty-five years old. Kids don't get adopted when they're thirty-five years old."

"They do if it takes that long," Hillary said hopefully.

There was a pause in which they all held their breath. Could this be happening? Addie wondered. The one thing she always wanted, which was so simple, yet so all-encompassing, the one peace she'd sought through all her trials, the one simple truth that always seemed to lie so elusively far away?

To be part of someone's family. To have a place in a family's home and hearts that no one could take away.

The Davises were saying it was within her reach. The impossible now lay in front of her.

Addie wept unashamedly. Tears spilled down her cheeks, and she tried to catch them by covering her eyes with her wrist. Warm tears continued to flow. Addie was shaking.

She felt Kate's arm around her and Hillary's hand, patting her shoulder, and Kris, reaching out to wrap an arm around her waist. And somehow, through all of it, she heard Linwood's voice. Still businesslike, but now emphatic with his own emotion.

"I have the papers right here. We talked to a lawyer. All you have to do is sign your name."

It seemed like magic. Like heaven bent down to gather

her up. And all it required was her signature.

Addie Randall Larsen.

Three simple words that hardly bought her anything in the past.

But this time she felt power as she formed the familiar letters. Her heart wouldn't stop pounding and she was filled with warmth inside. She watched, blinking away still more tears, as Kate and Linwood signed their names under hers. Although it wasn't required, Hillary and Kris had asked to sign, too.

Now the names were all there, together.

The whole family.

At last.

Kate couldn't believe the day had finally arrived, and that she, Linwood, and Addie were sitting here, together, at the back of the courtroom. Her heart was pounding too hard for her to listen to the other court proceedings taking place before the judge's bench. Instead, she looked around her—at the high ceiling, the flag, and at the judge, who was young and good-looking, as if he had been sent from Central Casting. And finally—she glanced over at Addie, whose big brown eyes brought back memories she had held in her heart for so many years now. She thought again of the first day she saw Addie—a girl who looked like a sad, little doll with raggedy clothes, toothpick legs, a poking-out tummy, and a crooked smile that tore at all of their hearts. She thought of the last day she saw Addie before she left their home—taller and suntanned, yet with that same questioning look in her eyes as if she wondered which hurt was headed her way next.

Now Addie still looked vulnerable, though she wore a dressy suit, her hair was combed perfectly, and a gold watch clasped her wrist. There was still that look in her eyes. Kate knew that this was why they were here today.

We've waited almost a quarter of a century for this day, Kate thought. A day we thought might never come.

"Davis?" the court clerk called out moments later. "Davis and Larsen?"

They stood, the three of them, in unison. There was a quick pause before all of them walked toward the clerk.

"The judge will hear your petition now." The clerk nodded. "You may sit in the front row, then you'll stand to address him."

More waiting. Kate sensed that her palms were cold. She tapped one foot. Did the judge even know they were here? she wondered, gazing at the silent young man in the black robe who gazed down at the paper on the podium in front of him. She felt herself breathe.

"Davis?" The judge finally looked up at them.

They nodded together. He looked at them and frowned.

"This is a petition for adoption. The decree requires that the child be present in the courtroom in order to finalize."

"I'm here." Addie raised her hand as she spoke.

"Are you the child's birth mother?" the judge asked.

Kate stepped forward. "She's the one we're planning to adopt."

Another frown as he peered at them through the glasses. "Adoption traditionally takes place up until the age of twenty-one." The judge's words were firm and definite, yet not unkind. "Most children are adopted under the age of five."

"We would have adopted her sooner," Kate said. "It just took us until now. See, when the state discovered we wanted to adopt, they took her—"

The judge held up a hand. "I'm not here to rule on past rulings. This is a petition to adopt starting today. Will the three of you please step forward?"

They stepped closer to the high, wooden podium.

"The adoptee?" He glanced down at them.

"That's me," said Addie.

The judge paused and stared. "While you are surely above the age of legal consent, I feel I must ask about your family. Do you have parents—a mother or father— who might object to these proceedings?"

"It wouldn't matter if they did. These people are my family now." The firmness in Addie's voice caught at Kate's heart.

The judge paused.

"And you—the parents who plan to adopt. I feel I must say that such a step creates entitlement. This young woman—Addie Larsen—will assume inheritance rights. She will be entitled to inherit assets from you."

"That's what we want." Kate's voice was a warm blanket in the chilly courtroom. "We've wanted to provide for her since she was five years old."

"It's one of the main purposes why we're here," said Linwood firmly.

Addie felt her heart beat.

"It will be just as if she were born to you. Although she is not a child, this will become a binding, legal alliance. You couldn't undo it if you wanted to."

"Not in a million years." Kate felt a tear on her cheek.

The judge gazed at them. "You've stated your position. I can think of no other reasons not to proceed." He sighed. "While your petition is a nontraditional one and probably not legally necessary, I nonetheless feel it is valid. I must say, that in this day and age, when I see so many partnerships and families dissolving, your desire to unify is heartening to me, and I see no reason to deny your request." He paused to look at them again. "The petition for Linwood and Kate Davis to adopt Addie Larsen is herewith granted." The judge's gavel hit the podium. Kate's hands were shaking as she rushed to fold Addie into her arms.

"Remember this reunion?" Sally's voice over called out. Then the camera focused on a light blue poster.

WHEN ADDIE MET SALLY said the poster. Below that were the words *a very happy ending to a very long story . . .*

The camera shifted to Sally Jessy Raphael, wearing her

trademark red-framed glasses and a cream-colored dress.
Her voice took on a thoughtful tone. "If I had to choose
a favorite story, this might very well be the one. A heart-
warming reunion story that literally moved most of us to
tears. Addie spent her first five years in foster homes. In
her case, they were awful. This isn't always what happens,
but it happened to her. Then she was placed in the home
of a wonderful, loving family. When they wanted to adopt
her, the state intervened." Sally paused, wiped her eye
discreetly. "As years passed, her dream was that this family would someday find her and adopt her." Again Sally
paused. "And today—on her thirty-sixth birthday—this
dream came true, and Addie got adopted. It's not usual to
adopt a thirty-six-year-old woman, but in this case, it was
what Addie and her family always wanted. They weren't
able to be here today, but they've sent us a tape from the
courthouse where the adoption took place."

Days later they looked like they'd always been together,
Kate thought, watching her homemade video as it now
appeared on the Sally show. Seeing them stand there, all
in a row, they looked like a family for life.

There she was, her arm around Addie, who called out
to the TV audience, "Thank you Sally, and Arliene, and
BigHugs.com. This is the best birthday I ever had since I
left these people."

They all smiled and cheered from the courthouse steps.

Kate heard her own voice call out, "And thank you for
my four new grandchildren. I never was a grandmother
before."

Kate played the tape again and again, still thinking of
how the group of them were a perfect blend after waiting
all those years. After the tape ended for about the tenth
time, Kate shut off the TV, removed the tape, and went
to get ready for her new granddaughter's first art lesson.

All those years, she thought, we were preparing for this.
The years she taught art to other children, the years she

spoke on the radio, the hours Hillary spent working to make a difference in the world. The years Kris worked in real estate, helping other people find homes.

Through all of it, they were a family, their stories interweaving, with laughter, tears, days of happiness, and days—like the one when Addie left—when they wondered if they even wanted to live one more day. But they made it this far—until now, the time when their family was finally complete.

In Search of the
Family She Lost

Chapter 1

❧

Friday night. Steve sighed and ran a hand through his blond hair before he turned and locked the shop behind him. It was late twilight. The summer heat was dying down and the cars in the parking lot in front of him were bathed in blue-gray light. He was still sweaty from the long day at work. If it were safe, he thought, he'd crash right here on the sidewalk, stay in his jumpsuit, set his toolbox next to him, and sleep until morning. He sighed. In some ways, it would be easier to just stay here, and not think of what he had to face at home.

But at the same time his heart pounded with anxiousness. Were the kids okay? He wondered every night as he drove home from work in his van. During the day he simply had to put his anxious thoughts aside or he knew he'd run instantly out of the drapery store, let the door bang behind him, and never come back. If he could, he'd be with his kids every single minute . . .

Steve looked forward to a hot bath and a dinner that he'd probably have to fix himself. He planned on going to bed early . . . unless there was trouble with Anna. He didn't want to think that tomorrow would be another day of drapes, followed by a night of work at Les's cleaners.

Driving up to his house, he felt the familiar pangs of apprehension and dread. His worry heightened when he saw only two lights in the upstairs bedrooms. It was getting increasingly difficult to know what Anna would be doing at any given time. He couldn't count on his wife doing anything consistently. He arrived home some nights to find her asleep with the TV blaring. Sometimes the children gathered in a scared little knot in front of the family-room TV until he got home. Other times he'd find them snacking in the kitchen, a haphazard assortment of plates, crackers, peanut butter, and bread looking some-how as sad and forlorn as their bewildered faces.

Now he walked through the silent house wondering where the children were, and if Anna was sleeping. What was it like to find out you had a lifelong illness at such a young age? He felt both sympathy and anger toward her, and anger at the changes her illness had brought to the life of his family.

The downstairs rooms were silent and empty. Where were the kids? Were they still playing outside, after dark? He trudged up the stairs, hoping the kids were asleep in their beds. As he passed his wife's room, he caught sight of Anna, sitting stiffly on the bed, surrounded by piles of clothes. She started at the sight of him, and he felt a shiver of fear as he stepped closer.

"What are you doing?" Worry penetrated past his con-fusion. How on earth could she make such a mess when she had so little energy? And why would she?

She glanced up for a moment, and he felt another stab of fear as their eyes met. Her face seemed to be etched with the same helpless pain he himself felt. She shook her head in anguish, then riffled though a pile of clothes.

"I need to tell you." She sighed, then reached into her drawer, pulling out a pile of underwear with trembling fingers.

"What are you doing?" he asked.

"I'm moving out."

"What?" He couldn't really be hearing those words, could he? "What do you mean?"

"I'm leaving." She looked up at him, eyes determined now. "I have to leave here."

He sat on the edge of the bed. He stared at her in dis-belief, then bent to touch her arm. When she moved away abruptly, he heard pained puzzlement in his own words. "This doesn't make sense. There's no way you can take care of yourself." The next words felt terrible and petty in his mouth. "You can barely walk."

"That's why I can't stay here. I can't do what needs to be done."

His heart thudded. "And how will it get done if you go?"

"You'll do fine by yourself." She looked up and caught his eye, and he sensed she was angry at him.

"What about the kids?"

She shook her head. "I can't take care of them. You can hire someone."

"With what money?"

"Well, I'm worthless to you. I'll never be the same. We both know that."

His sigh was heavy. "How will you possibly go any-where else?"

"I already arranged for the move."

"How will you drive? How will you get to work?"

"I'm going to work at Les's."

"But I already take us both there, every night."

"This will be full-time." Her eyelids fluttered, and she looked away. He sensed something.

"How will you—"

"Les will help me. He has the time."

A dark, sick feeling filled Steve. "You're leaving me for Les."

A heavy silence. He heard the bedside clock tick. Then her voice, rising in anger. "What do you want me to say?"

"How could you do something like this? You can hard-ly move." He felt sharp hurt for both of them.

"I'm sorry. But it isn't my fault."

"It's your fault you were cheating on me!"

"No one knew I was going to get sick. But Les will take care of me."

"You and Les . . ." His voice grew bitter with hurt and pain. "I thought you only got along good. But it was more than that."

She placed a pile of nylon stockings in a sack on the bed.

"How could you do this? I stayed with you the whole time you were sick."

"We shouldn't have married. We were too young. We should have divorced a long time ago."

"It's a little late to decide that. Four kids too late. And where are the kids now?"

"They're sleeping. They're safe here." Bitterness rose in her voice. "I'm not totally incompetent."

"No." Steve heard his voice grow louder. "Just selfish and thoughtless. Not thinking of what's good for your kids."

"I can't take care of them now. I'm leaving the kids with you."

" 'Cause Les won't take them. Does that tell you what he's like?"

She shook her head. "I was planning to be gone before you got home."

"I'm not going to help you pack." He stood up and slid a pile of clothes off the bed, onto the floor. "I'm not going to help you ruin our lives." He stomped out of the room, went downstairs to the living room, and lay down on the couch. It seemed like hours before his exhaustion yielded to sleep.

Opening her eyes, Amy feared she was probably already late for school. Her bedroom was filled with sunlight. She scrambled out of bed and ran to look at the clock.

Eight-twenty. School started in ten minutes. Dad was probably already at work. Where was Mom? Amy felt a familiar worry. She ran to her parents' bedroom and saw that the bed was made, but no one was there. She rushed to her brother's bedroom to try to shake him awake.

"Tom." She shook his shoulder. "It's time for school."

He gave her a bleary glance. "Mom didn't come to get me."

"I looked at the clock. It's eight-twenty. You gotta get up now!"

He yawned. "Where's Mom?"

"I don't know. I'm calling Dad." Amy fought a feeling of dread as she hurried to the kitchen. Did her mom leave a note on the table, like she sometimes did, saying where she had gone? The table was bare. Amy picked up the phone.

"Steve Gray," she said, the way Dad told her. Then she waited, listening to the sounds of Dad's drapery store. She pictured the racks of fabric, the industrial iron, the desk . . .

"Hello?" Dad's voice.

"Daddy, this is Amy." She felt the fear creep into her voice. "Mom's not here."

"You looked in the bedroom?"

"The bed's made, but she's gone."

"I hope she hasn't . . . I told her to talk to you first." Amy heard her father's sigh. Then he said, "I'll be right there."

Amy dressed herself. She got eight-year-old Tom out of bed and woke four-year-old Lauren and two-year-old Jennifer, glancing out of the house every few minutes, hoping that she would see either her mother's or her father's car. A shiver of fear filled her as she poured cereal and juice, then wiped up Jennifer's spills. Finally she heard the sound of Dad's van in the driveway.

His heavy footsteps on the front stairs calmed her pounding heart. Ever since she was little, Amy felt safe with Dad. But why wasn't Mom here?

Dad burst through the door. "Amy? Are you all right?"

"Yes," she said, wiping milk from Jennifer's chin. "Where's Mom?"

Amy saw her father's shoulders sag as he went to the phone. "I'll try to find her," he said, shaking his head. Knowing she should be gathering her books together for school, Amy stared at Dad's anxious face. What would happen now?

"Is Anna Gray in?"

Amy watched her father shake his head as he rocked back and forth impatiently.

"What are you doing there?" She heard both pain and panic in his voice.

"Well, you got four kids that need their mother this morning. You never said you wouldn't be here."

Dad waited. Amy caught shreds of her mother's angry voice.

"All right, all right!" Dad hung up the phone and turned to her. She saw panic and sadness in his eyes.

"Where's Mom?"

Dad pulled out a chair and sat at the table. He ran a hand along Jennifer's chin. "Guess I got something to tell you kids." He shook his head with frustrated anger.

"What do you mean?"

"Looks like—" Dad stopped to glance around at the four children seated at the table. His hand found Amy's shoulder. "Looks like your mom isn't going to be coming back for a while."

Tom asked, "Who will take care of us?"

"I'll take care of you," Dad said. Amy caught the sound of pain in her father's voice.

"Who'll get me ready for school?"

Amy heard her own voice say, "I will."

"I don't want you—I want Mama." Tom's voice broke.

"Mama's not going to be here for a while—maybe not ever." Dad's voice was soft. "So we'll have to take care of ourselves."

Tom broke into tears. "It's your fault—you always got in fights."

Amy's heart thudded as she looked at Dad's face. "It's not my fault," he said. "Or any of yours. Mama says it's her own fault. She decided to leave."

"She can't live without us!" Amy protested. She thought of Mama and how the multiple sclerosis had continued to progress, so that Mama now struggled just to walk.

"Doesn't she like us anymore?" Tom asked.

"She thinks—" Dad paused. "She thinks that because she got sick, she's not strong enough to be your mom here at home anymore and—"

"But who will drive her?" Tom asked. "How will she get home from work?"

"Looks like she's going to be staying with Les." Steve tried not to sound bitter, but his voice betrayed him.

"Tell her we don't like Les. And we don't care if she's sick. Tell her to come home," Tom pleaded.

Dad looked at them. Amy saw a hollow strange look cross his face. "I'll let you talk to her," he said. He turned and dialed the phone. "Anna Gray," he said flatly.

He handed Amy the phone. It felt warm against her face.

"Mama?"

"This is Anna," said her mother. Her voice sounded cold and faraway.

"Mama, why aren't you here with us?" Amy said.

She heard her mother sigh. "I told your dad. I'm not well enough to take care of a home and children."

Tears welled in Amy's eyes. "But we love you! We want you to come back."

"I'll visit you. And you can come visit me!"

"But you won't be here in the morning. You can't fix my hair."

"Your father will fix it."

"He doesn't know how to braid."

"Wear it down. It looks fine. I'll braid it for you when you come visit me."

"But you won't live here. You don't love us anymore!"

"I love you very much. But my illness—"

"If you loved us, you wouldn't leave us!" Amy's voice rose to a scream.

"You're just too young to understand," Mama said quietly. Then she hung up the phone, leaving Amy standing with the receiver in her hand and tears streaming down her face.

"Call her back, Daddy," she wailed.

He put his arm around her shoulders.

"I'll talk to her tonight."

"What if she doesn't come back?"

Dad's eyes closed quickly. "Then it will be just us. We'll talk about it later. I've got to get you guys to school. And the little ones—"

"Mom always leaves them down the hall at Mrs. Potter's," said Tom.

"Is that okay?" Dad stared into Amy's face.

"That's where she leaves them," said Tom.

Amy saw that her father's eyes held the same sharp pain she felt inside. What was going to happen now? She thought of the nagging worry she'd been feeling for the past months. She thought of how her mother had stopped braiding her hair in the mornings. She'd loved the warm calm feeling of her mother's hands working through her hair, patting her neck and shoulders. But lately Mama often hurriedly put her hair in pigtails or said, "Just wear it down today," and Amy had had to ask her to please braid it just this once. And there were the afternoons when she came home to a silent house. How could Mama leave Jennifer and Lauren with that scary Mrs. Potter. And now . . . wasn't Mama ever coming home?

Chapter 2

❧

What was he feeling, standing here on Mrs. Potter's doorstep? Panic, Steve realized. Sheer panic at the knowledge that his life was falling to pieces. He didn't want his wife to be gone, and he didn't want to leave his children with this woman.

Mrs. Potter answered the door, a baby on her hip.

"Oh. I didn't know they were coming today."

Steve emitted a long sigh. "I didn't either. But the truth is, I just left work to take care of a quick emergency and I've got to get back. The place could be full of customers with no one to help them."

Mrs. Potter sniffed and said contemptuously, "Where's Anna?"

Panic seized him in an iron grip. "She said she's leaving me. She's not here today—"

"Why didn't you tell her to take the kids with her?"

"She's . . . disabled . . ."

Mrs. Potter glanced at Steve, from his head to his toes, as if sizing him up. "She gets around all right when you're not here. Has someone to drive her places, too."

Steve raised his hands helplessly. "I didn't know this was going to happen, okay? I can't believe it either. But right now—"

"Anna owes me money. I shouldn't take the kids till I get paid."

Steve sighed in exasperation. "One day. Okay? Take them today and I'll pay you tonight."

Mrs. Potter gave him a look of distaste. "When are you getting home?"

"I'll leave as early as I can. Four-thirty or five o'clock."

"I'm not their grandma, you know. This isn't a place to just dump them and go on your way."

"Okay, okay. Five at the latest."

"Be here then, with the money, or I'll lock them out in the hall. Had too many people take advantage of me."

What kind of person is this? Steve thought. But what else could he do now?

Amy heard a loud crash from across the hall. Opening their apartment door, she forced her feet forward until she stood on Mrs. Potter's doorstep. She knocked. There was a fast, intense pause, before the woman, angry and red-faced, opened the door and whispered harshly. "Kids are napping. What do you want?"

"What was that noise?"

"I dropped a pan. It's not your concern."

Mrs. Potter reached to shut the door, but Amy thrust her arm out firmly.

"I'm here to pick up my sisters."

"Your dad said five o'clock. He's not getting out of paying me all the money he owes me because you're here early."

"I'm supposed to take them home when I get here after school."

"He didn't tell me that. And that one little girl—Lauren. She keeps crying. What's wrong with her?"

Amy swallowed. "She's just sad."

"I had to hold her for hours until she finally fell asleep."

Glancing down at the threshold, Amy said, "Our mom left yesterday."

Now Mrs. Potter sneered at her. "Where'd she go this time?"

Amy's throat filled. "I don't know," she said finally.

"Your mother left . . . and you don't where she is now." Mrs. Potter shook her head. "That woman is so irresponsible. It's no wonder that—"

"She's staying with Les," Amy said quickly.

"Oh . . . that boyfriend of hers. Well, you tell your dad he can't just dump his kids here anytime he feels like it. I don't just baby-sit for fun. This is a legitimate business and I have rules."

"I'll take care of them . . ." Amy's voice surprised her, bursting out when she thought she was as scared as she could be. "I'll hurry home every day after school."

Mrs. Potter's lips curled with contempt. "You're a kid. It's illegal for someone your age to watch other kids."

Amy drew herself up to her full height. "I'll be ten next month."

"You can't watch kids legally until you're twelve,"

Mrs. Potter said, as if she and Amy were in a contest and she'd just won.

"Well, I'll take my sisters home now. My dad will be there." Amy held her breath. She really wasn't sure whether Dad would be home now or not.

Mrs. Potter stared into her face, and Amy held her breath. Then the woman shut the door quickly, before Amy could step inside her apartment.

Seconds later Mrs. Potter appeared with a sleepy Lauren and a big-eyed, scared-looking Jennifer.

"Lauren was right in the middle of a nap. But you know best." Mrs. Potter's voice dripped sarcasm.

"Thank you," Amy managed, feeling the warm softness of her baby sister against her shoulder. She went home and lay on the bed next to Lauren, smelling her sweet baby smell and thinking it might be all that was left of the way their lives used to be. That night, Amy lay awake and wondered what would happen to their family. She listened to Lauren and Jennifer sleeping beside her and wondered why they weren't awake with worry like she was. Straining, she heard her father's familiar snore and stared at the gray blackness of the ceiling. How long would they be able to go on without Mama?

The next morning, she confronted Daddy at breakfast.

"You can't take the girls to Mrs. Potter anymore."

Daddy looked at her patiently. "Is that what she told you?"

Amy looked down. "No," she admitted. "But I don't like her. She's scary."

Now she and Daddy stared at each other. Daddy's voice was low and sad. "What am I going to do? You have to go to school. I have to go to work. And your mother isn't—"

"I'll stay home," Amy proclaimed.

"No. You can't miss school. But I'll tell you what. I'll look for another baby-sitter today. I'll find someone as soon as I can."

"Then let me stay here until you get one."

"I'll tell old lady Potter it's her last day," Dad said.

"Then who will you get?" Amy saw her own helplessness on her father's face.

"It might take me a day or two to find someone," he admitted. "I might have to ask her to watch them for a few more days," he conceded. "But I'll start looking right now."

"I can do it. Please, Daddy?" Amy's blue eyes looked questioningly into her father's.

"I'll tell her you have my permission to pick up the girls as soon as you get home."

Amy frowned. "She says I'm not legal."

"Tell her you're legal with me," said Dad. Somehow his hug couldn't reassure Amy, who, as days passed, felt like her family was slipping helplessly out of control. Mama came to visit a few times, sitting delicately on the couch for an hour or so until she said she was tired and phoned Les to come and get her. She didn't seem to be at home in their house anymore, Amy thought.

She thought of Mama again later as she scrambled upside down on the jungle gym at school, hanging by her knees. She planned to twirl around the bar, her knees conveniently catching with each revolution to keep her from falling. It was a trick she'd done lots of times. But this time her knees caught only empty air, instead of the solid metal bar. Panicked, she straightened her legs, only to feel her body zoom helplessly to the ground, where she crashed, her back slamming against the hard still-frozen earth.

For a moment she saw only black. Her lungs felt burned from the impact, and her vision blurred. It seemed like a full minute passed before air found its way down her jarred throat.

Faces above hers. She couldn't speak. It felt like she lay there forever, raw air and sunshine on her face, before someone knelt beside her and spoke.

"Amy? Are you okay?" It was her teacher. Amy scrambled to sit up, even as Mrs. Johnson ordered, "Sit still."

She was still dizzy, Amy realized, propping herself up on her arms. Mrs. Johnson knelt beside her. "Are you all right? How do you feel?"

"Dizzy," said Amy as her lip quivered. Her whole body ached, her back especially, where her spine had slammed against the ground.

"I'll call your mother," Mrs. Johnson said, rising to her feet.

Amy's thoughts foundered wildly. "My mom isn't there."

Mrs. Johnson paused, and Amy somehow sensed she knew that Mama wasn't just at the store or down the street. A frown creased the teacher's forehead.

"If she's not there, then who is taking care of you?"

Amy swallowed. "I take care of my myself after school. Then my dad comes home."

"So today, after school ends, you'll be staying home alone?"

"No, my brother and two little sisters will be there."

Mrs. Johnson stepped closer. For some reason, Amy felt afraid. Her fear heightened as Mrs. Johnson bent lower and stared into her face. "Listen to me. You are too young to baby-sit . . . and too young to be left alone."

"My dad said it's okay. He needs me."

"He needs to make appropriate arrangements."

"My mom just left us. He's looking for a new sitter."

"Your mother has left the household?"

Amy's nod was slow and pained.

"I'll need to let someone know about this."

"Please don't," Amy said. "Don't tell anybody."

"It isn't up to me." Her teacher's face turned serious. "There are guidelines I must follow."

Amy stared at her teacher's face. "Please—my dad feels so sad without my mom—"

"Please go back to class now. Or you may lie down in the school nurse's office."

"Tell me you're not going to tell anyone."

"I plan to do the right thing," said the teacher. "Now

what is right for you? The school nurse or your class?"

"My class," said Amy, who suddenly didn't want her teacher to think that anything was wrong at her house. Even though her back stung with pain, she sat all the rest of the afternoon in school, praying that everything would be all right when she got home.

"We're going to the beach," Dad announced, holding Jennifer in his arms after he arrived home from work. Amy sensed her father's smile was forced, and she searched his face for any sign that he felt as hopeful as his voice sounded. As they barbecued hot dogs, chased waves along the shore, and laughed together, worry hovered over her like an insistent cloud.

A few days later Dad was already there, sitting on the couch when Amy got home from school. He sat still, a vacant, haunted look on his face.

Amy felt her heart thud. "What's wrong?"

He shook his head and sighed.

"Dad!"

No answer.

"Are you all right?"

He waved her off with a hand.

"What is it? Tell me what's going on."

She saw his Adam's apple move as he swallowed. "Nothing that a little kid should worry about."

"I'm not a little kid."

"This isn't about you—" He looked away.

"Yes, it is," Amy said with a sudden, painful awareness that her whole life might be threatened.

"Didn't want to tell you—didn't know if I should . . ."

"What?"

A long sigh. Finally he turned to face her and his blue eyes met hers. "Someone made a complaint."

"A complaint? What do you mean?"

"Someone complained about me—"

"At work?" she asked, almost hopefully. As hard as

Dad worked, he sometimes talked about customers who gave him a hard time at his drapery business.

"No." He shook his head.

What else could it be? Amy wondered. "Tell me."

"Someone complained that I'm not taking care of you. That I'm not a good enough dad."

"Oh." Sadness flooded her and she reached out and she and Dad hugged each other. He held her tight as she felt tears fall on his stained work shirt, the shirt he wore when he measured and cut and delivered draperies. Now his shoulder was wet, and her vision was blurred, but she managed to look up at him.

"Daddy?"

"Mm-hmm."

"This is all my fault."

"No." The one word sounded anguished and dismissive.

"Yes. It is. I fell off the jungle gym and my teacher came—" She looked up to see that he was looking at her intently. "And she said she was going to call my mom and I had to tell her that Mom wasn't here. . . ."

She saw Dad's lips become thin with anger.

"And she said she would tell someone . . ."

Dad's hand was on her shoulder.

"I told her not to, but . . . maybe she did."

Now Dad squeezed her shoulder.

"And Mrs. Potter is mad at me, too. It could be her . . ."

"Whoever it was—it's not your fault. I just have to deal with it."

"I'll help you."

"Don't worry. You can help by not worrying."

A sudden thought assailed her. "But what are we going to do now?"

Dad shook his head. "I don't know."

"What about Lauren and Jennifer? Where will they go while I'm in school?"

Dad shook his head. "I don't know. I'm going to call the shop and tell them I have an emergency. Then we'll have to see."

"I'll stay home from school!" Amy said quickly.

"No." This time Dad's voice was firm. "I'll work something out. I just don't know what."

Feeling like she was about to cry again, Amy walked toward her room. Just as she was stepping through the doorway, Dad called her name.

She turned, hoping the pain would have somehow left his face.

"Amy—I might need your help."

"I'll help you, Daddy. You know that."

"I might need you—I will need you—to help with the kids. Just until we know what's going to happen. You're the mom now . . ." Dad paused. "Now that Mom is gone."

Amy struggled to speak. "I'll help you," she repeated. Then she rushed into her room and began to cry. Lying on her bed, she couldn't help but think that her life *looked* the same. There was the same bed with the lavender quilt, the dolls she used to play with, now dusty on the shelf, the row of books, the roller skates, and the soccer ball.

But would anything else around her ever be the same again?

Chapter 3

∽

Amy would wonder, forever after, what it was about the letter that had caught her eye. The envelope was plain, black and white, and it sat amid a sea of envelopes that came to their house. Advertisements, letters from salesmen who knew her father had a business, colorful flyers. Though the letter felt light in her hand, somehow holding it filled her with dread.

Los Angeles Department of Child Protective Services.

What did this mean? The letter was addressed to her father, and she felt a shiver of guilt as she slid her finger under the envelope flap. I shouldn't be doing this, she thought as her fingers anxiously tore at the paper. She knew she should stop, but she also knew, as surely as she knew she loved her dad, that she couldn't stop until she learned what he was facing now.

The letter looked official and important. Amy saw her father's name and address. Her eyes dipped below to a section of words that was typed rather than printed like the rest of the letter.

Allegations against you include neglect and sexual abuse of a child.

The words burned into her brain and caught at her heart. Sexual abuse? Even though she had just turned eleven, Amy knew what those words meant. Just a year before, when there was the McMartin Preschool scandal just a few miles away, she'd asked Dad what child sexual abuse meant. "It means that the teacher there touched the children's private parts," Daddy had said to her. Then he'd looked in her eyes. "If anything like that happens to you—*ever*—I want you to come and tell me. Right away."

Amy remembered how the thought of child sexual abuse had made her want to vomit. How could anyone do something like that? How could anyone think that Daddy—who took care of them, and made money for them and loved them—would do something like *that*? Just the thought made her heart hurt. She carried the pain with her as she went to pick up Jennifer and Lauren, set the table for dinner, then waited for Daddy to get home.

As the five of them ate spaghetti, Amy occasionally glanced at her father, who joked and laughed with them, even though his eyes still held the same lingering pain she'd seen in them since her mother had left.

It was after dinner, when the younger kids were watching TV and she and Daddy were clearing the table, that she suddenly couldn't keep the words inside her a moment longer.

"Daddy?"

"What?" he said, looking up as he walked to the sink with a handful of dinner plates.

"I read your letter that came today."

A noise of dishes clanking together as he put them in the sink. "I saw that it had been opened. I thought maybe you were the one."

"I couldn't help it. I'm really worried."

"I'm worried enough for both of us," Daddy admitted. "So you just try and let your worries fly away." He flipped a dish towel into the air.

"But it says . . . sexual abuse."

Daddy sighed and ran a hand through his hair. "I don't know who in this world would come up with something like that. All I know is that it must be someone who wants to get me—bad."

"But I'm here all the time, Daddy. And I know you'd never do anything like that. Ever."

"I know that . . . and you may have to tell it to someone else, too."

"Who?"

"A lawyer. We might have to go to court. But I've already told them I don't want my children to testify."

"What does *testify* mean?"

"It means tell the people in the courtroom what happened."

"Nothing like that happened. I'll tell them right away. Today."

"No." Now Daddy sighed in exasperation. "It's nothing like you think. And it's a long time away."

"I'll tell them," she insisted.

"I'll let you know." Daddy smiled at her. Suddenly it seemed that neither of them could say another word.

As the days passed, Amy helped with the other children, went to school, and waited. She hardly noticed when Mama came to visit or when her soccer team won a game.

Then, one evening, she heard Daddy on the telephone saying that he would be talking to his lawyer the next morning. She stayed awake nearly all that night, fearful that she would somehow fall asleep and miss his leaving in the morning. Yet near dawn, when she finally dozed off, she was startled awake with the realization that Daddy was now showering and getting ready to leave.

She waited until she heard the shower shut off. Seconds later, when Daddy emerged from the shower with a towel wrapped around him, Amy charged into his bedroom.

"I'm going to go with you," she told him vehemently.

She stood beside him, watching him take his work clothes out of the closet.

"I can't stay here," she said.

"You have school," he said, without looking down at her. She followed him to the bathroom and saw his careful, precise gestures as he shaved his face.

"This is more important than school. And I think I know who said those things about you. It was Mrs. Potter. Or Mrs. Johnson. Or maybe it was Mama," she said suddenly. "Or it might have been Les."

His eyes suddenly caught hers. "How do you know that? This isn't something for you to worry about. I'll handle it."

"I'm already worried, Daddy. I can't even think about my schoolwork."

He turned and knelt beside her so that their eyes met. "I'll take care of it. This isn't something for a kid to be concerned with." He stood to comb his hair.

"You said I'm the mom of the house now that Mom's gone."

Again, he turned. "I did. But you really shouldn't have to be the mom. You need to be a girl . . . with her own life. And I'm trying to get that for you."

"Then let me help you."

He stopped, the comb poised above his hair. "I have a lawyer. Lawyers go to school for years to learn the right thing to say in these situations."

Amy leaned against the bathroom door frame. "But I'm your daughter. I can tell him that you're a good father to me."

He reached out to touch her shoulder. Then his eyes closed. She saw his eyelids squeeze together. Was he holding back tears? Daddy hardly ever let her or the other children know when he was sad, but every once in a while she heard a dip in his voice or saw sorrow in his eyes. Now his words finally emerged, slow and rough-edged. "I'm glad you feel that way."

She stepped closer. "Then let me tell the judge."

He stared at her. "I don't want to take you into a courtroom. You're still a little girl. It could be very upsetting. People there might say bad things about me that would scare you."

"I'll just tell them those things aren't true."

He looked at her as if he were seeing her for the first time. "The lawyers who are trying to prosecute me could try to be mean to you. I told my lawyer I didn't want my kids on the stand."

"But I want to tell them you never hurt me."

He looked at her, then turned to adjust his tie.

"And when Mom left, you didn't leave us. You stayed here."

"I couldn't leave you like she did," he said, in that strange, tight voice. "I'll never understand how she could leave her kids."

"I'll tell him how you always take care of us. You have to work a lot, but you're still a good dad."

He ruffled her hair. "I'll ask my lawyer what he thinks," he said finally.

"No," she said firmly. "Let me go with you *today*. They might finish everything today and I wouldn't get another chance."

"I don't know if they'll ask you to speak. You're not on the list I gave my lawyer."

"Then put me on the list. I want to tell the judge I

already lost my mom; if I lose you, I won't have any-body."

He reached to give her a hug. "Get dressed," he said suddenly, "if you really want to go." He sighed. "I guess all they could do is tell me to take you back home."

"I'll tell them I told you to bring me . . . and they'll think you're a dad who listens to his kid."

He looked at her, smiled, and ruffled her hair again. "Get ready. We have to leave here in ten minutes."

Her heart pounding, Amy rushed to put on her best dress. Despite her firmness with her dad, she felt scared. Could a lawyer really be mean enough to scare her? It didn't matter, she decided. If Daddy needed help, she'd do whatever it took.

There were lots of people waiting outside the courtroom for their turn to appear before the judge. Amy saw the lawyer's frown as he sat next to Dad on the bench.

"I gotta tell you—this looks really bad."

"What do you mean?"

"Bringing your kid here. What were you thinking?"

Dad didn't answer.

"Is she going to sit out in the hall and wait for you?"

"I don't think so." Dad's voice was tight.

"You're charged with inappropriate behavior toward a child. You say you don't want your kids to testify. Then you show up here with *her*."

"She wanted to come with me."

"Do you let your kids have everything they want? I mean, do you know how serious these allegations are?"

"Maybe I could take her home—"

"It's too late." The lawyer shook head in disgusted an-ger. "We're in there"—he gestured with his head toward the courtroom—"in ten minutes. Fifteen tops." He looked at the ceiling and shook his head. "Do you know what this says? You bringing her here?"

"I don't—"

"It says inconsistency—and parenting is all about being consistent. It says not putting your kid first—putting you first and maybe behaving inappropriately toward your child. It says—"

"It wasn't my idea."

This time the lawyer bared his teeth. "What was the problem here, anyway? No cheap baby-sitter anywhere in sight?" He lifted his arms in an angry shrug.

"I told him to bring me." Amy's words emerged firm and solid as iron.

"So he let you tell him what to do?" The lawyer bent over so close she could see the rage in his eyes.

"I want to tell the judge about him."

"Listen, kid. Telling the judge isn't something you think you know how to do because Daddy here lets you stay up and watch *Perry Mason* on Friday night. If you're going to testify in a court of law, we have to meet. Plan your testimony. You have to understand what the prosecutor is going to say."

"I know my dad didn't molest Lauren. There's no way. I'm there twenty-four hours a day and he never hurts anybody."

Even the lawyer paused briefly. "Still, kid, you are a child. You aren't in your father's presence constantly."

"I'm the mother of our house since my own mother left. I dress the little girls in the morning. I stay with them at night when my dad works late. I fix dinner. I call the sitter if one of them is sick . . . I am like their mom."

Now the lawyer angled his head toward Dad. "That so?"

"Yes. My wife left and forced my daughter to become a substitute mother. I'm doing everything in my power to relieve her of this burden, because she should be able to just be a kid. But right now she helps take care of the other children."

"Hmm—I get mixed feelings about that," said the lawyer. "Her dedication is admirable. But saying that a girl her age is stuck giving child care—"

"I'm good at it," Amy insisted. "My sisters get to the

sitter on time every morning. And we don't have to have a stranger come to our house."

The lawyer paused. "Your daughter is articulate," he said.

"Yes."

"And she appears convinced of her opinion that your home is safe."

"It is," Amy broke in. "He spoils us, if anything."

The lawyer paused. "Did you bring her here with the purpose of testifying?"

"I want to," Amy said. "Daddy wouldn't hurt Lauren."

"I'm glad to hear her statements. I'll consider the possibility of her testifying," said the attorney. "I'll ask for a continuance."

Was she going to talk today?

Amy waited. When it was time, she went into the courtroom and sat next to Daddy on the hard wooden bench that felt cold against the back of her neck.

"Your Honor, certain matters have come to light that I wish to pursue further," Daddy's lawyer was saying. "And I therefore request a continuance."

"What are these matters?" said the judge, a huge black-robed man who filled his chair and stared at the courtroom with piercing blue eyes.

"The testimony of certain witnesses who have recently come to light," said the lawyer. "I would need time to prepare to bring these matters before the court."

"My feeling is that you have already had sufficient time to prepare your case."

"It has since become more complicated, Your Honor."

The judge frowned. "I can give you three weeks. No longer."

"Thank you, Your Honor," said Daddy's attorney.

Three weeks, thought Amy. What on earth could save them from this terrible trouble in just three weeks?

* * *

It was only one more week when Daddy said, "Amy, there's a woman who wants to talk to you."

Amy looked up in surprise. "Is she a lawyer?"

"I'm not sure . . . I don't think so," said Daddy.

"Does she work with your lawyer?"

"No . . ." Daddy paused. "She works for the state. They are the ones who are investigating."

"Then I won't talk to her."

Now Daddy sat by her. "You have to, sweetie. You said you wanted to help me. This is what you can do."

"But she wants me to say that you are bad and mean."

"You can tell her I'm not."

A woman stood outside the school, just where Daddy had said she would be waiting. She stood next to a bright, green car and smiled at Amy.

"Are you the lawyer?" Amy asked.

"No," the woman said. "I'm a police officer, actually."

"But you don't have a police car."

"This is a police car," the woman said. "Come here, and I'll show you. See this? Two antennas on the back? One of them goes to a police radio."

Amy stared at this woman, who looked pretty and nice. Why would she want to hurt Daddy?

"Do you want to go for a ride in my car, Amy? By the way, my name is Terry. Terry Rawlings, from the prosecutor's office."

When Amy didn't answer, Terry went over and opened the door to her car.

"Please get in, Amy."

She sat in the car that looked like any other car. She won't make me talk, Amy thought.

Terry sat beside her and drove.

"Amy, I just need to let you know that you are safe with me. Anything you want to tell me, you can."

Amy felt the sun beat through the window of Terry's car as the two of them drove.

"My dad didn't hurt me," she said suddenly.

"Okay . . . you feel like you are safe in your house?"

"Yes—all the time. He spoils me," Amy said.

"And how does he spoil you?"

"He takes me to the beach. He lets me help at his work. He says I get to be the mom—"

Terry interrupted quickly. "You get to be the mom?"

"I get to take care of the other kids sometimes. Because . . ."

"Because your mom has left the home."

"Yes. And Daddy feels really bad about it. He would never . . ."

"He felt sad when your mother left?"

"Yes."

"Do you know why she left?"

"I think she likes someone else now."

"Someone else? Another man?"

"Yes . . . a man she works with."

"But she didn't leave because your dad hurt you . . . or anyone else."

"No . . . she has a disease . . . multiple sclerosis . . . and she can hardly walk and she says that this other man can help her . . ."

"And your father couldn't help?"

"He could! She just said she couldn't take care of him and us, too."

"Did you agree with her?"

"No! No! I want her to come back."

Amy couldn't think of another word as Terry drove the car around the block, then drove into the school parking lot.

"Amy?"

"Yes?"

"If there's anything you want to tell me—maybe later—I'm going to give you this card."

Amy watched as Terry reached in her purse and handed her a small business card that looked a lot like the ones Daddy used for his drapery business. Gray Window Treatments. She took the card and held it in her hand.

"Call me anytime," Terry said, driving up to the school. "And I might need to talk to you again."

"My dad didn't do it," Amy said.

Terry didn't answer, but got out of the car and came to open the door beside Amy.

She said, "Keep that card in a safe place. Remember, I'm here."

Chapter 4

∞

It was the kitchen table he saw first. He was standing next to the table, talking to a client, when he noticed that the table was empty. No plates. No silverware. Still holding the phone, he edged over to the oven and opened the door. It was empty. Even as the client spoke to him, the silence in the apartment roared around him. Where were Amy and the kids?

" 'Scuse me," he said. "I need to get going. I'll call you back."

"But you told me the order would go in today."

"It will. I promise. I'll call you within half an hour."

"It's getting late for it to be today—"

"I'll get back to you. I promise. Maybe in five minutes."

"Okay. I'll be waiting here by the phone."

"Get right back to you," Steve said. He hung up, and the silence in the apartment seemed to shout at him.

"Amy!" he called out, his voice sounding throaty and scared. "Tom!"

No answer.

He ran from room to room. Where could they be? Amy always waited until he got home to—

Steve quickly ran across the hall and pounded on Mrs. Potter's door.

She threw the door open, angry as always.

"Where are my kids?"

"Haven't been here today. Haven't seen them in weeks."

Steve fought to calm his rising anxiousness. "I know they're not here to be baby-sat—but have you seen them . . . or heard anything from them?"

"No, and don't ever pound on my door again!" She slammed the door shut, and he found himself knocking on other doors, most of which remained closed. Finally a blond woman answered.

"I'm sorry," Steve said, realizing he was panting. "I'm just looking for my kids."

"The three girls and the boy? I always see you with them," said the woman. "But I didn't see them today."

"You'd recognize my kids?"

"Oh yes."

"But you didn't see them leave."

"No," she said.

Steve paused.

"Could I leave you my number, and if you do see them, or think of anyone else I could call, will you let me know?"

"Sure," the woman said. "You always seem like you're having so much fun together."

Steve smiled wanly and shook his head, thinking, There hasn't been much fun lately.

"I'm Pam," the woman said. "Sit down for a moment and I'll get a pencil."

Steve wrote his name, his phone number, and the number of the drapery business. He handed her the card. "I've gotta get going," he said. "I have to find them."

"I'll call you if I think of anything," Pam said.

Steve rang other apartment doorbells. The people who

answered had no idea who he was, let alone his children. Panic assailed him.

Where was Amy? Where was Tom? Where were Lauren and Jennifer?

Feeling dejected, he returned to the apartment, catching sight of Amy's book bag on the chair. It was a quarter to six. They always ate at six, saving some food for him if he called to say he planned to be late.

He called his customer back, then wrote up the order.

When his attorney answered the phone he said, "My kids are gone."

"Are you sure?"

"We always eat at six. They're not here."

"Did you try friends . . . their mother . . . stuff like that?"

Steve sighed. "I tried everybody here."

"Call everyone you can. But make it quick. If you don't find them, call the police."

Had he ever dialed so frantically? Les's. Neighbors. The other neighbor who baby-sat. Hanging up the phone, he ran down to the beach, his eyes combing the coastline for any sign of someone he knew.

No one.

He ran back to the apartment, his lungs burned with exhaustion. Panting, he picked up the phone.

"City police."

"I have an emergency. Someone stole my kids."

"Put you through to detectives." It felt like forever as he heard clicks on the phone.

"Lieutenant Hollis—"

"My kids are gone. Someone stole them."

"Name and address, please."

Feeling as if priceless seconds were passing, Steve gave the officer his information, then waited.

"So . . . you say two hours ago?"

"Yes, almost three."

"If you don't find them by ten, call us back."

Steve wanted to scream into the phone. How can they say I don't care about my kids when nobody cares about them *but* me?

Driving to his attorney's office, Steve decided that it must have been the state who took his children, and this was an example of what all the newscasters were discussing—a witch-hunt after the McMartin trial. Judges were pulling kids out of homes right and left just to avoid the possibility of anyone molesting a kid. But why him?

He waited a long time in the lawyer's office, resenting every minute that he was asked to spend away from his kids. Why didn't he—last week when he still could—bring them all here, he thought, and let the attorney see that they were a family who wanted to stay together.

"Mr. Gray?"

Was that a sympathetic look on the secretary's face? Did she know what had happened to him? He followed her down the long hall to his lawyer's office. The lawyer looked up at him and said, "There's something I need to let you know."

Somehow, the simple words bored into his mind and heart and filled him with anxiousness. What was going on?

"There isn't going to be a trial now. You won't have to go to court again."

"What happened?"

"The judge issued an ex parte order. To take your kids. They picked them up today, after school."

The words hit him like a sledgehammer.

"I'm sorry, man," his attorney was saying.

"What does this mean?"

"You lose custody—temporarily. While they finish investigating. Let's hope—"

"But nothing happened."

"In the hearing? You're right. Nothing was conclusive,

but they feel like they want to do a more thorough investigation . . . so they take the children just in case."

"In case of what? I love my kids. I work day and night to—"

"Hate to say it, but that's part of it."

"Part of what?"

"They think maybe you're gone too many hours. You don't really have time to be a dad."

"I'm trying to cut back. And the industry's changing. People are going to mini-blinds. Vertical blinds. Not as many drapes."

"You can tell all that to your caseworker."

"Who?"

"The social worker assigned to your case."

"Isn't there anything I can do to stop all this? To get my kids back?" Steve felt his voice rise in desperation.

"Not now. The judge has ruled. Go along with the order now, then just keep showing your social worker you're worthy to get the kids back."

"Who started this anyway?"

"I'm not sure, but they must have presented some evidence of—"

"There isn't any evidence." Steve was shouting now. "What do I have to do to make you see?"

"Apparently, there was more than one person who complained."

"Then they're all wrong."

"I believe you, man. But it's the judge's decision."

"This is so totally insane. What if I just find the kids and take them to Mexico?"

"Boy, I didn't even hear that one." His lawyer shook his head in exasperation. "Don't even think about it. It's not worth it. You'll lose them for good and you could go to prison for kidnapping."

"I just can't believe it. My wife leaves. I'm the only one that stays. And *I* lose the kids. I didn't deserve to lose them. My kids don't deserve to lose their only parent."

"Nobody deserves to have this happen. You just have

to consider this is just a battle . . . not the whole war. It isn't over yet."

"It might as well be," Steve said, holding his face in his hands.

"I gotta say, part of this is that you are a man. But things are changing."

"What do you mean?"

"They always think a dad isn't as good as a mom—but it's getting better. You just gotta hang in."

"Tell that to my kids."

The policeman and the woman with him both looked big and scary.

"You're coming with me now. I have orders to take you into custody," the man thundered at them.

"No!" Amy shouted. "Let us call our dad!"

"He couldn't stop these orders. Now I want all of you to come with me."

"No!" Lauren cried, not knowing why she was terrified. She ran and wrapped her arms around Amy, hugging her big sister and shaking with fright.

The policeman grasped Lauren's arm.

"Tell her to come with me," he ordered Amy. He said to the woman, "You bring the other little girl and follow me out to the car."

"What about our things?" Amy said as the policeman yanked Lauren out of Amy's arms. The smell of the policeman would stay with Lauren forever—tobacco and sweat. He squeezed her tight so that she couldn't move, yet her tears fell relentlessly onto his shoulder.

"Daddy!" Lauren called out. "I want Daddy."

The car roared away from their apartment, the two littlest girls clinging to each other as they watched the policeman order Amy into a different car.

"Amy!" Lauren called, turning and staring out the window at the same time that she grasped Jennifer's arm. "Bring Amy back!"

* * *

What was happening to the four of them? Amy stared
out at the long road ahead, unable to think of what might
be about to happen to her and her brother and sisters. And
what was Daddy thinking?

How far away from home was she? How many miles
had the social worker driven to reach this house?

Later, as Amy lay in a strange bed, in an unfamiliar
house, she wondered what she could do to get back home.
She felt as if her whole life had been instantly wrenched
away. The only reminder of her home and family was the
clothes she now wore. It was the first time in her life that
she had ever slept in Levi's and a T-shirt, but she clung
to them now as if they were precious mementos.

She watched as the curtains in the room appeared to
pale from dark blue to near white as the sun rose. She lay
in bed and listened to the sounds around her as this family
where she didn't belong talked, showered, and began their
day. Where was Daddy? Where were Tom, Lauren, and
Jennifer?

Her thoughts were interrupted when a blond woman
opened the door and turned on the light.

"There's cereal for you in the kitchen," the woman said,
without introducing herself. "Then you'd better get
dressed. They'll be here to pick you up in half an hour."

"Who?" Amy called, but the woman walked out of the
room and down the hall without looking back.

Amy slid out of the bed and walked down the hall,
turning to the only lighted room to find it was the kitchen.
She chose from among several boxes of cereal on the
table. She had eaten two spoonfuls when the doorbell
rang.

She heard someone answer the door, then moments
later, Frances Allen, the woman who had taken her from
her house the day before, stood at her side.

Amy swallowed. "Are you taking me home?" she asked
hopefully.

"Not to your family home."

"Who lives here?" Amy gestured at the unfamiliar kitchen. The sterile, white walls and spotless counter looked nothing like the jumble of belongings she was used to.

"This is a shelter home. Now you're going to a foster home."

A foster home. Fear crept over Amy as she thought of books and movies she'd seen where children were placed in foster homes. It seemed like they were never loved and sometimes were hurt and abused. She wanted to run away, right now, and hope that she could outrun Frances Allen. Instead, her words emerged fast and frightened. "Can't you just take me back to my house? I'll be all right."

"The judge has ordered you into foster care. He is the only one who can release you from state custody."

"But my dad . . . can I see him?" Amy pleaded.

"The court will rule on visitation."

"What about Jennifer . . . and Lauren . . . and Tom?"

"You and your brother will be placed in separate foster homes. The two little girls will be together."

"But they won't be with us—"

"Not in the current placement."

When they were in the car and driving away, Frances Allen's words continued to penetrate Amy's mind. They were all being taken away from Dad. She and Tom would be alone with strangers. Lauren and Jennifer would be together . . . but what good could that do them, both being so young and so small? They might forget all about us, Amy thought. They might have no memories of the nights on the beach, the long talks with Dad, and the hugs they all shared.

I won't let them forget, Amy suddenly told herself. I'll find them—all of them—and tell them myself.

There was a light in the apartment.

Steve saw it after a particularly long day at work. He'd

found himself working later and later, knowing that he would only return home to an apartment that was deadly dark and silent. He hadn't realized how comforting the sounds of his children were. Night after night, he drove home after dark, returning to his lonely apartment.

But now there was a light. Could the kids be back? Had they somehow found their way home to him? He dashed up the stairs, found the door to the apartment unlocked, and entered his living room . . . to find Anna sitting on the couch.

"You're too late," he said, his voice bitter. "I don't know why you're here. You can see that they're gone."

"This is still my home," Anna said primly. "I own half of everything in it and there are things that belong to me."

"Take them," Steve said, holding his hands out in frustrated surrender. "How are you going to carry them? Is Les here somewhere?"

Anna stared at him a long time. "I broke up with Les," she said.

"So that's why you're coming back here?"

She didn't answer.

"You can't come back like nothing's changed," he flung at her. "Too much has changed. We lost our kids."

He saw her hesitate, then straighten the afghan she'd piled over her legs. "Could the kids come back if I stayed here?"

"I told you—you're too late. The state already decided that they need to investigate me. Now I have to fight."

Chapter 5

∞

A teenage girl with long red hair and pale skin stared at Amy, then looked to Frances Allen. "Who's she?"

"This is Amy."

"Not stayin' here, is she?" The girl frowned.

"This is the placement where she's assigned."

"Thought they already said we had too many."

Frances Allen's voice was cold. "I don't need to discuss this with you. But because of your ages, more children are permitted in this home."

"Children—like we're little kids. I don't know where she'll sleep. Beds are all taken."

"I'll take that up with your foster mother."

"She isn't here."

"Oh? We had an appointment. I was scheduled to bring Amy now."

"Don't know where she went."

Frances sighed. "We'll wait a few minutes. Let's go back to the car, Amy."

Just take me home, Amy pleaded inside her mind. *I don't need to stay here. There's no room for me.*

Just then, a woman drove up in a station wagon filled with other teenage girls.

She got out of the car. "Think there's a mistake. County already brought me two more last week."

"You can have five," said Frances Allen.

"I already got six."

"I thought two of yours were transferred to other placements."

"They were—then County brought two more." The woman stared at Amy. "Guess she can stay here until you find her another place."

"Just take me home," Amy pleaded.

"This is your home right now," Frances Allen said.

"Can my dad come here?"

"That's up to him. He must petition the court." She turned to the woman. "I will have to see the room where she'll be staying."

"All the beds are full. She could stay with Tracy."

Who was Tracy? Amy wondered. She'd never missed her own bed and her own room more than at that moment.

"Each child has to have her own bed," said Frances.

"Haven't got one." The woman shrugged. "You keep bringing too many kids here."

"Show me what you've got."

"Not a whole bed just for her," the woman said, leading them into the cluttered, messy house. They walked up a flight of stairs to a bedroom with a double bed. "Here's Tracy's room. She could stay here—with Tracy."

"I could take her back to the shelter home," said Frances. "But it's full, too."

No one asked me what I want to do, Amy thought. Nobody here cares about me—who I am or what I want. No one cares.

"If I can promise a different placement by next week, she could stay?"

"Sure, what's one more?"

Amy sat alone on the bed after the two women left. Her despair was interrupted when a short, stocky black-haired girl entered the room.

"Oh, brother," she said. "Who are you?"

"I'm Amy. Are you Tracy?"

"Yeah, how'd you know?"

"They said I'd be sharing a room here . . . with you."

"No way. They told me everybody gets their own bed. That's all you get that's yours. What are you in here for, anyway?"

"I don't know," Amy said. "What about you?"
"Ran away from home. Put me in detention. Brought me here for six months."
"Then you get to go back home?"
"I don't know. I got kicked out of school. What about you?"
"Someone complained about my dad."
"What about him?"
"Said he wasn't taking care of us. Said maybe he was abusing my little sisters. But no way. I was there day and night."
"But you didn't get in any trouble?"
"I stayed home from school a few times. To take care of the kids after my mother left."
"That's all it takes." Tracy shrugged.
That's all it took, Amy thought, to rip me out of my home and put me here . . . in jail. She would get out of here someday, Amy promised herself. She would find Daddy, and Tom and the little girls. They'd be a family again if it was the last thing she did.

Every night, lying next to Jennifer, Lauren closed her eyes and pretended that she was back home. The familiar warmth of her sister beside her, and the memories of home that hovered inside her head, almost made her forget her fears for a moment. But only a few seconds would pass before something would remind her that she wasn't home, and might never be home again. The Speakmans' big dogs would bark, or the bed under this hard mattress would squeak, or one of the other kids would turn on the light and wake her up.
Every night, Lauren closed her eyes and prayed. "Please," she whispered. "Help my daddy find me."

Steve felt like he'd waited forever.
"Barbara Rabon." The social worker reached out to

shake Steve's hand. "What can I do for you?"

"It's been six months, and I haven't seen my kids."

"Did the court grant you visitation?"

"They took the kids one night and told me there was an investigation still going on. But that was months ago. I haven't heard a word."

"Let me look in your file and confer with a colleague."

More waiting. Steve studied the gold clock on her desk and the photo of her with a son and a daughter. He heard low voices talking outside in the hall. What were they saying about him?

Barbara Rabon returned to the room, a thick file in her hands.

"Apparently, the court has seen fit to grant visitation with your two older children—Amy, your daughter, and Tom, your son."

"Can I see them right now?"

"No. You will have to make an appointment."

"An appointment to see my own kids?"

"I'll give you the number of their foster homes. You can call there."

"I have to ask to see my kids? And what about Lauren? And Jennifer?"

Barbara Rabon stared at him for what felt like a full minute.

"They have had several placements. The court has not decided to return them to you. In fact, we would urge that you consider surrendering them for adoptive placement."

"No way! Give my girls to someone else?"

"We would suggest that you place them with someone who can give them what you cannot provide. A home with two parents. A home where there can be a parent with them most of the time. With someone who can afford . . ."

She handed him a bill. "What is this? I have to pay back the time my kids spent in state custody?"

"They are your children. The state has provided a service for you. Since you are unable to pay, you may wish to surrender the younger children."

"No. I'll never see them again if I do that."

"They will have normal lives with families who love them. They won't be shifted from one placement to another ever again."

"And they won't know I'm their dad."

Barbara Rabon clasped her hands on her desk. "Since that's how you feel, I would suggest you pursue the visitation with the older children."

"Give me the numbers and I'll call them today."

She handed him a small slip of paper and he rushed out of the office without looking back. He found his truck, then drove to where there was a pay phone.

The phone rang a lot of times before someone answered.

"Amy," he gasped. "Amy Gray."

"Just a minute . . ." A pause. "Who is this?"

"This is her dad."

"I don't know if—just a minute."

"Daddy?" Amy questioned cautiously.

"Amy." The tenseness in his body relaxed. "Where are you, honey? I miss you so much."

"I'm here . . . in this foster home. There are lots of kids here."

"Give me the address. And I'll come and see you."

"It's Forty-five—"

Steve heard a shuffling in the background.

"Your daughter is being transferred today," someone said.

"Daddy!" He heard Amy's cry in the background.

"Can I come and see her first? Can you give me the number of where she'll be later tonight?"

The phone clicked. When he called again, no one answered.

Putting another dime into the phone, he called the number for Tom's foster home. He let it ring at least thirty times before he hung up. He climbed into his car and drove back to the social worker's office.

"They've been moved again?" he asked.

Barbara Rabon hesitated. "Yes, Lauren and Jennifer are now in a new placement."

"What did they do this time?"

"It was nothing the children did, sir. Or the foster parents, really."

"Then why did you move them?"

"It wasn't our fault, either. These parents simply decided not to be foster parents any longer. It happens. They tried it out, and felt it didn't work for them."

"So they got rid of *my kids*. What is this doing to my children?"

Barbara Rabon stared. "I've already talked to you about that."

"Why don't you let me have them back? I can promise you I won't give them away."

"We've talked about this, too. Your income is now below the poverty line. You are still a single father. I understand that their mother only makes irregular visits. The court doesn't feel that you are able to care for them as yet."

"In the meantime, they go from house to house."

"Mr. Gray."

"Call me Steve."

"We've talked to you about this on previous occasions. With no income increase in sight, and the fact that you are still a single parent, we request that you place them for adoption." She stopped talking and met his blue eyes with her brown ones. "Give your kids the life they deserve, sir. You're not doing them any favors by leaving them in foster care."

"But I would never see them again."

"That's likely—but not definite. More and more adopted children seek reunions today."

"But there's no guarantee that I would—"

"There are no guarantees in life, sir. But it's a definite possibility."

"Their names could be changed. They could be sent anywhere."

"But their homes wouldn't be changed. Ever again. They would have one family—their own family."

"Oh—I don't know . . ." Steve sat back and ran a hand through his hair. "It just feels like I'm letting them down."

Barbara Rabon's voice turned gentle. "Not at all," she said. "It would be the greatest gift you could ever give them."

Steve felt his throat fill. "I always thought I would someday bring them home."

"This way you will give them a home."

"Will they hate me for giving them up?"

Barbara Rabon hesitated. "There might be some abandonment issues. But they already have those from being in foster care."

Steve sat back in his chair. He buried his face in his hands. "I guess it's all I can do," he said. "I don't see my life changing anytime soon."

"They won't see you to thank you," said Barbara. "But I can thank you. I can tell you that this will change their lives."

"If it will help them, I'll do it."

"I'll have the papers drawn up today for you to sign tomorrow."

That night, Steve floundered in a sea of emotion. What on earth could he possibly have been thinking, giving his kids to someone else? Thoughts of failure, despair, and sadness filled him. But the next morning, he felt a bleak and tenuous peace.

He signed the papers on Barbara Rabon's desk.

"Your children will be grateful to you," she said. Her hand found his shoulder. "And maybe they'll tell you someday."

"I'll always wait to hear from them," he said. He walked out of the office, knowing he would think about this day for a long time.

*   *   *

Would Daddy find her here? Would he really make it to this new foster home? Amy glanced out of the window on the Adamses' couch and looked for her father's familiar drapery truck, the ladders piled on the side and his logo painted on the door. She'd just about given up when the truck zoomed up the street, then slowed, and finally stopped in front of the Adamses' house.

Still wearing his work pants, Dad walked up to the porch and knocked.

Amy ran to the door, reached out, and hugged him. She closed her eyes and basked in the solid, warm, slightly sweaty feeling of his chest against her face. This is as close as I've been to home in a long time, she thought.

When they let each other go, Dad glanced around him. "Do we have to tell someone I'm taking you to lunch?"

"No." Amy shook her head. "The Adamses know all about it. They went to the store and told me to have a good time."

"They let you leave when you want, huh?" Dad said as they walked down the stairs out to the truck.

"As long as I'm home by six. Dinner is at six."

Dad started the truck then, and Amy heard the loud, shaking hum she still remembered. They drove onto the town's main street.

"Where would you like to go?" Dad asked. He pointed to a fancy-looking restaurant. "What about there?"

Amy glanced at the dark-tinted windows and gold-engraved lettering on the door.

"Take me where we used to go after the beach."

"Where is that?"

"McDonald's," she said, pointing. "Down there."

Sitting outside, on one of the McDonald's benches, she saw Dad's face suddenly grow serious.

"I probably should tell you," he began.

Worry filled her, and their eyes met.

"It's about the girls."

"Lauren and Jennifer? Did something happen to them?"

He reached out and wrapped a warm hand around her knee.

"Baby, I hope this won't be a bad thing. I just felt like I didn't have a choice. It was like the state forced me . . ."

Amy felt her voice rush. "Forced you to do what?"

"Now don't get all upset . . . maybe it's not the end of the world . . ."

"What happened to my sisters!"

"The state won't let me have them back . . . I'm still single and I'm still poor . . . and I don't know what whoever complained about me said, but—"

"Do you mean you're never going to get them back?"

"Well, the state asked me to place them for adoption."

"And you gave my sisters away!" Amy jumped off the bench and backed up in anger, still staring at her father. "I can't believe you!"

"I was tired of hearing about them being bounced around from house to house—like they'd never have a home."

"But now they'll never have you! We'll never see them again!"

"Maybe . . . when they're grown up."

"Oh, Dad." Amy sat back down on the bench and covered her face with her hands.

He sat beside her and put his arm around her. "I wasn't getting them back. There wasn't anything else for me to do."

Amy felt barren and bleak inside.

Chapter 6

❧

After six months passed, Amy decided that the Adamses were probably like typical grandparents. She herself retained only brief, fleeting memories of Mama's mother, a woman who had a greenhouse in her home and gave each of them sandwich bags full of caramels and pink mints. My family has lost each other, Amy thought. Grandma died, then Mama left, then Daddy gave Lauren and Jennifer away. Was there any way she could try to pull her family back together after everyone else had ripped it apart?

The Adams home was a good place to think, Amy decided. Mr. and Mrs. Adams seemed to believe the best way any child could behave was to be quiet. They were old, Amy thought, lots older than Dad or Mama, and their kids had their own kids already. But their house was peaceful. Her room had a rag rug that Mrs. Adams had made, and every dinner was composed of at least four different dishes—two vegetables, one of which was a potato, a meat dish, and some kind of salad. Mrs. Adams ironed Amy's clothes and washed her tennis shoes in the washer. She reminded Amy to brush her teeth, straighten her room, and do her homework. As clean as everything was, and as wonderful as Mrs. Adams's cooking was, Amy still longed for the days on the beach when she ate three hot dogs after tossing a Frisbee with Dad.

Now it was nearly Christmas. She and Mrs. Adams, and Tony and Trey, the two foster boys who also lived here, had decorated the Adamses' Christmas tree with perfectly coordinated red and gold ornaments. A sea of gold-wrapped presents lay beneath the tree, which twinkled with red and white lights.

It was long after dark, when Amy heard someone knocking on her bedroom door.

"Hey, Ame," She heard someone calling out in a harsh whisper.

What was this?

"Ame . . ."

She slid out of bed and tiptoed over to open her door. It was Trey.

"What are you—"

"Just come with us."

Without a sound, she followed the boys down the hall to the living room.

Tony and Trey sat by the presents. Tony lifted a gift and shook it. "Think this one's for you?" he asked Amy.

"These are their family's."

"Then where's ours?"

She hesitated. "Maybe there are presents there for you. I don't know."

"We're gonna look."

"Don't," Amy cried out, but before she could stop them, the boys began unwrapping the Adamses' carefully assembled gifts.

"You're going to get in trouble," Amy warned.

"What's going on here?" Mr. Adams sounded mad.

"I told them not to." Amy heard fear in her own voice.

"You're in for a spanking, that's what you're in for."

"You're not supposed to hit us."

"You've ruined our Christmas." Mr. Adams hauled Trey up by the arm and pushed the boy back down the hall to his bedroom.

"I'll wrap them back up again," Trey whimpered.

"You'll stay in here and think about what you did," Mr. Adams said, shoving Trey into his bedroom. Amy heard a slap, followed by Trey's scream, then a second slap and a louder scream.

Amy felt helpless and worried. It was at that moment

that she became sure, surer than she'd ever been, that Dad
had never hit her, or Lauren or Jennifer, or anybody else.

But what could she do about that now?

After he let a distraught Anna return to him twice and
she left him for the third time and became pregnant by
Les, Steve promised himself that never, never would he
date another woman in his life.

He would just be a dad, and that would be that.

But now the kids were gone.

Although he was allowed to make his weekly visits to
Amy and Tom, thoughts of his children left him feeling
a lingering, painful void. Why did he know that it
wouldn't get better? Barbara Rabon continued to promise
him that Lauren and Jennifer were happy and safe, but
how could he know that for sure? She did admit that the
girls hadn't been adopted together, but lived with two separate families.

Wasn't there a family who could love them enough to
take both of them? And what did their new families tell
them about him? Steve was unlocking the door to his
always empty apartment when he heard someone speak.

"Haven't seen you in a while."

He looked up to face a blond, blue-eyed woman in
jeans who was standing in her doorway. It was the
woman, Pam, who said she'd help him find his kids that
night when they were taken away.

"Wondered if you'd moved out," she said.

"No," he said, opening his door and stepping inside his
apartment.

"Seems like it's a lot quieter around your place these
days."

To his amazement the woman followed him in. "Yes,"
he said, walking to the kitchen.

"Wondered if you'd moved out."

"No." He was curious whether his face looked as sad
as he felt inside. "Still here—for a while anyway."

"Just you?" The woman frowned. "I got used to seeing lots of kids coming and going over here."

"Just me."

"Kids with the ex-wife?"

"Well, no. Not exactly."

"Oh."

"I never knew when we talked before . . . do you have kids?" he asked her.

"Nope. Never been married. Always liked to to watch you with your kids, though. You were really good with them."

"Some people didn't think so."

"Really? Who?" The woman pulled up a kitchen chair and sat down.

Steve sighed. "Don't know if I should tell you this— but somebody complained about me . . . about the way I acted with my kids."

"Who on earth would do something like that?"

He shook his head. "I'm not sure."

"But they're okay now? Your kids, I mean."

"I guess . . ." He flung up his hands in a shrug. "I don't have them anymore."

"And they're not with your wife?"

"No. I don't like to talk about it."

"I don't mean to be nosy. I just always noticed you with them. Riding bikes. Down on the beach. Carrying a pizza into your apartment."

"Yep. Those were the days."

"Do you mind if I ask . . . what happened?"

"They took away my kids even though I didn't do anything wrong."

"Any hopes you'll get them back?"

"I'm trying." He shrugged again. "But who knows? I never thought I'd lose them in the first place. I was a good father."

"Do you at least get to visit them?"

"The oldest ones."

"Why not the others?"

"They'll never admit they're through investigating me. And they keep saying I don't make enough money."

"You could fight this, you know."

"Oh yeah? With what money?"

"Sometimes it doesn't take money."

"This isn't one of those times," he said, and then he offered her a Coke, which she accepted, before he answered all of her questions and she told him not to give up.

At the time of their adoptions, Lauren watched as her foster mother packed Jennifer's things.

"Where is she going?"

The woman paused. "Jennifer has a new home, with a mommy and daddy."

"Am I going with her?"

"No . . . not today."

"Am I going there someday?"

Her foster mother, Mrs. Black, actually stopped packing and turned to look at Lauren. "I'm sorry. You won't be going there. But someday soon, you'll have a home, too."

"I want a home now. I want my daddy!"

Lauren saw Mrs. Black's face fill with pain and confusion. "You'll have a home someday, too, like Jennifer."

"I want a home now." Lauren kicked the side of the bed where she and Jennifer slept, and where she sensed she would now lie alone, night after night.

"Be quiet," her foster mother said. "Be quiet, and give Jennifer a hug. Tell her you love her."

Lauren hugged Jennifer, not letting go of her until the doorbell rang, and rough hands pried her sister away.

"Jennifer," she called out. "Why are they taking her?"

"Don't worry," said Mrs. Black. "Someday someone will take you, too."

* * *

Amy was getting ready to go skiing when the doorbell rang. The man who stood at the door was dressed in a khaki-colored uniform with a silver star over his heart. A woman in a gray winter coat stood by him. Amy watched him through the peephole until Mrs. Adams came to open the door.

"State of Colorado, ma'am. We have orders to take the children from this home."

No! Amy's heart sank. No! No! No!

"I'll get my husband," said Mrs. Adams. Amy watched Mrs. Adams's robe fly out behind her as she rushed to the bedroom.

What was going to happen to her now?

The woman in the gray coat stepped up to her. "Are you Amy Gray?"

"Yes . . ."

"Get your things. We've been instructed to arrange alternate placement."

What was wrong?

Amy rushed to her bedroom. For a moment she stared around the room, so calm, peaceful, and organized. Pictures in frames hung in perfect alignment on the walls. Serene floral wallpaper. Her chest of drawers, filled with folded clothes that she now flung haphazardly into a suitcase. The clothes in her closet—ironed and hung, all the skirts on one side, the blouses on another. Yet all this tranquillity couldn't still her beating heart.

She flung the suitcase ahead of her down the stairs.

"I'm calling my lawyer." Mr. Adams's voice thundered up the stairs as Amy dashed down. "You have no right to take these children."

"Oh, yes, we do," said the sheriff. "By the authority of the state of Colorado."

The social worker's hand found Amy's shoulder, which she knew was shaking.

"Just head on out to the car now," she said to Amy. While she walked to the social worker's car, Amy noticed that Trey and Tony were with the sheriff.

Her heart pounded all the way out of town, past houses, then farms, then fields.

Finally she asked, "Why are you taking me away? They were good foster parents."

The woman in front of her shook her head. "More than one report of corporal punishment. Those foster parents sign an agreement that says 'corporal punishment forbidden.'"

Amy hesitated. "What's corporal punishment?"

The social worker stopped the car. "Hitting. Beating. Any sort of discipline where they lay a hand on you. Did that happen to you?"

Amy recalled the Christmas-morning incident. "No. Not to me."

"Did you ever witness an occasion when they hit the boys?"

Now she swallowed and shifted on the car seat. "Yes. I'd be telling a lie if I said I didn't. But they were good parents!" she protested. "They gave us everything we needed."

"Amy. They violated the paper that they signed. They will probably lose their license."

"She was a good cook! She washed and ironed my clothes."

"Those things are important. But many children who are placed in foster care are victims of violence. They are sent to their foster homes to recover. The last thing they need is for a foster parent to become violent. It's too traumatic. We can't take the risk."

"They were just like grandparents," Amy said. "They told us if we did something wrong, we would get a spanking."

"That doesn't fly today. Not with abuse issues." The social worker sped out of town, leaving Amy wondering where she would end up now.

*　　*　　*

Pam sat next to Steve and waited. He was dressed in a clean shirt, and his hair was still shower-wet. The taut lines of his back and shoulders and the rigidity of his hands in his lap told her how nervous he was.

"Amy's old enough to drive?" she asked.

"Yes, she graduates high school in a few months." He shook his head. "I missed a lot of her life."

She watched as a blue car drove up to the McDonald's where they were waiting. The car eased to a stop, then a girl with long blond hair emerged.

She studied the easy stride of the girl who walked over to them.

"This is Pam," Steve said, and Pam eagerly watched the girl's face.

"Hi," Amy said, then, "Who are you?"

"Do you remember Pam? She lived down the hall from us at our apartment."

"I always thought your dad was a good dad," said Pam. "I used to watch him with you. It seemed like he was always riding bikes or taking you on a picnic."

"Those were the good old days," Amy said.

There was a silence before Steve reached over to take Pam's hand. "Pam and I have been dating. Thought she ought to meet you."

"Hello," Amy said stiffly, then walked around and sat by Steve.

"So what's going on with you?" Steve patted Amy's shoulder.

"Going to a new foster home. Still in shelter care."

"Tell them you want to come back to your old dad."

"They said maybe—after I graduate and turn eighteen, when I'm not a foster kid anymore."

"Really?" Steve smiled at Amy. "You finally get to escape?"

Amy made a face. "You know what I'm going to do?"

"Go to college? Join the army?" her dad joked.

"Nope."

"Travel to Europe?" said Pam.

"No, something else I have to do first."

"What's that?"

"I'm going to visit Tom. And I'm going to find Jennifer and Lauren. If it's the last thing I do."

"I bet you think of them all the time," Pam said.

Amy looked at her with fresh curiosity. "Have you ever had a child?" she asked.

"Never," Pam said. "I've never been married. But I used to watch you guys, with your dad, and think that maybe I'd like to have a family someday."

Amy stared at Pam, seeming to weigh her statement. "But my dad lost his family."

"Maybe you'll be able to get them back," Pam said gently.

Chapter 7

∞

"We'll get you a visit," Robyn was saying as she angled her Jeep Cherokee around the courthouse parking lot. "Don't you worry." Her hand found Amy's fingers and squeezed them a moment before she let go to steer into a parking place. When they got out of the car, Amy found it hard to keep up with Robyn as her foster mother charged across the parking lot, the braid down her back swinging against her gray sweater. She tried to imagine Robyn on the playground, blowing a whistle to catch the attention of the third graders she taught.

Robyn was a fireball.

Out of breath, Amy struggled to catch up, only reaching the shorter woman's side as she stood at the desk in the Family Services office.

"We have an appointment," Robyn said. "And I need to be back to work in an hour."

"Where do you work, ma'am?"

"Third-grade teacher. My principal said she'd sit in for me while I came to this appointment. But I have to get back."

"We'll get you in as soon as we can. Please have a seat." Amy sat and watched Robyn pace the room, stopping only briefly to look out the window or study posters on the wall. She didn't stand still to hear as each appointment was called. Every time the receptionist put down the phone, Robyn was right at the desk.

"Ma'am, I'll call you," the receptionist said in exasperation.

Amy was in the rest room when Robyn came in and pounded on the door with her small, tight fist.

"We're in, girl. Hurry up and come out here."

Robyn didn't give the social worker time to look through the file before she spoke. "I'm here to get visitation for my foster daughter here."

. The social worker stared from Robyn to Amy.

"She hasn't been seeing her parents?"

"Her dad, yeah, but her brother . . ."

"Siblings visits are often more complicated situations."

"Yeah, well, she hasn't had one yet and we're here to get one."

The social worker set down the file. "It's not that simple. It often depends on the status of both placements. Aren't you worried that such a visit might disrupt her placement with you?"

"Are you kidding? She's graduating from high school in four months. No more foster kid. I love her to death, but there's no use pretending . . ." Robyn reached out and hugged Amy with a strong, wiry arm.

"Then what is your interest in this, if she's not going to be with you much longer?"

"I'm here to see the kid get her rights. The right to see

her family members. Something we all do every day and don't even think about."

"I don't know what her brother's situation is."

"That's what we're here to find out. Where he is and how we get to see him."

"Just a moment, please . . ." The social worker opened a filing cabinet and drew out Amy's file.

"Wait a minute. It says adoption placement in here. No way can I give out any information on—"

"That's the two sisters!" Robyn jumped to her feet. "This is the brother. Tom."

"Wait a moment." The social worker dug in the filing cabinet again. She drew out a large file and set it on the desk.

"That his file?" Robyn leaned closer.

"Yes. But the information in it is confidential."

"We just need to know if he can meet us at McDonald's on Saturday."

"That's only three days away. I—"

"Time for him to clear his social calendar and meet sis here." Again, Robyn wrapped an arm around Amy's shoulder.

"There's no way I can let you know today."

"Can you file a petition or whatever? Can we sign anything? What about a phone call?"

"I'll talk to my supervisor. And I'll get back to you."

"When?" Robyn urged. "When will you get back to me?"

"Probably by the end of the week."

"That's not soon enough. I'll call back at the end of the day and you'll let me know."

"You can call, but I can't promise—"

"You'll hear from me at three-thirty."

"You may want to wait to—"

"There's not time for that."

Walking out of the parking lot with Robyn's arm around her shoulder, Amy felt a pang of loss—knowing that in all likelihood she would lose Robyn in four

months. This highly energetic woman was one of a kind—
the only foster mom who cared that she had a brother and
two sisters. The only foster mom who wasn't threatened
in the least that she wanted to see her family.

"Thanks, Robyn."

"Don't know if I did any good. We'll see."

Why did she feel nervous when she sat at the Abbotts'
table? Was it the cloth napkins, shiny silver, and fringed
place mats? Was it the fact that Mrs. Abbott always wore
a dress on Sunday and insisted she wear one, too?

"You were meant to be with us, Sarah. Let us thank
the Lord," said Mr. Abbott.

My name is Lauren. My name is Lauren, Lauren
thought to herself, all through the prayer. I wasn't meant
to be with you. I was meant to be with my dad, and
Jennifer and Tom and Amy.

After dinner, they read the Scriptures. Mr. Abbott
yelled when she began to nod off, tired after a long day
at school.

"This is God's word," said Mrs. Abbott.

"I'm tired," said Lauren.

"You must finish your Scripture study."

She knew better than to argue. Lauren read the verses the
Abbotts told her to read. After dinner, she went into her
room, with the clothes the Abbotts bought, the bedspread
they chose, and the books they said she should read.

Who am I? she wondered.

Lauren is lost. And I don't want to be Sarah.

Eight days later Amy introduced her father to Robyn.
"This is Robyn, Dad."

"Hello, Steve."

"Thanks for being good to my girl."

"She's a good girl . . . most of the time. Sometimes she
has a meltdown . . ."

Pam and Dad laughed. After their laughter died, there was silence in the car. Amy looked at the back of Dad's head, and saw that there were now a few gray strands mixed in with the blond. Pam, though, was all blond. A pretty woman. A calm woman. Someone who would stay with Dad and love him forever.

Like me, Amy thought. She's like our family.

The car zoomed off. Amy was still lost in thought when Dad pulled to a stop. The four of them got out, walked over to the merry-go-round, and waited.

"Bet I could still hang by my knees on that," Robyn said to Amy, pointing to the monkey bars. "Race you."

The two of them ran, scrambled up the bar, and hung upside down.

So Amy's first view of Tom was his tennis shoes.

"Hurry, squirt, that's him." Robyn swung around and landed hard on her feet.

Amy was slower. Slow enough to give Tom time to walk up and stand beside her for a full second before she threw her arms around him and felt the somehow familiar sensation of his shoulders and chest.

"Hi, Amy," he said.

"I missed you so much." She knew if she looked up, he'd see that she was crying.

"Same here," he said, his voice quavering.

"That's his sister?" said an unfamiliar voice.

Amy looked and saw an older couple, like the Adamses.

"Yes." Steve stood up from the bench he was sitting on. "I'm his dad, ma'am."

"We're his foster parents. He's been with us six months."

"Sounds like you've been in a couple of homes—like me," Amy said to Tom.

"More like fifteen or so," said Tom.

"Hey, you two, look up," Robyn called out. With identical blue eyes and the same shade of blond hair, Amy and Tom turned toward the camera.

"Lauren and Jennifer—were they with you?" Tom asked when they sat on the bench.

No one answered. Finally Robyn put her hand on Amy's knee and answered his question. "They did the adoption thing."

"I had to place them," Steve said.

"Oh." Tom looked down. "So there's no chance—"

"Don't ever say that. There could be lots of chance," said Robyn.

"I was sort of hoping you might help me look," said Amy.

"I'll help, too," said Pam, and Amy turned to look at her.

Lauren looked behind her as she climbed off the bus. She half expected someone to be following her. Mr. Abbott. Mrs. Abbott. One of them carrying a copy of the Ten Commandments, telling her to honor her father and her mother, which they never thought could be anyone but them.

She walked down the street, glancing back periodically to see if anyone was following her. Glancing upward, she found the address.

LEGAL AID SOCIETY.

"I want to talk to an attorney," Lauren said.

"Have a seat," said the red-suited receptionist, and for the first time Lauren realized that the room was crowded with waiting people. With each minute that passed, she kept expecting Mr. or Mrs. Abbott to confront her. Her tension didn't ease even as the wait grew long and tedious.

"You may go see Mr. Bush now," said the receptionist.

Lauren sighed and found her way down the hall and into Mr. Bush's office. He frowned at her slightly, obviously wondering what a girl her age was doing here without her parents.

"Lynn Bush," he said, extending a hand.

"Sarah Abbott," she said, thinking she'd better use her nearly legal name with an attorney.

"How can I help you?"

Lauren paused. She stared at Lynn Bush, trying to guess his reaction to her problem. Finally she said, "It's about my adoption."

"Oh, I couldn't help you seek your birth parents until you are twenty-one," he said.

"It's not that."

"What is it, then? Have you talked to your parents?"

"I can't. They are the problem."

"What do you mean?"

"I don't want to be adopted."

Mr. Bush's frown deepened. "I'm afraid there's been a misunderstanding. If you've been legally adopted, you can't just undo it, like having a fight with your best friend and making up."

"I'm not adopted yet. But I know I don't want to be."

"Sarah, if you're having a conflict with your parents, I would suggest that you go home and discuss it with them." His voice rose in anger. "You should go home and think about how lucky you are to have a home. There are thousands of foster children who won't ever have one."

"I want to go back to my dad."

"There is obviously something wrong here—very wrong, I might add—for you to have been placed for adoption. Now I think you are being terribly ungrateful—"

Lauren felt tears on her face. "I just can't be the daughter they want me to be. It's like they made up a daughter they wanted, and then wanted me to become her. And I can't do it."

"What is the problem?"

"They're Christians."

"What's wrong with that?"

"They want to force their beliefs on me. I believe in God. But I can't think about Him constantly the way they do. I have to wear a dress on Sunday, and read the Scriptures every day, and . . . it's just too much. I still remember my dad, and how we spent lots of time together on the beach. I want to go back to that."

"You can't. The court has decided."

"You really can't help me—even though the hearing is in two weeks?"

"No." The lawyer shook his head. "If these people have been given custody, you belong to them."

Lauren couldn't speak. She ran out of the office in tears.

Was there something wrong with her that she couldn't be Sarah Abbott? Something inside her told her that Sarah Abbott was a stranger to her, and always would be.

"Last night, huh?" Robyn said, studying the suitcases and boxes as Amy adjusted her white mortarboard on her head.

"No," Amy said quickly. "I'll be here a few more days."

"Don't know how your dad will feel about that." Robyn whisked a speck of dust from Amy's shoulder. "He's counting the minutes."

"I'm not in a big hurry."

"Why not? You only waited eight years."

Amy started to slide her watch onto her wrist, then hesitated. "When I leave—are you going to get somebody else?"

Robyn frowned at her. Amy smelled the smaller woman's perfume. "What do you mean? A boyfriend? I had enough of those."

"No, another foster kid."

Robyn shrugged. "I have no idea. Maybe . . . maybe not."

"You really should."

"You think so? I didn't ruin you in eight months?"

"You were the best . . ." Amy felt a lump in her throat.

"Hmm. Well, I'll tell them that when the social worker

gives me my evaluation. Don't know as they'll rank me very high. I'm too feisty."

"That's what kids need. Someone who fights for them."

"A fighter, that's me." Looking in the mirror, Robyn put a dangling gold earring through one ear.

"But maybe you don't need another foster kid . . ."

"Oh no?" Robyn stood next to her, then stood on her toes so that they were almost equal in height. "I'm not tall enough, huh?"

"No, maybe you need a permanent kid."

"A perma-kid, huh? What a concept."

"I think maybe you need to adopt."

Amy watched as Robyn set her lipstick down. Puzzled, she looked again and saw that Robyn's lip was quivering now, with the lipstick spread only halfway across her bottom lip.

"I—" Robyn started to speak, then stopped.

Amy reached out to hug her, but Robyn held out a restraining hand. "I didn't dig out my iron and work on that gown for hours for nothing. You're not ruining it by giving me a hug."

"But you're crying."

"You didn't see that. Didn't happen."

Amy felt her own eyes fill.

"See"—Robyn struggled—"I can do the other parts. The cooking part. The cleaning part. And especially the school part. But it's this part I don't I think I can take again."

"What's that?"

"The good-bye part," Robyn said, and this time, pushing aside Robyn's protesting arms, Amy hugged her foster mother for a long time, until Robyn finally spoke.

"I'm not making you late for your own graduation. Now let's get cracking."

Steve sat between Pam and Robyn.

"You know what your kid told me this morning?" Robyn asked him.

Steve smiled at her. "No, what?"

"Twenty-two."

"Twenty-two what?"

"Schools. That's how many the kid's been to. Lucky this is the last."

"And they kept saying she was so much better off. You know, away from me. Anywhere as long as she was away from me."

"Well now, you got her back," Robyn said.

Steve watched her swallow.

"You're not getting out of her life this easy," he said. "I'm lucky she wants to come back."

"Sounds like you get Tom, too, lucky guy. And she really wants to find those sisters . . ." Robyn couldn't believe she had to fumble for the names.

"Lauren and Jennifer," said Pam.

"She'll do it," said Robyn, who planned to go on and say how she'd help, and to keep in touch. But her throat closed again when she caught sight of Amy, up there, at the beginning of the line of graduates, ready to walk toward them.

Chapter 8

∞

The next day Amy and Pam visited the social worker's office where Amy and Robyn had been regular visitors.

"I'm no longer a foster child and I want to know about my sisters," she said.

"They are foster children?"

"No . . ." Amy looked down. "They were adopted."

"Oh." The social worker sat back. "Then I wouldn't have any information for you."

"Not . . . anything?"

"Nothing I can give you. Your father could file for non-identifying information, and we could see if there is anything in the file that we could give to him. But I doubt it."

Pam spoke up. "I'm her father's wife. Her stepmother. Could you release it to me?"

"The files are sealed," said the social worker. "It takes a court order to open them."

Amy paused. "Could I just see where the files are kept?"

The social worker looked at her as if she were crazy. "We keep them in a vault downstairs."

"Could I see the vault?"

Now the social worker stared. "No one's ever asked to see *that* before." Moments later she led Amy down a flight of dark stairs to the basement. After a moment Amy's eyes adjusted to the darkness.

"Over there," said the social worker.

Amy stared. There was a huge closetlike room filled with manila folds that were crisscrossed with wires.

"Our alarms are activated twenty-four hours a day," said the social worker.

My sisters are in there, Amy thought. I'd have to electrocute myself to get to them.

"If there were a message for me—from one of them—you'd tell me, wouldn't you?"

"If you made a written request to open your file."

"I'll make one today." When she didn't hear back after several months passed, Amy became increasingly convinced that her file was empty. It was as if her sisters had dropped off the face of the earth.

Lauren quivered with fear as the guard unlocked her cell at the detention center.

"Your parents are waiting for you in the visitation room."

"They're not my parents." Lauren shrugged aside the guard's arm.

"You are Sarah Abbott?"

"That's not my name."

"It's the name on your intake form."

"It's not my name legally."

"It's who you are while you are here."

Lauren's anger rose inside her. Yet her anger turned to fear as soon as she saw that the Abbotts didn't smile at the sight of her.

"We have something to tell you," Mrs. Abbott said. "Although you are still struggling with adjustment problems, we still felt it best that we let you know."

"What?" asked Lauren, biting the word off quickly.

"Someone called for you. She said she was your sister. From your first family. Here is the number."

"What was her name?" Lauren sensed she shouldn't act too interested.

"We didn't write it down. We thought you didn't need to know any information that is best left in the past," said Mr. Abbott.

"But we could not lie to you. Here is the number."

Lauren took the piece of paper, and crumpled it as if she planned to throw it away. But she put it in her drawer that night. Maybe she'd call it someday, she decided, when she was finally alone and safe.

Chapter 9

∞

Amy would remember the day forever. The world around
Dad's apartment looked washed after a morning rain-
storm, and now the sun outside was soothing as she
walked home from the store. The kitchen phone was already ringing as she opened the door.

"Hello?" She realized she sounded out of breath. She
could hear Dad and Pam talking with a drapery client in
the living room.

"Steve Gray, please."

She remembered the phone techniques he'd taught her
all her life when answering calls for the business. They
were especially fresh in her mind now that she was working for Dad. The caller sounded far away, as if calling
long distance, and she felt her curiosity rise.

"May I tell him who's calling?"

"This is Mary Margaret Hansen from the San Francisco
Division of Child and Family Services."

The words penetrated to the bone and made her shiver.
Even though she was legally an adult and no one could
uproot her and her brothers from their home ever again,
fear and tension filled her. Her legs felt fluid and weak.
She clung to the phone limply. "And you wanted . . . ?"

"To speak to Mr. Steve Gray." Now the voice sounded
rushed, irritated.

"Just a moment." From the living room, she heard her
dad's calm recitation of his price list and available fabric
options.

"Dad . . ."

He looked up at her and frowned slightly. "Can you take a message?"

Her head shook quickly. "Don't think I'd better. This sounds really important."

He glanced from Pam to the client, then said quickly, "Excuse me."

Amy watched her dad retreat to the bedroom to pick up the extension. With only a second's hesitation, she rushed to the kitchen and placed the receiver to her ear. Tension hummed inside her.

"Who did you say you were looking for?" Confusion in Dad's voice.

"Mr. Steve Gray."

"That's me, but I don't know anything about that other name you were asking about."

"Sarah Vilardi?" The woman's voice asked. "That name is not familiar to you?"

"Not at all," Dad said, "Now, if you'll excuse me, I'm in the middle of—"

"Wait!" Amy's voice burned as it burst from her throat and interrupted their conversation.

"Amy?" Dad's voice sounded puzzled.

The woman from Family Services waited.

"Who are you asking about?" Amy was surprised at the steeliness of her own words.

"This is confidential."

"Give my daughter the information. Maybe she knows about the person you are looking for." Neither of them stopped to explain that they'd spent half of their lives apart and could not ever take for granted the calm peace of being together.

"Sir, you wouldn't—"

"Give my daughter the name." Now Dad's iron resolve matched her own.

The woman cleared her throat. "It's Sarah Vilardi."

The name was totally unfamiliar. Yet what was this rising feeling inside her that wouldn't let go? Amy racked her brain. She held her breath. "What is her birth date?" she asked suddenly.

"June twenty-first, 1978," said the social worker.

Chills at her back. "Dad, it's Lauren!"

"What?" Confusion in her father's voice.

"That's Lauren's birthday!" Now tears streamed down Amy's face.

"My daughter?" Amy heard emotion in Dad's voice, too. But at the same time she knew she couldn't stop to explain. This could be the most important phone call of her—and Lauren's—life.

"We know Sarah Vilardi," she said quickly. "Her name used to be Lauren, and she is my sister."

The social worker paused. "She lives there, then? May I speak to her?"

For a moment Amy was stunned silent. "No," she said. "I haven't seen her since she was five years old. When she was placed for adoption."

"Oh, excuse me, then," the social worker said. "Sorry to have bothered—"

"Wait!" Amy insisted. "Why are you calling about Lauren . . . Sarah?"

"I shouldn't be talking to you. This is a serious error."

"Why did you think Lauren might be here with us?"

"I really can't say any more about this. We just thought possibly . . ."

"What did you think?" Each word emerged rock-hard.

"Mr. Gray—your father—is her birth father?"

"My dad is her dad." Now puzzlement mixed with her fury.

"We thought she may have sought out Mr. Gray."

"Why would you call us about that?"

"We are searching for Ms. Vilardi . . ."

"You're looking for Lauren? Have you called the family that adopted her?"

"Yes." the social worker sighed. "We spoke with them. Now I really must—"

"What did they say?"

"Miss? What is your name?"

"Amy," she said, thinking oh so briefly how grateful she was that her name had stayed the same throughout her life. "I'm Lauren's—Sarah's—older sister. I took care of her when she was a baby. And I'm worried about her now. Where is she?"

"I shouldn't give out this information."

Amy gripped the phone. "I am her sister. You have reached her family. Tell me where she is."

"That's just it, Ms. Gray. We don't know."

"Tell me what's going on."

"I can't. I've already gone beyond the bounds of confidentiality."

"Now that you've told me too much, just tell me that she's safe."

"I can't tell you because I don't know that. I really should have consulted with our lawyer, Mr Siegel, before making this call. But you would probably have found out sooner or later. Ms. Vilardi is missing."

"What? You don't know where she is?" There was a long pause, but Amy's anxiousness rose until she could wait no longer. "Where do you think she is?"

"We're searching for her. We feel sure we'll find her within the week."

"But how long has she been gone?"

"I can't release that information."

"Where is she missing from?"

"I'm sorry, Ms. Gray. We made an error in contacting you. Sorry to have disturbed—" The woman hung up without finishing her sentence.

"Wait—" Amy called out, but her voice reached only the dial tone.

Lauren was gone. Amy's mind swam as she tried to process the implications of the phone call. Now her sister was actually missing—not just adopted and living somewhere else. The magnitude of this realization filled her with a flood of helplessness. What could she do now?

The Child and Family Services phone call haunted

Amy as days passed. Where was Lauren? Was she in danger? Was she actually trying somehow to find her way home to their family? Why didn't the Child and Family Services organization know where she was?

One night at dinner, Amy broke the heavy silence that filled the room. "I'm going to find Lauren."

Dad pressed his lips together, and she saw concern fill his face as he smiled wanly. "You know I think that would be great . . . but I don't want you to spend a lot of time and then end up disappointed and upset. If the authorities can't find her—"

"If they can't find her, then I will."

Dad's gaze was level. "I'd like to see her as much as you would. But these people—from the state—they've been trained, and they're connected with the police and the FBI."

"But they don't care about Lauren," Amy protested.

Dad paused. "I still find it strange that they lost her . . . an agency charged with caring for children."

"It's just that they did a bad job this time . . . like some of our foster homes were bad. This time, they weren't willing to look hard enough."

"They found us, though, didn't they?"

"And look how crazy that was. They should know Lauren was adopted somewhere else and we haven't seen her!"

Dad's hand found her shoulder. "If you want to look, I'll help you. But where would we look—if those people don't know where she is?"

"San Francisco!" Amy pounded the table with her fork. "That's where they were calling from."

"Who would we call for information?"

"We have to go there," she said to Dad. "I can't stop thinking about it. What if this is our one chance to find Lauren?"

Chapter 10

∞

Amy and Dad set out on a rainy Friday, *after she looked up* the address of the main San Francisco police station in a phone book at the library. "Shouldn't we call first?" Dad asked as he slid on his loafers. Amy glanced with affection at Dad's shoes, work-worn and covered with snippets of thread. As she looked up to his face, he asked "Maybe there's someone we need to make an appointment with?"

"No." Amy shook her head vehemently. "They don't want to talk to us. It's too easy for them to hang up the phone. We have to confront them in person."

Her father looked as if he wanted to say something more, but stopped when he saw the determined look on her face. The two of them went out to Dad's car and said nothing as they drove to the gas station and filled the tank with gas. Dad came out and handed Amy a bottle of 7UP, his unspoken admission that this could be a long journey. They spoke little as miles of freeway surged past, and the sun brightened from early morning half-light into full noon blaze. A mixture of fear and hope hovered inside Amy. What did she hope to find? Wouldn't Child and Family Services know everything that the police knew? Still, she couldn't go on without asking. You didn't throw away your only chance.

She knew they had reached San Francisco by the sudden increase in traffic and tall buildings bordering both sides of the freeway, along with the breathtaking view of the Golden Gate Bridge, like a graceful, rust-colored dinosaur basking in the bay. Her father veered off into the exit lane at the main downtown exit.

"Now where do we go?" Dad asked her.

"I don't know," she admitted, swallowing with worry as he pulled over to the side of the road, stopped the car, and stared at her. "The address is 1001 Franklin Street. I just need to find where that is."

Her heart thudded.

"You got me to drive all the way up here and now we'll find it whatever it takes." His words sounded angry, yet she knew that rather than being directed toward her, his emotion was generated by the frustration they both felt.

"We shouldn't have to do this," Amy said. "We should be able to walk up to Lauren or call her on the phone anytime we want."

"It was the most unfair thing in my life." Dad shook his head in angry despair, yet his hand on Amy's shoulder emphasized the underlying gentleness of his words. She felt her throat catch. She wanted to comfort him, yet sensed her voice would break if she spoke. Then a thought struck.

"Just a minute." She leaped out of the car before he could say another word. It seemed like unexplainable luck that she caught sight of a policeman right then. At the officer's curious look, she gasped, "The police station. Main one downtown. Franklin Street. I need to find it."

The officer studied her a moment, then half smiled. "Haven't been there before, have you? You're practically standing on the steps. It's right over there."

Amy nodded a breathless thanks, then went back to the car.

"One block north." She pointed with her finger, still unable to meet Dad's gaze.

From the corner of her eye, she watched him shake his head. "You got some kinda luck. Franklin Street could have been miles from here. Don't know how you did it."

"Let's just hope my luck continues," Amy said quietly, feeling her heart beat fast. Her pulse stayed quick as her

father drove around and around what seemed like an endless parking lot. Finally he found an empty space and the
two of them wordlessly climbed out of the car. The car
doors slammed with a bang that echoed in Amy's ears.

She strode on, ahead of Dad, down a long walkway
and through the heavy glass doors at the San Francisco
Municipal Building. Feeling like a criminal, she put her
purse on the conveyor belt and watched it slide beneath
the X-ray machine. Moments later they both walked
through. I never imagined we'd be here, Amy thought.

A woman in a blue uniform sat, bored, behind a desk
with a sign that said INFORMATION.

"I need to find a police report," Amy told her.

"Public computer's over there." The woman waved her
off.

Amy sat at the computer, clicked on a square that said
Police Reports. There were so many requests for infor-
mation for which she had no answers. Case number. Date.
Address. Phone number.

Still, Amy typed.

The screen turned to gray, and the machine clicked. In
the long wait that followed, she stared outside at the gray
San Francisco day. Crowds of people wearing jackets and
raincoats and carrying umbrellas walked by. She felt the
rhythm of her own breath. Finally a form flashed on the
screen.

Missing Persons Report.

Amy stared at the screen. There it was. Sarah Vilardi.
Even the unfamiliar name caught at her heart. Lauren was
here. She scrolled down the computer screen past blank
spaces without information—lines that requested information about dates, addresses, etc. She paid a quarter to
print the report, and it wasn't until the printed copy, still
warm from the machine, fell into her hand that a crucial
bit of information seemingly leaped out at her.

"Lauren's a runaway!" she exclaimed. Dad slid his
chair closer beside hers.

Amy scanned the form. In the space that said *Person*

Filing This Report, there were two words, *Pacific Palisades.*

"What could this be?" she asked Dad, touching the line with her finger.

He shook his head. "Not a person's name. Sounds like a hotel."

Another line said *girl has been reported missing.*

But the rest of the form was depressingly, mysteriously blank. There was no picture of a teenage Lauren, or a phone number, or any kind of notation.

The only other line filled in was the date: 1995.

"Three years ago!" Amy exclaimed. "How could she be gone that long and they just called us last week. We've got to talk to somebody." She thrust her chair under the computer desk and rushed to the information counter.

A bored clerk. "Help you?"

"I need to know what happened to my sister!"

The woman looked down at the report in Amy's hand. "This is all the information we furnish to the public."

"But she's missing! She's still gone!"

"If there is a report, the matter is under investigation."

"Then let me talk to an investigator."

The woman sighed, picked up a phone, and said words that were practically unintelligible. The only words Amy could understand were "public" and "report." Moments later the woman gestured for Amy to hand her the copy of the police report. Then the woman paused, the phone to her ear. Seconds later she said, "Have a seat over there. Officer Barker will be with you."

The wait seemed interminable before a tall officer in a navy-blue uniform gestured for them to follow him. "We'll go in the conference room."

After they reached the room and sat down, Amy glimpsed a manila folder on the conference table.

"How can I help you today?" the officer said.

"I need to know about my sister." Amy tried to calm the urgency in her voice.

"Your sister is . . . ?"

"Lauren—Sarah Vilardi. Is that her file?"

"This is the file that corresponds to the police-report number you gave."

"Then it's hers. It says she's missing."

With a sigh, the officer opened the file and thumbed through the pages. "It is a missing persons' file," the officer acknowledged.

"I need to know what happened to her. We didn't know she was gone until last week."

"She is your sister—and you don't know what happened to her?"

Amy sighed. "It's a long story. Please just tell me what it says in her file."

When the officer stared, Amy felt obligated to explain. "My dad"—she gestured fumblingly toward her father—"was forced to give her up for adoption."

"Forced?" the officer questioned. "Legal adoption is voluntary."

"She was taken away unjustly. But that isn't why I'm here. Someone called us. Someone from the Division of Child and Family Services. They were looking for Lauren—Sarah. Now our family is worried sick and we need to know why Lauren is gone."

"Hmm." The officer looked at more of the papers in the file. Amy fought the urge to grab the documents from his hands. "There isn't anything I can tell you that isn't on the police report."

"But it's three years old!"

"The investigation is still ongoing."

"But how did she get to be missing to start with? And where is she now?"

"That's what the police are trying to find out."

"It's taken three years—to get nowhere?"

The officer shrugged. "They haven't given up. They're still pursuing the leads that they have. The case isn't closed."

Suddenly the color drained from Amy's face as a frightening realization filled her. "You're saying that you have no idea where Lauren is? She could be dead."

The officer hesitated and then nodded. "I'd have to say we don't know. There hasn't been an update on the case since"—he flipped through the pages—"last May."

"Why did it take the Division of Child and Family Services three years to contact us?" Amy felt her voice rising. "Didn't anyone care enough about her before now? Not even last May?"

The policeman weighed his words. "You aren't the family she lived with, am I correct?"

"Yes." Amy felt impatient.

"Then it would take some time for the investigation to reach you. And I must say that is a highly unusual procedure, to contact the family who has given someone up—"

"We didn't exactly give her up."

"Placed. Is that the word they use? Placed her for adoption."

"My dad was forced—and we never forgot her. And we want to find her again."

Now the policeman held up his hands in a half shrug. "I wish I could tell you. I honestly do. But the truth is, we haven't found any promising leads."

Amy's voice broke. "You must not be trying very hard. Maybe we're the only people who care about her. Maybe I need to try to find her myself." She felt Dad's hand on her arm, sensed he was cautioning her.

The policeman pressed his lips together, then closed the file. "More power to you," he said simply. Then he stood. "I'm sorry I can't tell you more."

Amy couldn't resist. "You couldn't be as sorry as I am," she said.

"Take care." The officer nodded at her curtly, then strode to the door and left Amy and her father sitting in sad puzzlement in the conference room. Another long, silent drive followed. Yet even as the car logged mile after mile, Amy's brain was racing. So now they knew. Lauren was missing, and even the police couldn't find her.

Chapter 11

∞

*Pacific Palisades. Like a tongue twister, the name kept re-*peating in Amy's brain. It brought visions of an amusement park—roller coasters, concession stands, game booths. What was Lauren doing and why had she run away from a place like that?

A week later Amy was home alone when she decided to call directory assistance in San Francisco.

"Pacific Palisades, please."

'The hotel's main number is—"

"Wait—not the hotel. Is there another Pacific Palisades?"

"I never heard of one."

"Could you check?"

"Sure." Another long pause. "Ma'am?"

"Yes."

"I don't know if this is what you're looking for. I've always heard that name, Pacific Palisades, associated with the hotel. But—there is something else. Again, I'm not at all sure if it's what you're seeking."

"What is it?"

"I think it's some kind of reformatory. A home for wayward teens, or something like that. Or maybe it's an orphanage. I'm not sure."

"Thank you," Amy said, hanging up after she got the number. What had happened to Lauren? If she was adopted from a foster home, what was she doing in an orphanage? Or a reformatory?

She hesitated, then dialed the number.

"Pacific Palisades."

"Is this an orphanage?"

"A boarding home."

"I'd like to speak to my sister. I believe she's staying there."

"Her name?"

"Laur—Sarah Vilardi."

She heard the operator speaking to someone else before returning to her.

"She's no longer a resident here."

"Do you know where I could reach her?"

"I can't give out any information."

"This is her sister."

"Under privacy laws, I can't release—"

"Is she missing from there?"

"I can't—"

"Can I speak to your supervisor?"

"Certainly. I'll put you through."

Moments later a voice said: "This is Ms. Wells."

"Ms. Wells? This is Sarah Vilardi's sister." Amy paused. She held her breath. "You know, of course, that she is still missing—"

"I can't give out any information."

"We've been to the police, and they told us that Pacific Palisades was where she was last seen."

"It sounds as if you've done what we've done. We also went to the police."

"I'd like to look for Sarah."

"Perhaps the police could give you some suggestions."

"Could you tell me why she was residing at your facility?"

"You say you are her sister? And you need to ask that question?"

"All I know is that it says 'runaway' on the police report. So she must have run away from—"

"I have another call. But I'll say yes. She ran away from her adoptive home and then she ran away from here.

And I suppose she may have run away from somewhere else, which is why you are calling."

"No—I just—"

"My other call. I've said all I can say. Good-bye."

Amy waited on the phone after Ms. Wells had hung up. What on earth had happened to Lauren? She picked up the phone and dialed.

"Pacific Palisades."

"May I speak to the manager?"

"Do you mean the director?"

"Yes."

"May I tell her what this is regarding?"

"My sister . . . who ran away."

"Didn't we just talk to you?"

"Yes . . ." Amy felt her heart pound. "I just had another thought. I wanted to run it past the director."

"I'm not sure if she'll speak with you."

"I'll wait."

This time the wait seemed interminable. Amy fought her instinct to hang up. Suddenly a voice on the phone said, "This is Mrs. Flynn."

"This is Amy Gray. I'm looking for my sister."

"You know that our records are confidential. These are juveniles who are housed here."

"I haven't seen her since she was five years old. And now I hear that she's missing."

"Who is your sister?"

"Sarah Vilardi."

"Oh." A long silence.

Amy's voice, high and thin: "Is she still missing?"

"Since you already know that fact, I will confirm it. Yes. Both the school and the police have been unable to locate her. We believe she has run away."

"Is there anything, anything at all, that you could tell me to help me find her?"

Again, a long silence. Amy thought the woman had hung up.

"She called here . . ." Mrs. Flynn said, softly, under her breath.

"What?"

"She phoned a friend. Twice. The calls were traced to a pay phone."

"Could you give my number to that friend? And tell her about me? Just in case?"

"Surely."

Amy thought about the phone call again and again as the next two years passed. Had Lauren ever called Pacific Palisades again? Had her friend lost Amy's number? Where was Lauren now?

Her thoughts were interrupted as a tall black-haired woman and an even taller young man—her son?—entered Gray Window Treatments.

"May I help you?" Though she looked at the woman, something about the young man caught her eye. It was like a voice inside her said, *You know him.*

"I'm here to pick up my drapes."

"Have you arranged for an installation appointment?"

Amy felt Dad walk up in back of her.

"No, Phil will just put them up." The woman gestured toward her son.

"We really recommend professional installation," said Dad. "So that they will look their best."

"I'll do it okay," said the boy. Amy noticed that while he spoke to her father he looked at her. After they left, she continued to think of him as she answered the phone and put metal hooks into new draperies.

Two hours later mother and son were back. This time Dad walked past Amy and smiled at them. "Got a question?" he asked.

"Yes. I wanted to see about ordering miniblinds for my kitchen."

"What about the drapes you took home today?"

"Oh, I already got those up." The son smiled.

Dad stepped forward. "Those drapes are already hanging in your living room?"

"Sure."

"Would you like a job here?"

The boy looked at Amy. "As a matter of fact, I would."

"I mean, I don't know that I'd send you out on an installation assignment the first week or two, but . . . could you start Monday?"

The boy said yes, and Amy realized her heart was pounding.

Sarah walked past the pet store about five times before she thought she'd dare walk in. For the past week each time she got off the bus, she checked to see that the sign was still there. HELP WANTED. They still needed somebody. And she still needed work. There were nights when she wondered how long she would make it alone. She was three days away from her limit of nights at the shelter. She would not be allowed to occupy a bed after Friday. She imagined a night when she'd actually turn herself in to the police.

I can't take it anymore, she realized. I need a home. I know that's what I need even though I haven't had a real one since I was five. Did kids who ran away think they knew how it would be without parents? No one to help you buy a car when you turned sixteen. No one whose insurance paid your medical bills when you got sick. No one to tell your teacher that you didn't understand that last algebra problem. No one to tell you it would be all right when you felt like crying when you broke up with your first boyfriend. Before she started to cry herself, Sarah drew herself to her full height, walked inside the door of the pet store, and came face-to-face with a blond woman who was sweating and looked exhausted as she bathed a schnauzer in a tub.

"Help you?" the woman said, pouring suds over the dog's back.

Sarah and the soapy dog stared at each other.

"Do you have an appointment?" The woman held a sponge in midair, and Sarah watched sudsy water drip back into the tub.

"No. I need—"

"You'll have to make an appointment."

Now making eye contact with only the schnauzer, Sarah said, "I'd like to apply for the job."

"I usually ask people to make an appointment for that, too." The woman began to rinse the dog. "You can see I'm swamped." She gestured around the room, where Sarah saw other dogs waiting in cages.

"I rode the bus here." Sarah sensed her voice sounded plaintive. "Don't know when I'll get back this way."

"There's another bus heads back the way you came in fifteen minutes." The woman wrung out her sponge. "So maybe we can get this over quick. I'll try to talk while I wash."

"Thank you." Sarah breathed.

The woman sneezed and suds flew. "You look pretty young. Had any experience working with dogs?"

Did she dare lie? Sarah thought that if she did, the woman could question her and find out the truth right away. "No," she admitted.

The woman lifted the dog onto a table and turned to Sarah. "We don't even need to interview you, then. You don't qualify."

Somehow the words struck Sarah like a punch in the stomach. "I'm willing to learn," she said. "I'll work hard."

"I need someone who can step right in here now—so I can get done by the end of the day. People are getting impatient with me." The woman shook her head, then turned back to the schnauzer.

"I could start now—today . . ." Sarah bravely took a step closer to the woman.

"You're just not what we're looking for." More head shaking. "But if the owner knew I turned someone away . . ." This time she flung her hand up. "Guy's just totally unrealistic . . ."

"Could I talk to him?" Sarah now stood inches from the woman.

"He's in there." The woman pointed to a doorway through which Sarah glimpsed cages, aquariums, and displays.

She walked in, at first thinking the place was empty, then she caught sight of a lean, efficient-looking man with salt-and-pepper hair who was meticulously dusting a row of aquariums with a feather duster.

"Sir," she said timidly.

"Not open yet. Come back at ten," he said, without looking at her.

"I'm not here to buy anything."

The feather duster paused in midswish and he looked at her through bifocals. "What can I help you with?"

"I want to apply for the job."

"The store clerk? We ask that you be at least eighteen."

"No, the grooming job." Sarah held her breath.

Now the man stepped down from a stool on which he was standing. "Have you had any experience?"

Sarah breathed. "I like dogs. I love animals."

"But in actually grooming a dog?"

"I never have." Her gaze dropped.

"This probably isn't the right position for you, then. Grooming a dog actually requires a great deal of skill."

"I'm willing to learn."

"And I'm sure you know that there are different styles for different dogs. The schnauzer cut. The poodle."

"Animals like me. I can always make friends with them."

He looked at her. "I would recommend, then, that you pursue studying about animals in school. You can take biology, anatomy, and other classes to learn about animals."

"I don't go to school. I dropped out when I was fourteen."

The man stood straighter and sighed. "You could read about them, then, from books at the library. They have some really great ones now with—"

"Will you give me the job if I promise to read about the animals?"

"The job would require training—from a groomer."

"Could I take the training?"

"We really need someone who already knows how to groom . . . now. Angie"—he turned toward the grooming room—"is terribly overscheduled." He lowered his voice. "Sometimes she doesn't finish by the end of the day and our customers get very upset."

"I could help with that. I could shampoo while she's grooming."

Now the man shook his head. "Even that takes training. To keep soap out of their eyes and ears, and make sure that you are washing the whole—"

"I could do it. I know how dogs feel."

The man paused. He stared at her, then laughed. "Oh, really?"

"Yes. I was a foster child since I was five. I know how it feels to live with someone who doesn't really care *about* you, but feels like they have to care *for* you. Sometimes they feed you bad food, or beat you if they're in a bad mood, or leave you alone for hours. Some dogs have lives like that."

The man continued to stare at her.

"And sometimes you're in a really good home and you think you are going to live there forever—then the next day you're dumped in a bad home with no explanation. That happens to dogs, too."

"It does," he admitted.

"And some homes that people think are the best really aren't," she said, thinking of the Abbotts.

He nodded, then looked off wistfully.

"I know how it is to have no one—" She cringed as her voice broke. She tried to swallow as quickly as she could. "And some dogs have no one."

She watched the man breathe. He sighed, leaning the feather duster against his hip. "I agree—your understanding might be helpful. But you still would need training."

"I'll do it."

"I'd have to ask Angie. And I don't know where she'd find the time."

"I'd come early. Or stay late. Or even go over to her house."

"That would be up to her. She'd have to agree."

Sarah waited. "Could we ask her now?"

"Sure." The man gestured for her to lead the way back to the grooming room.

Now Angie was washing a gray poodle. "Angie, I'd like you to meet someone. This girl, uh . . ."

"Sarah," Sarah supplied.

"Would like to begin training as a groomer."

Angie threw up her hands. "Since when do we need a beginner?"

"She's told me about some . . . well . . . sort of experiences she's had with knowing how dogs feel."

Angie laughed bitterly. "What does that have to do with shampoos and poodle cuts?"

Sarah spoke up. "I know I'll catch on fast."

"I thought we were trying to move this whole operation faster," Angie said. "Not stop to train a new person."

"You don't have to stop. I'll watch for a while first and you can tell me what you're doing."

"Wait a minute." Now the man suddenly turned to Sarah. "I need to tell you that I can't pay you while you train. So if it takes time—it will be a while before you get a paycheck."

No paycheck until she was through training. And here she stood—three days away from being kicked out of the shelter. Sarah looked up to see the man giving her a questioning look. "So do you think you'd rather—"

"I'll take the job," she said, feeling more uncertain than she'd ever felt in her life.

"She'll take it." Angie frowned. "I didn't hear you offer it to her."

"So you understand that the pay doesn't start until after you're through training?"

"Yes."

"Can you start Monday?"

"Yes," Sarah said. "What time?"

"Nine A.M." The man extended his hand to her. "Daniel McCann—and you are?"

"Sarah Vilardi."

"See you Monday, Sarah."

Chapter 12

∽

She fumbled in her purse for the pad where she'd written the attorney's name. There it was. Siegel. Lawrence Siegel. Alone in the house on a rare Friday off work, Amy called San Francisco directory assistance. "Lawrence Siegel, please," she told the operator.

"Residence or business?"

"Business." She looked down to see that the hand that held her pen over a spiral notebook was shaking.

The operator's voice was coolly professional.

She stared at the number a long time, trying to think of the right words to say. I love my sister. I've missed her for more than a dozen years. I'll never forget her.

"Siegel and Associates."

"Lawrence Siegel, please."

"I'll connect you to his secretary."

The receptionist transferred her quicker than she could reply. Amy held her breath.

"Lawrence Siegel's office."

"Is he in? May I speak to him?"

"Who's calling please?"

"This is Amy Gray. He called me last week."

"What is this regarding?"

"He called me about my sister. Lauren Gray. Wait." Her mind rushed. "He called me about Sarah Vilardi."

A long pause. "Please hold."

Amy finally let out her breath as she heard the phone click. There was a long, vacant silence.

"Lawrence Siegel," said a man's voice.

"Mr. Siegel . . . this is Amy Gray. You called my house last week . . . about Sarah Vilardi."

"Yes. I recall. We determined that you had no knowledge of where she is now. Thank you for speaking with us. Good—"

"Wait!" Amy jumped in before he could hang up. "I want you to tell me where Sarah is."

"I couldn't comment on that."

"Could you just tell me if she's safe? You got my family all worried."

"My client is the Department of Social Services. I have no obligation to you and—"

"Yes, you do," Amy practically shouted. "You told us that my sister is still missing. Now we need to know what's wrong. Is she in trouble? Is she on drugs? Can we help find her?"

"All of that would be covered under attorney-client privileges. I have no information to give you."

Amy inhaled. "But—"

"Good day," the man said firmly, hanging up the phone.

Sarah was sitting on the park bench, waiting for Matt, when a well of sadness surged inside her. Staring out at the bleak, empty coastline where a few seagulls flew, Sarah felt a bleak, empty ache. She could hardly bear to think about her life, even though her path ahead seemed

clear. She wanted the job at the pet store. She wanted to
start training, the way Mr. McCann said. But how could
she do it? She had no money, no parents . . . nothing but
herself. She half listened as seagulls cried out on the beach
in front of her. What could she tell Mr. McCann? How
could she make herself say no to this when nothing else
lay ahead in her life. Maybe she should—

With a smile, her boyfriend Matt flung himself onto the
iron bench beside her. His arm looped across her shoulders as his smile flashed. "What's going on?"

Sarah shook her head as her throat suddenly filled.

"You're starting training next week? What is the name
of the place? That New Pet?"

She felt her lip quiver. "Don't know if I can . . ."

Now Matt turned to face her. "Didn't he say you could?
The guy?"

For a moment she just stared at Matt. How could she
explain that having permission to start work was the least
of her problems? When she didn't answer right away, his
blue eyes searched her face. "Don't you want to do it
anymore?" he asked.

"You know I want to! I don't have any money! I don't
have any parents! I don't have a home! How can I do it?"
He blinked as she flung her doubts at him as if they were
his fault.

"Why can't you do it?" His brow furrowed in confusion.

"Because the store won't pay me while I train," she
said as anger filled her. "And without money, how can I
live?"

He turned away, looking out to the barren shore and
the seagulls, their feet etching delicate lines in the sandy
coastline. She stared at the side of his face, and for just a
moment her problems lifted as she realized how handsome
he was.

"I could say you could live with me," he said, grinning
at her.

She shook her head. "No one really wants me to live with them. Not my whole life—"

His eyes suddenly flashed. "I know someone. The perfect place."

She looked at him skeptically. "Who—a movie star? Someone rich and famous who will let me live in his mansion?"

Now he paused, smiling at her, as he watched her out of the corner of his eye. "My grandmother," he said slowly.

She shook her head, realizing that for a moment there, she'd held hope. Her laugh was bitter. "Sure." She gave his shoulder an exaggerated pat.

"No, really," he said.

"She wouldn't want an extra person taking up room in her house."

"She would. She's done it before. Lots of times. Lots and lots." He stopped and took her hand. "She's done it for me."

"But I don't have money to pay her. Not if I have to quit the store."

"She'd do it just to help you."

Sarah shook her head in frustrated sadness. "No one's ever let me live with them just to help me. Not since I was little. The state has had to pay people to take me since I was five years old."

"Not her. She'll see you and fall in love with you— just like I did."

"No one has before—my life just isn't like that." She stood, stretched, and yawned. "But I hate to tell That New Pet that I can't start training."

"Then come with me. This is Mexican night."

What did he mean? Sarah fought not to cling to a shred of hope as Matt took her hand and led her away.

Chapter 13

∽

"Amy . . . I need you back here for a minute."

Amy gulped. She knew that tone in Dad's voice. The hardest thing for both of them now that they were back together was to disagree.

"Ame . . . I need to talk to you."

Amy studied her father's tired-looking face. His hair was disheveled and his shirt was rumpled. It was another typical day at Gray Window Treatments.

Amy folded her arms and waited.

"You and Phil . . ." her father began.

A blush found its way onto Amy's face.

"You know what I'm talking about."

Now a trickle of sweat at her side.

"I just can't have you fraternizing with the help. He's my best installer."

Amy stood. "I'm not fraternizing," she insisted.

"I see you. You talk all the time. Even when you're supposed to be—"

"We're getting married."

Dad stopped. "What?"

"In three months. In July."

"But you don't even really know him."

"We've gone on about ten dates."

"That's not enough. Part of my conflicts with your mother happened because we were too young." Her father stared. "How long have you felt you were in love with him?"

"It only took us a week to fall in love. Both of us."

"Then you can't be sure yet."

"We're more than sure . . . we're positive. We thought you would be happy."

"It's just . . . so soon. You're too young."

"I'm twenty-three. I'm old enough. You just forgot to count the missing years."

A sad, bleak look filtered over Dad's face. "My little girl. I just got her back and now . . ."

"You won't lose me. I'll still be here. I'll still work with you every day."

"Still . . ."

"I want you to give me away."

"I feel like I gave you away once already . . . when you were eleven . . ."

"Someone took me then. You didn't give—"

Her father's finger pointed at her. "If you really mean this, I'll give you away this time. If you're getting married, you can be sure I'm not going to miss it. I already missed a bunch of Christmases and Halloweens. Your high-school prom. I'm not about to let you get married without me."

The house they approached was medium-sized and gray brick. Sarah pictured a gentle, gray-haired elderly lady who really hoped to be left alone in peace. She wondered if she herself would ever know the luxury of living alone, in a place that belonged just to her. She knew she wished that would happen someday.

A Hispanic man in a blue auto mechanic's overalls answered the door. "There you are, Matthew." The man reached out and ruffled Matt's hair. "We hoped you wouldn't miss dinner. Not tonight." He nodded at Sarah.

"Sarah Vilardi, this is my grandpa, Victor," said Matt.

Sarah shyly extended a hand, and the man shook it firmly.

"Where is Grandma?" asked Matt.

"Where else?" Victor laughed. "You know where she is."

Matt smiled and reached for her hand. "Come on," he said.

As soon as he took her hand to lead her down a dark hall, Sarah smelled heaven. Someone was cooking a delightful concoction of meat, cheese, and peppers. Her stomach growled. It was a long time since she had last eaten.

As they entered a kitchen that seemed to be filled with heat and steam, Sarah nearly tripped over a tiny, thin woman who moved like lightning from the counter to the stove to the kitchen table. The stove was piled with Mexican dishes—she recognized enchiladas and tacos—and the table was filled with salads, tortilla chips . . . and people waiting to eat.

"This"—Matt playfully grabbed the little woman after she set the enchiladas on the table—"Is my grandma, Pilar."

The woman stopped, stock-still, took a glove-shaped pot holder off her hand, and hugged Sarah. "Hello, dear," she said. "Welcome to my home. Please sit down and have dinner. This is my Mexican night."

Who were all these people sitting at the table? A variety of ages, from adults to teens. Pilar placed a steaming plate heaped with food in front of Sarah, who felt her stomach growl again. Helpless to resist, she was reaching for her fork when Matt caught at her arm. "Wait a sec," he said as Victor bent his head and said a short prayer in Spanish. Though praying before dinner reminded her of the Abbotts, Sarah had to admit the circumstances here were totally different. She waited a moment longer, let everyone start eating, then suddenly Pilar asked, "Matt, your friend? Is something wrong with her food?"

Now Matt looked at Sarah. "Go ahead. Dig in. Quick, before someone else around here grabs your plate."

Her stomach growled again even as he spoke.

She dipped her fork through layers of melted cheese. Steam rose, along with the scent of spicy beef. With the first bite in her mouth, the flavors of olives, lettuce, cheese, and meat joined in a delightful blend. She ate ravenously, only half aware of the gazes of the others at the table. Her stomach eagerly welcomed the food, and before she knew it, her plate was scraped clean.

"Look, Mama," said Matt's grandpa, "once again, your food is a hit!"

The little woman turned from the stove and beamed. Seconds later she rushed over to Sarah.

"What else can I get for you?" Her brown eyes blinked as her hand, still warm from the stove, reached comfortingly to touch Sarah's shoulder.

Sarah felt a sudden lump in her throat. When was the last time she felt such peace? "Come on," said Pilar, "you're still starving. Look." She gestured at Sarah's empty plate.

She could eat about a billion plates more. Home cooking was something she had experienced rarely in her life. "Just a little more of . . . whatever you have," she said.

Pilar nodded, took her plate, and returned with another as highly heaped as the first. Sarah ate it all, every last crumb. She looked up to find that only Matt and Pilar were left at the table and they were watching her. To her embarrassment, she burped. "Excuse me . . . I'm sorry . . . I ate so much . . ."

They smiled at her.

"It was so good." She blinked at them.

"Grandma, Sarah is the girl I've been telling you about. She needs a place to stay." Matt smiled at his grandmother, and Sarah cringed, too ashamed to say a word. How could he ask a favor like this right while she herself was sitting there? Did he know how humiliating this was?

Pilar stared at her, a long, gentle look.

"Please." Sarah's voice broke through suddenly. "I couldn't stay here. I don't have any money—"

Pilar's soft voice was firm. "What's important isn't your money. What's important is getting you off the street."

Pilar's warm, understanding words somehow penetrated the ache inside her, the core of pain that came from years of feeling like she wasn't really wanted. To have someone care about her was such a rare occurrence that she burst into tears.

"I'm sorry," said Pilar. "I didn't mean to make you cry."

Sarah sobbed. "It's just been hard—"

"Of course it has," Pilar said calmly. "Did Matt tell you that lots of people stay here? People who need a home?"

"Who are they?" Sarah asked.

"Mostly they're friends of my grandchildren. Just kids who need help for a while. I'd like to help you." Pilar's small warm hand reached out and took Sarah's.

Sarah shook her head as a sob filled her throat. "I don't know when I could ever pay you back. I'm training to become a dog groomer, and they don't pay you while you train."

"That's fine. I understand," said Pilar. "Matt, do you think she could share the room upstairs with Yvette?"

"No, I don't want to put anyone out."

Now Pilar squeezed her hand harshly. "Stop with the worrying. Yvette is a college student. Friend of my oldest granddaughter. She's been here three years. Matt, show Sarah the room."

It was a big bedroom with pale peach flowered wall-paper. From the moment she stepped through the door-way, Sarah felt bathed by the peace in this room. The bed looked big and soft and the room felt airy and calm and spacious.

"It's beautiful. It really is—but I can't just move in and take advantage of these people."

"No more saying why you can't do it. This is your room," said Matt. "Grandma wants it that way."

Sarah breathed. She glanced around the room again. Even shared with an unknown college student named Yvette, this would be the biggest amount of space she ever called her own in her life. How could she say no?

"Just for a little while," she said. "Just until I can afford my own apartment."

"Until you finish training," Matt insisted. "Until you know how to groom dogs. Or maybe"—he gave her a sidelong glance—"until we get married."

Sarah looked around the room again. Where would she go if she didn't stay here. "I should go to a shelter. I have no money to pay."

"This is your shelter. I stayed here with Grandma for two years and she never mentioned money. Please stay here—for her sake. Helping people is her life."

Suddenly there was nothing more to say. The next day, Matt helped bring her suitcases and boxes in his car. When they reached Pilar's house, there was a banner in front that said WELCOME SARAH.

Tears flooded her face. Welcome was a feeling she'd never really felt before.

Chapter 14

୭ଧ

It was later the next day when she found Amy's number, tucked inside the Bible Mrs. Abbott had given her all those years ago. There it was: 555-679-8220. Her sister. Her big sister, who took care of her when she was little and they all lived in the same house. Before her mother left. And after, too.

I can't call her now, Sarah thought. She felt she couldn't interrupt this brief peace in her life with any possible trauma. Not now. As a flood of guilt filled her, she folded the small slip of paper and tucked it back in the Bible.

Someday, she promised herself. Someday she would call Amy and tell her she still loved her. She would confess that somewhere, in the dark recesses of her mind, there were memories of Amy, who was the one who was really her mom. But no one seemed like a mom to her now, except Pilar.

Amy's thoughts rushed from work to her wedding to the letter she was writing as she cleared the table after dinner. Piling a stack of dishes, she picked up the phone.

"I'm looking for Amy Gray."

She turned on the cold water, added some hot, and poured in the soap.

"This is Amy . . ."

"Hi, Amy. This is Matt."

She racked her brain. The name didn't ring a bell. "This is my home number. Did you mean to call the store?"

"Oh . . . you have a store?"

"My dad's store. Gray Window Treatments."

"Then this is Amy Gray."

"Yes . . . did you need my dad?"

"Hmm . . . just a minute."

Matt, whoever he was, left the phone. Amy sloshed the dishes in the hot water and scraped a particularly stubborn stain with her fingernails. Should she hang up the phone?

"Hello . . ." This time a girl's voice.

"I was speaking with Matt." Amy felt annoyed. What was going on here? Was this a prank call?

"Is this still Amy?"

Amy sighed. "This is me." She *would* hang up now if her hands weren't submerged in dishwater.

"Amy . . . it's Sarah."

Amy's heart stopped. Chills rushed over body, despite the hot dishwater. There had to be some mistake.

"You're . . . Sarah."

"Yeah."

"Sarah . . ." Amy ventured cautiously. "Vilardi?"

"Yes."

Amy took a breath. "Is this . . . Lauren?"

"That was my birth name."

Amy backed away from the sink. Water dripped onto the floor. She sat on a kitchen chair and waited, not knowing what to say . . . though part of her wanted to drop the phone and scream and shout and run for Dad.

"Amy? You still there?"

"Yeah."

"I don't know how to say this. I think I used to be your sister. I mean—*am* your sister."

Amy dropped the phone then. When she tried to retrieve it, it slid along the floor. She scrambled and slid on the wet kitchen floor and then reached under the table. With a gasp, she grabbed the phone.

"Lauren?"

"This is Matt. She thought maybe you hung up."

"No . . . never. I looked for her for years . . . my dad and me."

"Well, she's right here."

"Where are you?" Amy asked.

"Northern California. What about you?"

"Southern. Can you come down here and see us?"

"Uh . . . just a minute." She heard the two of them talking, but she couldn't make out their words.

"Amy . . . this is Sarah again. Matt said you mentioned something about coming there to visit. I don't know how to explain this. But I ran away twice and now I'm sort of homeless."

"Do you live in a shelter?" Amy's heart ached for Sarah.

"No—with Matt's grandmother. But I don't have a car and I just got a new job . . . so traveling's not something I can do right now."

"It's a huge relief to know you're all right. And we can talk on the phone, right?" Drying her hands off, Amy reached for a pen. "Why don't you give me your phone number?"

* * *

Amy sat at her desk at the drapery shop. This was her break. She needed to write this letter fast. Dear Big-Hugs.com, she wrote.

> My dream is for all four of us to be together, just one time. My two sisters, Lauren and Jennifer, and my brother, Tom. She paused. We've been separated most of our lives. Back then, I tried to keep our family together. But it didn't work. All four of us went in different directions. We've all been in a lot of foster homes since then. We've spent a lot of time apart. Now I feel like it's time for us to get back together. I'm willing to do anything I can to help with the search. I've been searching by myself for a long time, and I have a lot of information. Please help me.
> Sincerely,
> Amy Gray

She sealed the envelope, and that night, dropped it off in the after-hours slot at the post office. Please, she thought. I don't know if there's any other hope.

It was after dinner, after a long day at the drapery shop. Now there was a silent, restful calm in her apartment as Amy cleared the table following a pizza dinner with Phil. The phone rang.

Amy heard a pause, followed by a rush of air. "May I speak with Amy Gray?"

The voice sounded official. Did someone from the drapery store somehow get her home number? "This is she."

"Amy, this is JoAnn from *Maury Povich*."

"Really?"

"I'm calling about the letter you sent . . ."

"You got my letter?" Did she dare get excited? Was there any way she even dared hope?

"Yes. We did. Amy, I need to tell you that our producers found your story to be very interesting."

Amy laughed ironically. "We've been separated for so long . . ."

"I'm calling to ask if you are available to fly to New York on Friday."

"This week?" It was already Tuesday. And she'd have to ask to get off work, and buy a dress to wear, and . . .

"Yes . . . Friday the tenth."

A surge of hope suddenly filled her. "Did you find Jennifer?"

A long pause.

"Amy. I have to tell you. We didn't find Jennifer. But we feel like we might if you were somehow able to come back here and make a plea. You would be a guest, and you and Maury would tell your story. Then we feel it's highly likely that someone who knows your sister—or maybe she'll even see the show herself—would be able to help us contact her."

"Well, I'll do it. But you want me to come all the way to New York, just to—"

"You have a very sympathetic story, Amy. And we feel that if the audience sees you—and any photos you might have of when you were together when you were young—there is a chance."

"Well . . ." The possibility made her mind spin.

Chapter 15

∽

Amy decided that New York smelled completely different from California. There was no salty ocean tang, but instead, a more dignified, city smell of smoke, fog, and high-density living.

Amy and Dad followed the producer, whose name was Natalie, down the hall to a room near the soundstage.

"You can watch the show here for a few minutes," she said. "Then we'll be calling you."

"How would it be," Maury was saying, "to know that you had a long-lost brother or sister . . . out there . . . somewhere . . . that you might never see again?

"Our guests today have that experience. They know that they have a sibling they were separated from. While most of us can get in touch with our family in just a few seconds by calling on a cell phone, some people aren't that lucky. So we decided to help out."

Amy jumped as Natalie touched her shoulder. "It's time now," she said. "He's waiting for you."

Amy took a long breath and stepped out into the sea of lights and applause. Maury's smile caught at her heart, which was thudding like it would never stop.

"Right out here. Audience, I'd like you to meet Amy." He smiled at her. "Amy wrote to us with a special wish." Maury's smile broadened. "Can you tell our audience what you are hoping for, Amy?"

"I'd like to find my sister."

"And as I understand it, your whole family was separated for a while."

"We were. They took us away from our dad when we were really little."

Maury paused. "I understand there was a court hearing."

"Yes . . . someone made false allegations against him."

"Regarding neglect and abuse, am I right, Amy?"

"Yes. No one ever proved anything, but they took us anyway."

"And you waited all this time."

"Fourteen years."

"How many children are there altogether?"

"Four of us. Me, my brother, my sister Lauren, who I just talked to after fourteen years . . . and Jennifer, who is still missing."

"As I understand it, you know where Lauren is, but you haven't seen her, am I right?"

"Yes."

"Amy, how would you like to able to ask Lauren to help you make this plea to find Jennifer?"

"She can't travel right now." Amy felt flustered.

"Oh, I think she might be willing to help you. Would you like to ask her?"

Maury pointed, and Amy's jaw dropped.

A beautiful blond girl, hair swinging and eyes smiling, was walking rapidly toward her.

"Lauren?" Amy breathed, not waiting for an answer before the girl held her arms out and Amy rushed to hug her.

"I looked for you so long." Amy felt tears.

"I wondered if you would even remember me. I thought you might forget . . ."

"No . . . never . . . we wanted to find you so much."

"Amy?" Maury stepped closer to the two of them. "I believe there was someone else who was supposed to be here today . . . someone who couldn't get off work."

"Tom!" Amy exclaimed as her brother walked out on the stage, grinning broadly.

"How did you . . . ?"

"The miracle of separate flights." Maury laughed.

"Now, audience, while this reunion is amazing in itself, I'm sorry to say it isn't complete." Amy watched as Tom and Lauren turned to look at Maury.

"There is another sister in this family. And you—all three of you—came to make a plea to find her. Tell us, Amy."

"Jennifer was the baby sister," Amy began. "Dad and I always used to talk about her, and wonder where she was. We hope she's safe out there somewhere, that she's alive and safe . . ."

"And you're here to ask the audience . . . ?"

"If anyone out there knows my sister or how to find her, if they would please call in."

Abruptly, a young woman stood in the audience.

"I might know where she is," the girl called out.

Amy stared out into the audience, unable to see the girl because of the blindingly bright lights.

Maury stood. "There's Jennifer! Jennifer, come up here and meet your family."

Amy stared through her tears as another young girl, as blond and beautiful as Lauren, walked up onto the stage.

Amy ran to hug Jennifer, and instantly felt other pairs of arms—Tom, Dad, and Lauren—enfold them both.

"Have you ever seen so much love in one place?" Maury asked the audience. "I think we need to give these folks some time alone. Here is another family reunited thanks to BigHugs.com."

Ahead of Amy, the frame of logs was draped with a canopy of frothy white fabric. She held a bouquet of white flowers in her hand and stepped forward across the warm, sunbaked sand. She lifted her bouquet briefly to savor the scent of daisies, roses, and sunshine. Glancing over her shoulder, she caught sight of Jennifer and Lauren walking behind her, in perfect rhythm to the "Wedding March" being played on guitars. She gazed at the fresh flowers in their hair, their reassuring smiles, and the colorful bouquets they held.

When she looked ahead once again, her eyes met Dad's. He didn't look tired today, Amy realized. Instead of a wrinkled golf shirt, he wore the first tuxedo of his life, complete with a bow tie. His blond hair was neatly combed and still shower-wet. He winked at Amy, and her heart beat.

I did it, she thought. We're here, all of us, at my wedding. My whole family is with me, after all these years. She stepped forward, and then glanced up at Phil, who smiled at her.

A few more steps. Strains of music, played by a guitarist who sat on a nearby rock, drifted out across the ocean waves as Amy stepped closer. Finally her hand found Phil's.

The pastor spoke, "Do you, Amy Michelle Gray, take Phillip Alexander Mitchell, to be your lawfully wedded husband . . . for richer or poorer, in sickness and in health . . ."

The words fell on her lightly, like raindrops in a warm spring storm.

"I do," she said.

"Do you, Phillip Alexander Mitchell, take Amy Michelle Gray, to be your lawfully wedded wife . . ."

"I do."

The pastor paused. "Along with witnessing the joy of new love, this is a family who has recently discovered the happiness of being together after a long separation. The joining of this couple is a new, special joy that is now added to the delight this family has recently received."

The pastor smiled. "Amy and Phillip, I now pronounce you man and wife."

Phillip kissed her. Dad hugged her first, and then Lauren, Jennifer, Tom, and Pam.

"Thank you, everybody, for being here today," said Amy. "This was my life's dream . . . for all of us to be together on the beach, once again. I was about to give up when my dream came true, showing me that we should never give up."

"You did it," Dad said, minutes later, as he handed her a hot dog.

"You did, too. You made me want to bring us together," said Amy. "All those years . . . you worked so hard."

"It was my dream, too," Dad said.

They sat there, all of them, as the afternoon dimmed to twilight, and the fire needed to be rebuilt again and again. In a way, it felt like their days on the beach long ago had never been interrupted. Dad cooked hot dogs and marshmallows, and the girls talked and laughed together. As the fire gradually died, they stayed there, seated in a circle on the sand, as if they wanted to stay on the beach forever.

WHO WOULD YOU LIKE TO FIND?

 My name is Troy Dunn, and I am the CEO of BigHugs.com, the organization who helped to reunite all of the wonderful people you just read about. Over the past decade, we have reunited thousands of families worldwide and continue to do so at this very moment. We would like to help you find a lost friend or family member as well. Who knows, you might be our next great story!

I feel everybody has somebody they have lost touch with. Someone who they would love to see one more time in this short life we live. Who is that person for you? Is it an old classmate, a teacher, someone in the military or perhaps a former coworker or neighbor? Perhaps you are one of the twenty-seven-million Americans affected by adoption (our specialty), and you want to find your biological family?

Whatever the case may be, we can help you find that special someone and bring closure, answers and, hopefully, joy to your life and the life of your family. Contact us and see if we can help you. We will evaluate your situation and recommend the best, fastest and least expensive route to help you find that missing person.

There are several ways to contact us. Pick your preference:
BY TELEPHONE: Call our world headquarters at (941) 574-1799
Our toll-free information line is (800) BigHugs
BY INTERNET: Visit our Web site at http://www.BigHugs.com
(While there, check out our FREE reunion registry!)
BY MAIL: Write to us at BigHugs.com
2503 Del Prado Blvd.
Cape Coral, FL 33904
(This is the slowest way to correspond with us, so be patient.)

Thank you for reading this wonderful book by our good friend Carolyn Campbell. Look for the other books in this series coming soon to your favorite bookstore. I wish you the best of luck in your search for friends and family, and encourage you to never give up. We have a saying in our office, "You can't find peace until you find all the pieces."

God Bless,
Troy Dunn
CEO, BigHugs.com